White Apples
and the Taste *of* Stone

Exiles and Marriages (1955)

The Dark Houses (1958)

A Roof of Tiger Lilies (1964)

The Alligator Bride (1969)

The Yellow Room (1971)

The Town of Hill (1975)

Kicking the Leaves (1978)

The Happy Man (1986)

The One Day (1988)

Old and New Poems (1990)

The Museum of Clear Ideas (1993)

The Old Life (1996)

Without (1998)

The Painted Bed (2002)

White Apples and the Taste of Stone (2006)

White Apples
and the Taste *of* Stone

DONALD HALL SELECTED POEMS
1946–2006

Houghton Mifflin Company

BOSTON   NEW YORK

Copyright © 2006 by Donald Hall

For information about permission to reproduce selections from
this book, write to Permissions, Houghton Mifflin Company,
215 Park Avenue South, New York, New York 10003.

Visit our Web site: www.houghtonmifflinbooks.com.

Library of Congress Cataloging-in-Publication Data

Hall, Donald, 1928–
    White apples and the taste of stone : selected poems, 1946–2006 / Donald Hall.
        p. cm.
    ISBN-13: 978-0-618-53721-1
    ISBN-10: 0-618-53721-x
    I. Title.
    PS3515.A3152A6 2006
    811'.54—dc22   2005020047

Book design by Anne Chalmers
Typeface: Filosofia (Emigre)

Printed in the United States of America
QUM 10 9 8 7 6 5 4 3 2

Poems published here for the first time in book form previously appeared in the
following publications: *American Poetry Review:* "Safe Sex," "Usage," "Tea," "The
Master." *Chicago Athenaeum:* "Gospel." *New Republic:* "The Angels." *The New Yorker:*
"Tennis Ball," "Secrets," "The Hunkering," "1943." *New York Times* (op-ed page):
"Witness's House." *Ploughshares* (vol. 30, no. 4): "Fishing for Cats, 1944." *Poetry:*
"Olives" (July 2005), "After Horace" (August 2005), "North South" (March 2006).

For Linda Kunhardt

Contents

4. Root Cellar

12. ALL

13. LETTERS WITHOUT ADDRESSES

14. THROWING AWAY

15. RECENT POEMS

1 *Early Poems*

Old Home Day

Old man remembers to old man
    How bat struck ball upon this plain,
Seventy years ago, before
    The batter's box washed out in rain.

Love Is Like Sounds

Late snow fell this early morning of spring.
At dawn I rose from bed, restless, and looked
Out of my window, to wonder if there the snow
Fell outside your bedroom, and you watching.

I played my game of solitaire. The cards
Came out the same the third time through the deck.
The game was stuck. I threw the cards together,
And watched the snow that could not do but fall.

Love is like sounds, whose last reverberations
Hang on the leaves of strange trees, on mountains
As distant as the curving of the earth,
Where the snow hangs still in the middle of the air.

Wedding Party

The pockmarked player of the accordion
Empties and fills his squeezebox in the corner,

Kin to the tiny man who pours champagne,
Kin to the caterer. These solemn men,
Amid the sounds of silk and popping corks,
Stand like pillars. And the white bride
Moves through the crowd as a chaired relic moves.

We are the guest invited yesterday,
Friend to the bride's rejected suitor, come
On sudden visit unexpectedly.
And so we chat, on best behavior, with
The Uncle, Aunt, and unattractive girl;
And watch the summer twilight slide away
As thunder gathers head to end the day.

Now all at once the pockmarked player grows
Immense and terrible beside the bride
Whose marriage withers to a rind of years
And curling photographs in a dry box;
And in the storm that hurls upon the room
Above the crowd he holds his breathing box
That only empties, fills, empties, fills.

EXILE

Each of us waking to the window's light
Has found the curtains changed, our pictures gone;
Our furniture has vanished in the night
And left us to an unfamiliar dawn;
Even the contours of the room are strange
And everything is change.
Waking, our minds construct of memory
What figure stretched beside us, or what voice
Shouted to pull us from our luxury—
And all the mornings leaning to our choice.

To put away—both child and murderer—
The toys we played with just a month ago,
That wisdom come, and make our progress sure,
Began our exile with our lust to grow.
(Remembering a train I tore apart
Because it knew my heart.)
We move to move, and this perversity
Betrays us into loving only loss.
We seek betrayal. When we cross the sea,
It is the distance from our past we cross.

Not only from the intellectual child
Time has removed us, but unyieldingly
Cuts down the groves in which our Indians filed
And where the black of pines was mystery.
(I walked the streets of where I lived and grew,
And all the streets were new.)
The room of love is always rearranged.
Someone has torn the corner of a chair
So that the past we call upon has changed,
The scene deprived by an intruding tear.

Exiled by death from people we have known,
We are reduced again by years, and try
To call them back and clothe the barren bone,
Not to admit that people ever die.
(A boy who talked and read and grew with me
Fell from a maple tree.)
But we are still alone, who love the dead,
And always miss their action's character,
Caught in the cage of living, visited
By no faint ghosts, by no gray men that were.

In years, and in the numbering of space,
Moving away from what we grew to know,

We stray like paper blown from place to place,
Impelled by every element to go.
(I think of haying on an August day,
Forking the stacks of hay.)
We can remember trees and attitudes
That foreign landscapes do not imitate;
They grow distinct within the interludes
Of memory beneath a stranger state.

The favorite toy was banished, and our act
Was banishment of the self; then growing, we
Betrayed the girls we loved, for our love lacked
Self-knowledge of its real perversity.
(I loved her, but I told her I did not,
And grew, and then forgot.)
It was mechanical, and in our age,
That cruelty should be our way of speech;
Our movement is a single pilgrimage,
Never returning; action does not teach.

In isolation from our present love
We make her up, consulting memory,
Imagining to watch her image move
On daily avenues across a sea.
(All day I saw her daydreamed figure stand
Out of the reach of hand.)
Each door and window is a spectral frame
In which her shape is for the moment found;
Each lucky scrap of paper bears her name,
And half-heard phrases imitate its sound.

Imagining, by exile kept from fact,
We build of distance mental rock and tree,
And make of memory creative act,
Persons and worlds no waking eye can see.

(From lacking her, I built her new again,
And loved the image then.)
The manufactured country is so green
The eyes of sleep are blinded by its shine;
We spend our lust in that imagined scene
But never wake to cross its borderline.

No man can knock his human fist upon
The door built by his mind, or hear the voice
He meditated come again if gone;
We live outside the country of our choice.
(I wanted X. When X moved in with me,
I could not wait to flee.)
Our humanness betrays us to the cage
Within whose limits each is free to walk,
But where no one can hear our prayers or rage
And none of us can break the walls to talk.

Exiled by years, by death no dream conceals,
By worlds that must remain unvisited,
And by the wounds that growing never heals,
We are as solitary as the dead,
Wanting to king it in that perfect land
We make and understand.
And in this world whose pattern is unmade,
Phases of splintered light and shapeless sand,
We shatter through our motions and evade
Whatever hand might reach and touch our hand.

Newdigate Prize, Oxford, 1953

EXILE (1968)

A boy who played and talked and read with me
Fell from a maple tree.

I loved her, but I told her I did not,
And wept, and then forgot.

I walked the streets where I was born and grew,
And all the streets were new.

Elegy for Wesley Wells

Against the clapboards and the window panes
The loud March whines with rain and heavy wind,
In dark New Hampshire where his widow wakes.
She cannot sleep. The familiar length is gone.
I think across the clamorous Atlantic
To where the farm lies hard against the foot
Of Ragged Mountain, underneath Kearsarge.
The storm and hooded wind of equinox
Contend against New England's bolted door
Across the sea and set the signals out
Eastport to Block Island.
I speak his name against the beating sea.

The farmer dead, his horse will run to fat,
Go stiff and lame and whinny from his stall,
His dogs will whimper through the webby barn,
Where spiders close his tools in a pale gauze
And wait for flies. The nervous woodchuck now
Will waddle plumply through the garden weeds,
Eating wild peas as if he owned the land,
And the fat hedgehog pick the apple trees.
When next October's frosts harden the ground
And fasten in the year's catastrophe,
The farm will come undone—
The farmer dead, and deep in his plowed earth.

Before the Civil War the land was used,
And railroads came to all the villages;
Before the war, a man with land was rich;
He cleared a dozen or two dozen acres,
Burning the timber, stacking up the stones,
And cultivated all his acreage
And planted it to vegetables to sell.
But then the war took off the hired men;
The fields grew up, to weeds and bushes first,
And then the fields were thick with ashy pine.
The faces of prosperity and luck
Turned westward with the railroads from New England.
Poverty settled, and the first went off,
Leaving their fathers' forty-acre farms,
To Manchester and Nashua and Lowell,
And traded the Lyceum for the block.
Now the white houses fell, among the wars,
From eighteen sixty-five, for eighty years,
The Georgian firmness sagged, and the paint chipped,
And the white houses rotted to the ground.
Great growths of timber felled grew up again
On what had once been cultivated land,
On lawns and meadows, and from cellarholes.
Deep in the forest now, half covered up,
The reddened track of an abandoned railroad
Heaved in the frosts, in roots of the tall pines;
A locomotive stood
Like a strange rock, red as the fallen needles.

The farmer worked from four and milking time
To nine o'clock and shutting up the hens.
The heavy winter fattened him: The spring
Required his work and left his muscles lame.
By nineteen forty, only the timid young

Remained to plough or sell.
He was the noble man in the sick place.

I number out the virtues that are dead,
Remembering the soft consistent voice
And bone that showed in each deliberate word.
I walk along old England's crowded shore
Where storm has driven everyone inside.
Soon I will leave, to cross the hilly sea
And walk again among familiar hills
In dark New Hampshire where his widow wakes.
The length of Wesley Wells, old man I loved,
Today was carried to the lettered plain
In Andover
While March bent down the cemetery trees.

My Son My Executioner

My son, my executioner,
    I take you in my arms,
Quiet and small and just astir
    And whom my body warms.

Sweet death, small son, our instrument
    Of immortality,
Your cries and hungers document
    Our bodily decay.

We twenty-five and twenty-two,
    Who seemed to live forever,
Observe enduring life in you
    And start to die together.

THE SLEEPING GIANT

a hill in Connecticut

The whole day long, under the walking sun
That poised an eye on me from its high floor,
Holding my toy beside the clapboard house
I looked for him, the summer I was four.

I was afraid the waking arm would break
From the loose earth and rub against his eyes
A fist of trees, and the whole country tremble
In the exultant labor of his rise;

Then he with giant steps in the small streets
Would stagger, cutting off the sky, to seize
The roofs from house and home because we had
Covered his shape with dirt and planted trees;

And then kneel down and rip with fingernails
A trench to pour the enemy Atlantic
Into our basin, and the water rush,
With the streets full and all the voices frantic.

That was the summer I expected him.
Later the high and watchful sun instead
Walked low behind the house, and school began,
And winter pulled a sheet over his head.

JE SUIS UNE TABLE

It has happened suddenly,
by surprise, in an arbor,
or while drinking good coffee,
after speaking, or before,

that I dumbly inhabit
a density; in language,
there is nothing to stop it,
for nothing retains an edge.

Simple ignorance presents,
later, words for a function,
but it is common pretense
of speech, by a convention,

and there is nothing at all
but inner silence, nothing
to relieve on principle
now this intense thickening.

DANCERS

Bowing he asks her the favor;
    Blushing she answers she will;
Waltzing they turn through the ballroom
      Swift in their skill.

Blinder than buffers of autumn,
    Deaf but to music's delight,
They dance like the puppets of music
      All through the night.

Out of the ball they come dancing
    And into the marketing day,
Waltzing through ignorant traffic,
      Bound to be gay.

They slacken and stoop, they are tired,
    They walk in a weather of pain;

Now wrinkles dig into their faces,
    Harsh as the rain.

They walk by identical houses
    And enter the one that they know.
They are old, and their children like houses
    Stand in a row.

By the Exeter River

"What is it you're mumbling, old Father, my Dad?
Come drink up your soup and I'll put you to bed."

"By the Exeter River, by the river, I said."

"Stop dreaming of rivers, old Father, my Dad,
Or save all your dreaming till you're tucked in bed."

"It was cold by the river. We came in a sled."

"It's colder to think of, old Father, my Dad,
Than blankets and bolsters and pillows of bed."

"We took off his dress and the cap from his head."

"Outside? In the winter? Old Father, my Dad,
What can you be thinking? Let's get off to bed."

"And Sally, poor Sally I reckon is dead."

"Was she your old sweetheart, old Father, my Dad?
Now lean on my shoulder and come up to bed."

"We drowned the baby. I remember we did."

T. R.

Granted that what we summon is absurd:
Mustaches and the stick, the New York fake
In cowboy costume grinning for the sake
Of cameras that always just occurred;
Granted that his Rough Riders fought a third-
Rate army badly run, and had to make
Headlines to fatten Hearst; that one can take
Trust-busting not precisely at its word;

Robinson, who was drunken and unread,
Received a letter with a White House frank.
To court the Muse, T.R. might well have killed her,
And had her stuffed, yet here this mountebank
Chose to belaurel Robinson instead
Of famous men like Richard Watson Gilder.

THE HOLE

He could remember that in the past, seven months ago,
and much of the time for fifty years before that,
his body walked without pain. He breathed in and out
without knowing that he was breathing, and he woke up
each day to the day's process
as if it were nothing to wake and dress in the morning.

When the doctor confided that his body would flake away
like a statue of rust, he looked into the long mirror
at his own strong shoulders with the skin smooth over them
and at his leg muscles which continued to be firm.
He announced to his body,
"We have resolved, and we will hold to our purpose."

Then eyes faded, limbs dwindled, skin puckered, lungs filled.
He dug himself into the private hole of his dying
and when he talked to his wife his voice came from a distance
as if he had married his pain, and lived alone with her.
He kept himself cold
and lay and twisted and slept, until nobody called him.

RELIGIOUS ARTICLES

By the road to church, Shaker Village
glints with prosperity in an age
lacking Shakers. New signs hosannah:
RELIGIOUS ARTICLES RELIGIEUX,
and a new Ford waits to be drawn for,
in the Bishop's Fund, in November.

"I come to the garden alone," where
old women's voices strain and quiver
to the organ one of them has played
for sixty years. The house which was made
for the farm Sunday lacks a preacher.
Ten women, two old men, and I hear

a boy in the pulpit measure out
a brutal sermon. His sky-blue suit
took the diploma from high school just
two months ago. The watch on his wrist
his cousin gave him ticks the time he
must wait for college, cloth, and city.

Among the dead of this village church
the old women's voices use the pitch
of the pumping organ to lean on;
light comes through the trees and the dark green

curtains speckled with holes, and light hits
the frayed red cloth of the cushioned seats.

I stand among the relics of childhood
and the century before. My dead
crowd into the pew; I hear their thin
voices complain in a reedy hymn
of parch in the garden, of hunger
for rest, and of the words that I hear:

"We who do not exist make noises
only in you. Your illusion says
that we who are cheated and broken
croon our words to the living again.
You must not believe in anything;
you who feel cheated are crooning."

The Foundations of American Industry

In the Ford plant
at Ypsilanti
men named for their
fathers work at steel
machines named Bliss,
Olaffson, Smith-Grieg,
and Safety.

In the Ford plant
the generators
move quickly on
belts, a thousand now
an hour. New men
move to the belt when
the shift comes.

For the most part
the men are young, and
go home to their
Fords, and drive around,
or watch TV,
sleep, and then go work,
toward payday;

when they walk home
they walk on sidewalks
marked W
P A 38;
their old men made
them, and they walk on
their fathers.

COPS AND ROBBERS

When I go west you wear a marshal's star,
    Persistent as a curse;
    And when I steal a purse
A note inside says, "I know who you are."

In England I am awfully on my guard.
    With a new mustache I live
    In Soho as a spiv
Until you drop around from Scotland Yard.

In Paris with a black beret I sell
    Disgusting pictures to
    Americans; but you
Appear disguised among my clientele.

In far Antarctica with Admiral Byrd
    I feel secure, though chilly,

Till toward me with a billy
An outsize penguin lumbers from the herd.

SESTINA

Hang it all, Ezra Pound, there is only the one sestina,
Or so I thought before, always supposing
The subject of them invariably themselves.
That is not true. Perhaps they are nearly a circle,
And they tell their motifs like party conversation,
Formally repetitious, wilfully dull,

But who are we to call recurrence dull?
It is not exact recurrence that makes a sestina,
But a compromise between a conversation
And absolute repetition. It comes from supposing
That there is a meaning to the almost-circle,
And that laws of proportion speak of more than themselves.

I think of the types of men who have loved themselves,
Who studious of their faces made them dull
To find them subtle; for the nearly-a-circle,
This is the danger. The introvert sestina
May lose its voice by childishly supposing
It holds a hearer with self-conversation.

When we are bound to a tedious conversation,
We pay attention to the words themselves
Until they lose their sense, perhaps supposing
Such nonsense is at very least less dull.
Yet if the tongue is held by a sestina,
It affirms not words but the shape of the unclosed circle.

The analogy: not the precise circle,
Nor the loose patching of a conversation
Describes the repetition of a sestina;
Predictable, yet not repeating themselves
Exactly, they are like life, and hardly dull,
And not destroyed by critical supposing.

Since there is nothing precise (always supposing)
Consider the spiraling, circular, not full-circle
As the type of existence, the dull and never dull,
Predictable, general movement of conversation,
Where things seem often more, slightly, than themselves,
And make us wait for the coming, like a sestina.

And so we name the sestina's subject, supposing
Our lives themselves dwindle, an incomplete circle;
About which, conversation is not dull.

WAITING ON THE CORNERS

Glass, air, ice, light,
and winter cold.
They stand on all the corners,
waiting alone, or in
groups that talk like the air
moving branches. It
is Christmas, and a red dummy
laughs in the window
of a store. Although
the trolleys come,
no one boards them,
but everyone moves
up and down, stamping his feet,

so unemployed.
They are talking, each of them,
but it is sticks and stones
that hear them,
their plans,
exultations,
and memories of the old time.
The words fly out, over
the roads and onto
the big, idle farms, on the hills,
forests, and rivers
of America, to mix into silence
of glass, air, ice, light,
and winter cold.

"MARAT'S DEATH"

Charlotte, "the angel of assas-
sination," is unrelaxed.
She is not deep but she is tall.

Marat is dead. The people
of France will endure his death,
l'ami du peuple and no man.

Charlotte, the will begins to
revise you to leather. How
volition hurts the skin of girls!

Marat had skin which boiled like
water on a stove. His wet
and cruel skin has one wound more.

Charlotte is standing naked
and simple above the bed.
Her body is an alphabet.

Edvard Munch

"THE KISS"

The backs twist with the kiss
and the mouth which is the hurt
and the green depth of it
holds plainly the hour.

The aim loses its lie.
We are victims, and we shift
in the cloyed wind, the dark
harm. No, in the thick

of rubbed numbness, and we
are the winter of the air,
and the not-nothing, blurred,
bound, motion declared.

At night, wound in the clothes
of the groomed and unendured,
where the five hands of wire
rasp, hurt me, and fold,

we love. Love is a kiss
which adheres like the feet
of a green lizard to walls
whole days, and is gone.

Edvard Munch

"BETWEEN THE CLOCK AND THE BED"

In the yellow light, an old man
stands between the clock and the bed.
While he paints the picture, this old
painter lives among clock and bed
as if three elderly brothers
still inhabited the house where
they were born. But the grandfather's
clock annoys the painter; it keeps on
measuring its pendulum back
and forth, insistent, repeating
itself as if he heard nothing.
He becomes angry, and decides
to shut the clock up. He thinks: What
can I use, in this furnished room?
He remembers putting a gun
among his linen handkerchiefs
but when he looks, it is not there.
Perhaps it is in the locker
by the wall. He kneels beside it
but the clasps are too difficult.
He feels extremely tired. He crawls
up to the narrow bed, and sleeps
in the clock's light which is yellow.

Edvard Munch

CHRIST CHURCH MEADOWS, OXFORD

Often I saw, as on my balcony
   I stirred the afternoon into my tea,
Enameled swards descending to the *Thames*,
   Called *Isis* here, and flowers that were gems,
Cattle in herds, and great senescent trees,

Through which, as Pope predicted, ran the breeze.
Ad sinistram, where limpid *Cherwell* flows,
  Often I saw the punts of gallant beaux
Who sang like shepherds to each gentle love
  Quaint tales of Trojan warriors to prove
That loving Maidens are rewarded here
  With bastards and with pints of watered beer.
Here too I saw my countrymen at large,
  Expending *Kodachrome* upon a barge.
From chauffeured *Car*, or touring *Omnibus*,
  They leered at me, calling me "them," not "us."
A jutting woman came to me and said,
  "Your *Highness*, can those big white geese be fed?"
"*Yankee* go home," I snarled. "Of course the *Swans*,
  As the *Bard* puts it, are reserved for *Dons*."
She fainted then, beside two *Christ Church* porters,
  Who cast her, as I told them, on the waters.

CHRISTMAS EVE IN WHITNEYVILLE

December, and the closing of the year;
The momentary carolers complete
Their Christmas Eves, and quickly disappear
Into their houses on each lighted street.

Each car is put away in each garage;
Each husband home from work, to celebrate,
Has closed his house around him like a cage,
And wedged the tree until the tree stood straight.

Tonight you lie in Whitneyville again,
Near where you lived, and near the woods or farms
Which Eli Whitney settled with the men
Who worked at mass-producing firearms.

The main street, which was nothing after all
Except a school, a stable, and two stores,
Was improvised and individual,
Picking its way alone, among the wars.

Now Whitneyville is like the other places,
Ranch houses stretching flat beyond the square,
Same stores and movie, same composite faces
Speaking the language of the public air.

Old houses of brown shingle still surround
This graveyard where you wept when you were ten
And helped to set a coffin in the ground.
You left a friend from school behind you then,

And now return, a man of fifty-two.
Talk to the boy. Tell him about the years
When Whitneyville quadrupled, and how you
And all his friends went on to make careers,

Had cars as long as hayracks, boarded planes
For Rome or Paris where the pace was slow
And took the time to think how yearly gains,
Profit and volume made the business grow.

"The things I had to miss," you said last week,
"Or thought I had to, take my breath away."
You propped yourself on pillows, where your cheek
Was hollow, stubbled lightly with new gray.

This love is jail; another sets us free.
Tonight the houses and their noise distort
The thin rewards of solidarity.
The houses lean together for support.

The noises fail, and lights go on upstairs.
The men and women are undressing now
To go to sleep. They put their clothes on chairs
To take them up again. I think of how,

All over Whitneyville, when midnight comes,
They lie together and are quieted,
To sleep as children sleep, who suck their thumbs,
Cramped in the narrow rumple of each bed.

They will not have unpleasant thoughts tonight.
They make their houses jails, and they will take
No risk of freedom for the appetite,
Or knowledge of it, when they are awake.

The lights go out and it is Christmas Day.
The stones are white, the grass is black and deep.
I will go back and leave you here to stay
Where the dark houses harden into sleep.

2   The Musk Ox

The Long River

The musk ox smells
in his long head
my boat coming. When
I feel him there,
intent, heavy,

the oars make wings
in the white night,
and deep woods are close
on either side
where trees darken.

I rowed past towns
in their black sleep
to come here. I passed
the northern grass
and cold mountains.

The musk ox moves
when the boat stops,
in hard thickets. Now
the wood is dark
with old pleasures.

The Snow

Snow is in the oak.
Behind the thick, whitening

air which the wind drives,
the weight of the sun
presses the snow
on the pane of my window.

I remember snows and my walking
through their first fall in cities,
asleep or drunk
with the slow, desperate falling.
The snow blurs in my eyes
with other snows.

Snow is what must
come down, even if it struggles
to stay in the air with the strength
of the wind. Like an old man,
whatever I touch I turn
to the story of death.

Snow is what fills
the oak, and what covers
the grass and the bare garden.
Snow is what reverses
the sidewalk and the lawn
into the substance of whiteness.

So the watcher sleeps himself
back to the baby's eyes.
The tree, the breast, and the floor
are limbs of him, and from
his eyes he extends a skin
which grows over the world.

The baby is what must
have fallen, like snow. He resisted,

the way the old man
struggles inside the airy tent
to keep on breathing.
Birth is the fear of death.

Snow is what melts.
I cannot open the door
to the cycles of water.
The sun has withdrawn itself
and the snow keeps falling,
and something will always be falling.

THE FARM

Standing on top of the hay
in a good sweat,
I felt the wind from the lake
dry on my back,
where the chaff
grew like the down on my face.

At night on the bare boards
of the kitchen,
we stood while the old man
in his nightshirt gummed
the stale crusts
of his bread and milk.

Up on the gray hill
behind the barn, the stones
had fallen away
where the Penacook marked
a way to go
south from the narrow river.

By the side of the lake
my dead uncle's rowboat rots
in heavy bushes.
Slim pickerel glint
in the water. Black horned pout
doze on the bottom.

THE MOON

A woman who lived
in a tree caught
the moon in a kettle.

The wind on the roof
of the tree thumped
while she built her fire.

She boiled it down
to a flat bean
to set on her plate.

She swallowed the moon
and the moon grew
like a child inside her.

When the wind flew away
she mounted
the steps of the air

to bear the moon
on a dark bed
in the house of the night.

She nurses him
while the wind perches
like a heavy bird

in the void branches
of a tree, beside
a cold kettle.

THE CHILD

He lives among a dog,
a tricycle, and a friend.
Nobody owns him.

He walks by himself, beside
the black pool, in the cave
where icicles of rock

rain hard water,
and the walls are rough
with the light of stone.

He hears low talking
without words.
The hand of a wind touches him.

He walks until he is tired
or somebody calls him.
He leaves right away.

When he plays with his friend
he stops suddenly
to hear the black water.

The Poem

It discovers by night
what the day hid from it.
Sometimes it turns itself
into an animal.
In summer it takes long walks
by itself where meadows
fold back from ditches.
Once it stood still
in a quiet row of machines.
Who knows
what it is thinking?

Wells

I lived in a dry well
under the rank grass of a meadow.

A white ladder leaned out of it
but I was afraid of the sounds

of animals grazing.
I crouched by the wall ten years

until the circle of a woman's darkness
moved over mine like a mouth.

The ladder broke out in leaves
and fruit hung from the branches.

I climbed to the meadow grass.
I drink from the well of cattle.

An Airstrip in England, 1960

It is a lost road into the air.
It is a desert
among sugar beets.
The tiny wings
of the Spitfires of nineteen forty-one
flake in the mud of the Channel.

Near the road a brick pillbox
totters under a load of grass,
where Home Guards waited
in the white fogs of the invasion winter.

Good night, old ruined war.

In Poland the wind rides on a jagged wall.
Smoke rises from the stones; no, it is mist.

New Hampshire

A bear sleeps in a cellarhole; pine needles
heap over a granite doorstep; a well brims
with acorns and the broken leaves of an oak
which grew where an anvil rusted in a forge.

Inside an anvil, inside a bear, inside a leaf,
a bark of rust grows on the tree of a gas pump;
EAT signs gather like leaves in the shallow
cellars of diners; a wildcat waits for deer

on the roof of a car. Blacktop buckled by frost
starts goldenrod from the highway. Fat honey bees
meander among raspberries, where a quarrel
of vines crawls into the spilled body of a plane.

Self-Portrait as a Bear

Here is a fat animal, a bear
that is partly a dodo.
Ridiculous wings hang at his shoulders
as if they were collarbones
while he plods in the bad brickyards
at the edge of the city, smiling
and eating flowers. He eats them
because he loves them
because they are beautiful
because they love him.
It is eating flowers which makes him so fat.
He carries his huge stomach
over the gutters of damp leaves
in the parking lots in October,
but inside that paunch
he knows there are fields of lupine
and meadows of mustard and poppy.
He encloses sunshine.
Winds bend the flowers
in combers across the valley,
birds hang on the stiff wind,
at night there are showers, and the sun
lifts through a haze every morning
of the summer in the stomach.

Orange Knee Socks

When he lies in the night away from her,
the backs of his eyelids burn.
He turns in the darkness as if it were an oven.
The flesh parches and he lies awake
thinking of everything wrong.

In the morning when he goes to meet her,
his heart struggles at his ribs
like an animal trapped in its burrow.
Then he sees her running to meet him,
red-faced with hurry and cold.

She stumbles over the snow.
Her knees above orange knee socks
bob in a froth of the hems
of skirt and coat and petticoat.
Her eyes have not shut all night.

SLEEPING

The avenue rises toward a city of white marble.
I am not meeting anyone. The capitol is empty.
I enter the dome of sleep.
. . .
I was lying on the sofa to rest, to sleep
a few minutes, perhaps.
I felt my body sag into the hole of sleep.
All at once I was awake and frightened.
My own death was drifting near me
in the middle of life. The strong body
blurred and diminished into the waters.
The flesh floated away.
. . .
The shadow is a tight passage
that no one will be spared
who goes down
to the deep well.
In sleep, something remembers.
Three times since I woke
from the first sleep,
it has drunk that water.
Awake, it is still sleeping.

"King and Queen"

As they grew older,
the land which had grown wheat
washed down the hill,
and the river
carried the land into the sea.

The priest with the horned
mask, who brought meat
from the altar,
turned into a bird
and flew among mountains.

The people of the markets,
who touched their heads to the ground,
changed into clumps of weed
among the gutters
of the bare hill.

The King and Queen rule
over the dark nation
of thrones. As slowly
as a river builds a delta,
they have become still.

Henry Moore

"Reclining Figure"

Then the knee of the wave
turned to stone.

By the cliff of her flank
I anchored,

in the darkness of harbors
laid-by.

   Henry Moore

Digging

One midnight, after a day when lilies
lift themselves out of the ground while you watch them,
and you come into the house at dark
your fingers grubby with digging, your eyes
vague with the pleasure of digging,

let a wind raised from the South
climb through your bedroom window, lift you in its arms
—you have become as small as a seed—
and carry you out of the house, over the black garden,
spinning and fluttering,

and drop you in cracked ground.
The dirt will be cool, rough to your clasped skin
like a man you have never known.
You will die into the ground
in a dead sleep, surrendered to water.

You will wake suffering
a widening pain in your side, a breach
gapped in your tight ribs
where a green shoot struggles to lift itself upward
through the tomb of your dead flesh

to the sun, to the air of your garden
where you will blossom
in the shape of your own self, thoughtless
with flowers, speaking
to bees, in the language of green and yellow, white and red.

39

THE PILOT OF 1918

He discovers himself on an old airfield.
He thinks he was there before,
but rain has washed out the lettering of a sign.
A single biplane, all struts and wires,
stands in the long grass and wildflowers.
He pulls himself into the narrow cockpit
although his muscles are stiff
and sits like an egg in a nest of canvas.
He sees that the machine gun has rusted.
The glass over the instruments
has broken, and the red arrows are gone
from his gas gauge and his altimeter.
When he looks up, his propeller is turning,
although no one was there to snap it.
He lets out the throttle. The engine catches
and the propeller spins into the wind.
He bumps over holes in the grass,
and he remembers to pull back on the stick.
He rises from the land in a high bounce
which gets higher, and suddenly he is flying again.
He feels the old fear, and rising over the fields
the old gratitude. In the distance, circling
in a beam of late sun like birds migrating,
there are the wings of a thousand biplanes.

LETTER TO AN ENGLISH POET

Your letter describes
    what you see from your window. You chose,
among the council
    houses and gray cities, to observe

a destroyed abbey
    whose stones you touch for their proportion,
the lines of a mind
    although the mind is dead. I write you

from an old attic
    where the green of maples like a storm
cuts off my winter
    prospect of square blocks of the same house.

Maples are the past,
    for the settlers liked a good shade tree.
On the older blocks,
    ugly frame houses like ours recall

the German merchants
    who left their country to avoid war.
Rural Michigan
    took them in. It is sentimental

to love their houses
    for being burly like them, and trees
too are evasions.
    In America, the past exists

in the library.
    It is not the wind on the old stone.
The wind blows in you
    like power, and the blades of the mill turn.

Unmeasured voices
    shed lies in their vying to utter
like leaves from maples.
    Yet the loose roads and the twelve seasons

allow us to move.
    It is what we like most in ourselves.
Most of your country
    envies our worst houses, and would sell

abbeys if they could
    to Americans who collect. Some
here try to construct
    a new abbey without architects

or an idea,
    except to represent the shapeless
shape of a nation.
    All of them scatter with the dry leaves.

But the best of us
    have resembled instead the raiding
millionaires; without
    history, we pillage history.

Although museums
    glass-in our inheritance, how else
shall we inherit?
    Without parents we adopt the world.

STUMP

1

Today they cut down the oak.
Strong men climbed with ropes
in the brittle tree.
The exhaust of a gasoline saw
was blue in the branches.

The oak had been dead a year.
I remember the great sails of its branches
rolling out green, a hundred and twenty feet up,
and acorns thick on the lawn.
Nine cities of squirrels lived in that tree.

Yet I was happy that it was coming down.
"Let it come down!" I kept saying to myself
with a joy that was strange to me.
Though the oak was the shade of old summers,
I loved the guttural saw.

2

By night a bare trunk stands up fifteen feet
and cords of firewood press
on the twiggy frozen grass of the yard.
One man works every afternoon for a week
to cut the trunk gradually down.

Bluish stains spread through the wood
and make it harder to cut.
He says they are the nails of a trapper
who dried his pelts on the oak
when badgers dug in the lawn.

Near the ground he hacks for two days,
knuckles scraping the stiff snow.
His chain saw breaks three teeth.
He cannot make the trunk smooth. He leaves
one night after dark.

3

Roots stiffen under the ground
and the frozen street, coiled around pipes and wires.
The stump is a platform of blond wood

in the gray winter. It is nearly level
with the snow that covers the little garden around it.
It is a door into the underground of old summers,
but if I bend down to it, I am lost
in crags and buttes of a harsh landscape
that goes on forever. When snow melts
the wood darkens into the ground;
rain and thawed snow move deeply into the stump,
backward along the disused tunnels.

    4
The edges of the trunk turn black.
In the middle there is a pale overlay,
like a wash of chalk on darkness.
The desert of the winter
has moved inside.
I do not step on it now; I am used to it,
like a rock, or a bush that does not grow.

There is a sailing ship
beached in the cove of a small island
where the warm water is turquoise.
The hulk leans over, full of rain and sand,
and shore flowers grow from it.
Then it is under full sail in the Atlantic,
on a blue day, heading for the island.

She has planted sweet alyssum
in the holes where the wood was rotten.
It grows thick, it bulges
like flowers contending from a tight vase.
Now the stump sinks downward into its roots
with a cargo of rain
and white blossoms that last into October.

In the Kitchen of the Old House

In the kitchen of the old house, late,
I was making some coffee
   and I daydreamed sleepily of friends.
Then the dream turned. I waited.
   I walked alone all day in the town
where I was born. It was cold,
   a Saturday in January
when nothing happens. The streets
   changed as the sky grew dark around me.
The lamps in the small houses
   had tassels on them, and the black cars
at the curb were old and square.
   A ragman passed with his horse, their breaths
blooming like white peonies,
   when I turned into a darker street
and I recognized the house
   from snapshots. I felt as separate
as if the city and the house
   were closed inside a globe which I shook
to make it snow. No sooner
   did I think of snow, but snow started
to fill the heavy darkness
   around me. It reflected the glare
of the streetlight as it fell
   melting on the warmth of the sidewalk
and frozen on frozen grass.
   Then I heard out of the dark the sound
of steps on the bare cement
   in a familiar rhythm. Under
the streetlight, bent to the snow,
   hatless, younger than I, so young that
I was not born, my father
   walked home to his bride and his supper.

A shout gathered inside me
   like a cold wind, to break the rhythm,
to keep him from entering
   that heavy door—but I stood under
a tree, closed in by the snow,
   and did not shout, to tell what happened
in twenty years, in winter,
   when his early death grew inside him
like snow piling on the grass.
   He opened the door and met the young
woman who waited for him.

THE DAYS

Ten years ago this minute, he possibly sat
in the sunlight, in Connecticut, in an old chair;
a car may have stopped in the street outside;
he may have turned his head; his ear may have itched.
Since it was September, he probably saw
single leaves dropping from the maple tree.
If he was reading, he turned back to his book,
and perhaps the smell of roses in a pot
came together with the smell of cheese sandwiches
and the smell of a cigarette
smoked by his brother who was not dead then.

The moments of that day dwindled
to the small notations of clocks,
and the day busily became another day,
and another, and today, when his hand moves
from his ear which still itches
to rest on his leg, it is marked with the passage
of ten years. Suddenly he has the idea
that thousands and thousands of his days

lie stacked into the ground
like leaves, or like that pressure of green
which turns into coal in a million years.

Though leaves rot, or leaves burn in the gutter;
though the complications of this morning's breakfast
dissolve in faint shudders of light
at a great distance, he continues to daydream
that the past is a country under the ground
where the days practice their old habits
over and over, as faint and persistent
as cigarette smoke in an airless room.
He wishes he could travel there like a tourist
and photograph the unseizable days
in the sunlight, in Connecticut, in an old chair.

SWAN

1
December, nightfall at three-thirty.
I climb Mill Hill
past hawthorn and wild cherry,
mist in the hedgerows.
Smoke blows
from the orange edges of fire
working the wheat
stubble. "Putting
the goodness back,
into the soil."

2
Driving; the fog
matted around the headlights;
suddenly, a thudding

white shape in the whiteness,
running huge and frightened, lost
from its slow stream . . .

   3

The windmill drew up to power
the dark underneath it
through tunnels like the roots of a beech
up from the center of the earth.
Fire breaks out in the fields
because the wheel of the mill
does not turn.

Fog stacked in the hedges.

The windmill
flies, clattering its huge wings, to the swamp.
I make out cliffs of the church,
houses drifting like glaciers.

   4

I envy the man hedging and ditching,
trimming the hawthorn, burning branches
while wasps circle in the smoke of their nest,
clearing a mile of lane, patches of soot
like closed holes to a cave of fire,
the man in his cottage
who smokes his pipe in the winter, in summer
digging his garden in ten o'clock light,
the man grafted entirely to rain and air,
stained dark
by years of hedging and ditching.

5

The close-packed surface of the roots
of a root-bound plant
when I break the pot away,
the edges white
and sleek as a swan...

THE MAN IN THE DEAD MACHINE

High on a slope in New Guinea
the Grumman Hellcat
lodges among bright vines
as thick as arms. In nineteen forty-three,
the clenched hand of a pilot
glided it here
where no one has ever been.

In the cockpit the helmeted
skeleton sits
upright, held
by dry sinews at neck
and shoulder, and by webbing
that straps the pelvic cross
to the cracked
leather of the seat, and the breastbone
to the canvas cover
of the parachute.

Or say that the shrapnel
missed me, I flew
back to the carrier, and every morning
take the train, my pale
hands on a black case, and sit
upright, held
by the firm webbing.

3

I Am the Fox

The Alligator Bride

The clock of my days winds down.
The cat eats sparrows outside my window.
Once, she brought me a small rabbit
which we devoured together, under
the Empire table
while the men shrieked
repossessing the gold umbrella.

Now the beard on my clock turns white.
My cat stares into dark corners
missing her gold umbrella.
She is in love
with the Alligator Bride.

Ah, the tiny fine white
teeth! The Bride, propped on her tail
in white lace
stares from the holes
of her eyes. Her stuck-open mouth
laughs at minister and people.

On bare new wood
fourteen tomatoes,
a dozen ears of corn,
six bottles of white wine,
a melon,
a cat,

broccoli,
and the Alligator Bride.

The color of bubble gum,
the consistency of petroleum jelly,
wickedness oozes
from the palm of my left hand.
My cat licks it.
I watch the Alligator Bride.

Big houses like shabby boulders
hold themselves tight
in gelatin.
I am unable to daydream.
The sky is a gun aimed at me.
I pull the trigger.
The skull of my promises
leans in a black closet, gapes
with its good mouth
for a teat to suck.

A bird flies back and forth
in my house that is covered by gelatin
and the cat leaps at it,
missing. Under the Empire table
the Alligator Bride
lies in her bridal shroud.
My left hand
leaks on the Chinese carpet.

SEW

She kneels on the floor, snip snip
in the church of scraps,

tissue like moth's wings,
pins in the cushion of her mouth,
basting and hemming
until it stands up like a person
made out of whole cloth.

Still, I lie folded
on the bolt in the dark warehouse,
dreaming my shapes.

THE COAL FIRE

A coal fire burned in a basket grate.
We lay in front of it
while ash collected on the firebrick
like snow. The fire was tight and small
and endured
when we added a chunk every hour.
The new piece blazed at first
from the bulky shadow of fire,
turning us bright and dark.
Old coals red at the center
warmed us all night.
If we watched all night
we could not tell the new coal
when it flaked into ash.

THE BLUE WING

She is all around me
like a rainy day,
and though I walk bareheaded
I am not wet. I walk

on a bare path
singing light songs
about women.

A blue wing tilts at the edge of the sea.

The wreck of the small
airplane sleeps
drifted to the high-tide line,
tangled in seaweed, green
glass from the sea.

The tiny skeleton inside
remembers the falter of engines,
a cry without
answer, the long dying
into
and out of the sea.

WOOLWORTH'S

My whole life has led me here.

Daisies made out of resin,
hairnets and motor oil,
Barbie dolls, green
garden chairs,
and forty-one brands of deodorant.

Three hundred years ago
I was hedging and ditching in Devon.
I lacked freedom of worship,
and freedom to trade molasses
for rum, for slaves, for molasses.

"I will sail to Massachusetts
to build the Kingdom
of Heaven on Earth!"

The side of a hill
swung open.
It was Woolworth's!

I followed this vision to Boston.

THE REPEATED SHAPES

I have visited men's rooms
in several bars
with the rows
of urinals like old men
and the six-sided odor

of disinfectant.
I have felt the sadness
of the small white tiles,
the repeated shapes
and the unavoidable whiteness.

They are my uncles,
these old men
who are only plumbing,
who throb with tears all night
and doze in the morning.

CREWCUTS

Men with crewcuts
are impossible, like
ice shows. In airport bars, all winter,
holding standby tickets,
they wait for a plane into the next territory
and confess
to puzzlement
over the Oriental mind.

Later, they want to drop eggs on the Russians.
Later, they want
to keep violence out of the streets
by installing a machine-gun nest on every corner.
When they talk about women, they are discussing
a subjugated race
rumored to have cached away
huge quantities of ammunition.
They lounge on the porch of the Planters' Club,
in darkest Africa,
pith helmets over their crewcuts, drinking pink gins,
and laughing at jokes about the stupid natives,

while the tom-toms start to beat
in a million kitchens,
and the sky lightens
with a storm of Russians with hair
down to their shoulders,
as inscrutable as the Chinese,
as merciless
as women.

TALL WOMEN

If I said, "Tall women,
shut in your dark
houses, an enormous
tiger lily splits
the roof of each house

in the night, and arranges
the moon to itself,
and only withdraws
just at dawn,"
you would smile,

and think about bright
flowers, and forget
the money and the shopping,
but if I went on, "I only
see your lilies grow

in my happy sleep,
because you have made no gardens
in your blocks of houses
for flowers that come
in oblivious night,"

you would suddenly
cry, or pick up a book,
or walk by yourselves
all night long
on the white sidewalks.

Walking back to the farm from the depot,
Riley slapped flies with his tail.
Twilight. Crickets scraped
in the green standing hay by the road.
The voice of my grandfather
spoke through a motion of gnats.
I held his hand. I entered
the sway of a horse.
                  At the brown table
I propped books on each other.
All morning in the room my skin
took into itself small discs
of coolness.
Then I walked in the cut hayfield
by the barn, and lay alone
in the little valley of noon heat,
in the village of little sounds.
Grasshoppers
tickled my neck and I let them.
I turned into the other world
that lives in the air. Clouds passed
like motes.
              My grandfather
clanked up the road on his mowing machine,
behind Riley dark with sweat.
I ran to the barn
and carried a bucket of water
to the loose jaws working
in the dark stall. For lunch
I sliced an onion.
Then we raked hay into mounds
and my grandfather pitched it up
where I tucked it in place on the hayrack.

My skin dried in the sun. Wind
caught me in clover.
The slow ride
back to the barn, I dangled
legs over split-pole rails
while my grandfather talked forever
in a voice that wrapped me around
with love that asked for nothing.
In my room I drank well water
that whitened the sides of a tumbler
and coolness gathered like dark
inside my stomach.
                This morning
I walk to the shaded bedroom and lean
on the drop-leaf table.
                The table hums
a song to itself without sense
and I hear the voice of the heaving
ribs of Riley
and grasshoppers
haying the fields of the air.

MOUNT KEARSARGE

Great blue mountain! Ghost.
I look at you
from the porch of the farmhouse
where I watched you all summer
as a boy. Steep sides, narrow flat
patch on top—
you are clear to me
like the memory of one day.
Blue! Blue!
The top of the mountain floats

61

in haze.
I will not rock on this porch
when I am old. I turn my back on you,
Kearsarge, I close
my eyes, and you rise inside me,
blue ghost.

The Young Watch Us

The young girls look up
as we walk past the line at the movie,
and go back to examining their fingernails.

Their boyfriends are combing their hair,
and chew gum
as if they meant to insult us.

Today we made love all day.
I look at you. You are smiling at the sidewalk,
dear wrinkled face.

Gold

Pale gold of the walls, gold
of the centers of daisies, yellow roses
pressing from a clear bowl. All day
we lay on the bed, my hand
stroking the deep
gold of your thighs and your back.
We slept and woke
entering the golden room together,
lay down in it breathing
quickly, then

slowly again,
caressing and dozing, your hand sleepily
touching my hair now.

We made in those days
tiny identical rooms inside our bodies
which the men who uncover our graves
will find in a thousand years,
shining and whole.

WATERS

A rock drops in a bucket;
quick fierce
waves exhaust themselves
against the tin circle.

A rock in a pool;
a fast

splash, and ripples move out
interrupted by weeds.

The lake enormous and calm;
a stone falls;
for an hour the surface
moves, holding to itself the frail

shudders of its skin. Stones
on the dark bottom
make the lake calm,
the life worth living.

Nose

it is an accurate nose
like an adding machine
powered by perfect electricity

yet it has no cord
it does not run on batteries

it is an observatory
for observing moons and planets
I watch it revolve

it is a birchbark canoe

it is a snail
that hesitates on a hedge

it is the fist of a new child

it is the egg
of a demonstrable bird
do not sit on this nose

Stones

Now it is gone, all of it.
No, it is there,
a rock island twelve miles offshore
in the Atlantic. Straight cliffs,
salt grass on top,
rabbits, snipe.

At lowest tide,
a scrap of sand; maybe once a year

the sea is so calm
that an island man beaches his coracle,
wedges the anchor in stone,
and rock-climbs to the top.

He traps small game,
listening to the wind, fearful
of skull island.
Monks in the Middle Ages
lived in a stone house here
whole lives.

THE DUMP

The trolley has stopped long since.
There is no motorman.
The passenger thinks
he is at the end of the line.
No, he is past the end. Around him
is the graveyard of trolleys,
thousands of oblongs tilted
at angles to each other,
yellow paint chipped.
Stepping outside, he sees smoke rising
from holes in roofs.
Old men live here, in narrow houses full of rugs,
in this last place.

THE HIGH PASTURE

I am the hounds,
I am the fox.

I wake reassembling
torn muscle and fur

to run again
over raw fields

to a corner of stone.
I twitch

awake with the crazy
intolerable scent

of me in my nostrils.
Yet I am also the leaf

that breathes
slowly in sun

by the wooden bridge
at the end of the pond

in the high pasture.

THE GREEN SHELF

Driving back from the market,
bags of groceries beside me,
I saw on a lawn
the body of a gray-haired man
twisted beside his power mower.

A woman twisted
her hands above him, mouth wide
with a cry.

She bent close to him, straightened,
bent again, straightened,

and an ambulance
stopped at the curb.
I drove past them slowly
while helpers
kneeled by the man.

Over the stretcher
the lawnmower continued to throb
and absently
the hand of the old woman
caressed the shuddering

handle. Back,
I put the soup cans in order
on the green shelves—
pickles, canned milk, peas,
basil, and tarragon.

ADULTERY AT FORTY

At the shower's head, high over the porcelain moonscape,
a water drop gathers itself darkly, hangs, shakes, trembles,
and hesitates, uncertain in which direction to hurl itself.

TO A WATERFOWL

Women with hats like the rear ends of pink ducks
applauded you, my poems.
These are the women whose husbands I meet on airplanes,
who close their briefcases and ask, "What are *you* in?"
I look in their eyes, I tell them I am in poetry,

and their eyes fill with anxiety, and with little tears.
"Oh, yeah?" they say, developing an interest in clouds.
"My wife, she likes that sort of thing? Hah-hah?
I guess maybe I'd better watch my grammar, huh?"
I leave them in airports, watching their grammar,

and take a limousine to the Women's Goodness Club
where I drink Harvey's Bristol Cream with their wives,
and eat chicken salad with capers, with little tomato wedges,
and I read them "The Erotic Crocodile," and "Eating You."
Ah, when I have concluded the disbursement of sonorities,

crooning, "High on thy thigh I cry, Hi!"—and so forth—
they spank their wide hands, they smile like Jell-O,
and they say, "Hah-hah? My goodness, Mr. Hall,
but you certainly do have an imagination, huh?"
"Thank you, indeed," I say; "it brings in the bacon."

But now, my poems, now I have returned to the motel,
returned to *l'éternel retour* of the Holiday Inn,
naked, lying on the bed, watching *Godzilla Sucks Mount Fuji*,
addressing my poems, feeling superior, and drinking bourbon
from a flask disguised to look like a transistor radio.

And what about you? You, laughing? You, in the bluejeans,
laughing at your mother who wears hats, and at your father
who rides airplanes with a briefcase watching his grammar?
Will you ever be old and dumb, like your creepy parents?
Not you, not you, not you, not you, not you, not you.

FÊTE

Festival lights go on
in villages throughout

68

the province, from Toe
Harbor, past the
    Elbow Lakes, to Eyelid Hill
when you touch me, there.

ELEANOR'S LETTERS

I who picked up the neat
Old letters never knew
The last names to complete
"Aunt Eleanor" or "Lew."

She talked about the weather,
And canning, and a trip
Which they might take together
"If we don't lose our grip."

But "Lew has got a growth
Which might turn out, they say,
Benign, or shrink, or both."
Then, "Lewis passed away."

He didn't *die.* That word
Seemed harsh and arbitrary
And thus was not preferred
In her vocabulary.

"Everything's for the better,"
She wrote, and what is more,
She signed her dying letter
"As ever, Eleanor."

The Raisin

I drank cool water from the fountain
in the undertaker's parlor
near the body of a ninety-two-year-old man.

Harry loved horses and work.
He curried the flanks of his Morgan;
he loaded crates twelve hours—to fill in
when his foreman got drunk—
never kicking a horse,
never kind to a son.

He sobbed on the sofa ten years ago,
when Sally died.
We heard of him dancing
with widows in Florida, cheek
to cheek, and of scented
letters that came to Connecticut
all summer.

When he was old he made up for the weeping
he failed to do earlier:
grandchildren, zinnias,
Morgans, great-grandchildren.
He wept over everything. His only
advice: "Keep your health."
He told old stories, laughing slowly.
He sang old songs.

Forty years ago his son
who was parked making love in the country
noticed Harry parked making love
in a car up ahead.

When he was ninety he wanted to die.
He couldn't ride or grow flowers
or dance
or tend the plots in the graveyard
that he had kept up
faithfully, since Sally died.

This morning I looked into the pale
raisin of Harry's face.

THE TOWN OF HILL

Back of the dam, under
a flat pad

of water, church
bells ring

in the ears of lilies,
a child's swing

curls in the current
of a yard, horned

pout sleep
in a green

mailbox, and
a boy walks

from a screened
porch beneath

the man-shaped
leaves of an oak

down the street looking
at the town

of Hill that water
covered forty

years ago,
and the screen

door shuts
under dream water.

White Apples

when my father had been dead a week
I woke
with his voice in my ear
                              I sat up in bed
and held my breath
and stared at the pale closed door

white apples and the taste of stone

if he called again
I would put on my coat and galoshes

4 *Root Cellar*

Maple Syrup

August, goldenrod blowing. We walk
into the graveyard, to find
my grandfather's grave. Ten years ago
I came here last, bringing
marigolds from the round garden
outside the kitchen.
I didn't know you then.
                              We walk
among carved names that go with photographs
on top of the piano at the farm:
Keneston, Wells, Fowler, Batchelder, Buck.
We pause at the new grave
of Grace Fenton, my grandfather's
sister. Last summer
we called on her at the nursing home,
eighty-seven, and nodding
in a blue housedress. We cannot find
my grandfather's grave.
                              Back at the house
where no one lives, we potter
and explore the back chamber
where everything comes to rest: spinning wheels,
pretty boxes, quilts,
bottles, books, albums of postcards.
Then with a flashlight we descend
frail steps to the root cellar—black,
cobwebby, huge,

with dirt floors and fieldstone walls,
and above the walls, holding the hewn
sills of the house, enormous
granite foundation stones.
Past the empty bins
for squash, apples, carrots, and potatoes,
we discover the shelves for canning, a few
pale pints
of tomato left, and—what
is this?—syrup, maple syrup
in a quart jar, syrup
my grandfather made twenty-five
years ago
for the last time.
               I remember
coming to the farm in March
in sugaring time, as a small boy.
He carried the pails of sap, sixteen-quart
buckets, dangling from each end
of a wooden yoke
that lay across his shoulders, and emptied them
into a vat in the saphouse
where fire burned day and night
for a week.
              Now the saphouse
tilts, nearly to the ground,
like someone exhausted
to the point of death, and next winter
when snow piles three feet thick
on the roofs of the cold farm,
the saphouse will shudder and slide
with the snow to the ground.
                  Today
we take my grandfather's last
quart of syrup

upstairs, holding it gingerly,
and we wash off twenty-five years
of dirt, and we pull
and pry the lid up, cutting the stiff,
dried rubber gasket, and dip our fingers
in, you and I both, and taste
the sweetness, you for the first time,
the sweetness preserved, of a dead man
in the kitchen he left
when his body slid
like anyone's into the ground.

THE TOY BONE

Looking through boxes
in the attic of my mother's house in Hamden,
I find a model airplane, snapshots
of a dog wearing baby clothes,
a catcher's mitt—the oiled
pocket eaten
by mice—and I discover
the toy bone.

        ∾

I sat alone each day
after school, in the living room
of my parents' house in Hamden, ten
years old, eating
slices of plain white bread.
I listened to the record, Connee
Boswell singing
again and again, her voice
turning like a heel, "The Kerry Dancers,"
and I knew she was crippled, and sang
from a wheelchair. I played

with Zippy, my red and white
Shetland collie, throwing
his toy bone
into the air and catching it, or letting it fall,
while he watched me
with intent, curious eyes.

I was happy
in the room dark with the shades drawn.

O CHEESE

In the pantry the dear dense cheeses, Cheddars and harsh
Lancashires; Gorgonzola with its magnanimous manner;
the clipped speech of Roquefort; and a head of Stilton
that speaks in a sensuous riddling tongue like Druids.

O cheeses of gravity, cheeses of wistfulness, cheeses
that weep continually because they know they will die.
O cheeses of victory, cheeses wise in defeat, cheeses
fat as a cushion, lolling in bed until noon.

Liederkranz ebullient, jumping like a small dog, noisy;
Pont l'Évêque intellectual, and quite well informed; Emmentaler
decent and loyal, a little deaf in the right ear;
and Brie the revealing experience, instantaneous and profound.

O cheeses that dance in the moonlight, cheeses
that mingle with sausages, cheeses of Stonehenge.
O cheeses that are shy, that linger in the doorway,
eyes looking down, cheeses spectacular as fireworks.

Reblochon openly sexual; Caerphilly like pine trees, small
at the timberline; Port-du-Salut in love; Camembert

eloquent, tactful, like a thousand-year-old hostess;
and Dolcelatte, always generous to a fault.

O village of cheeses, I make you this poem of cheeses,
O family of cheeses, living together in pantries,
O cheeses that keep to your own nature, like a lucky couple,
this solitude, this energy, these bodies slowly dying.

KICKING THE LEAVES

1

Kicking the leaves, October, as we walk home together
from the game, in Ann Arbor,
on a day the color of soot, rain in the air;
I kick at the leaves of maples,
reds of seventy different shades, yellow
like old paper; and poplar leaves, fragile and pale;
and elm leaves, flags of a doomed race.
I kick at the leaves, making a sound I remember
as the leaves swirl upward from my boot,
and flutter; and I remember
Octobers walking to school in Connecticut,
wearing corduroy knickers that swished
with a sound like leaves; and a Sunday buying
a cup of cider at a roadside stand
on a dirt road in New Hampshire; and kicking the leaves,
autumn 1955 in Massachusetts, knowing
my father would die when the leaves were gone.

2

Each fall in New Hampshire, on the farm
where my mother grew up, a girl in the country,
my grandfather and grandmother
finished the autumn work, taking the last vegetables in

from the cold fields, canning, storing roots and apples
in the cellar under the kitchen. Then my grandfather
raked leaves against the house
as the final chore of autumn.
One November I drove up from college to see them.
We pulled big rakes, as we did when we hayed in summer,
pulling the leaves against the granite foundations
around the house, on every side of the house,
and then, to keep them in place, we cut spruce boughs
and laid them across the leaves,
green on red, until the house
was tucked up, ready for snow
that would freeze the leaves in tight, like a stiff skirt.
Then we puffed through the shed door,
taking off boots and overcoats, slapping our hands,
and sat in the kitchen, rocking, and drank
black coffee my grandmother made,
three of us sitting together, silent, in gray November.

3

One Saturday when I was little, before the war,
my father came home at noon from his half day at the office
and wore his Bates sweater, black on red,
with the crossed hockey sticks on it, and raked beside me
in the back yard, and tumbled in the leaves with me,
laughing, and carried me, laughing, my hair full of leaves,
to the kitchen window
where my mother could see us, and smile, and motion
to set me down, afraid I would fall and be hurt.

4

Kicking the leaves today, as we walk home together
from the game, among crowds of people
with their bright pennants, as many and bright as leaves,
my daughter's hair is the red-yellow color

of birch leaves, and she is tall like a birch,
growing up, fifteen, growing older; and my son
flamboyant as maple, twenty,
visits from college, and walks ahead of us, his step
springing, impatient to travel
the woods of the earth. Now I watch them
from a pile of leaves beside this clapboard house
in Ann Arbor, across from the school
where they learned to read,
as their shapes grow small with distance, waving,
and I know that I
diminish, not them, as I go first
into the leaves, taking
the way they will follow, Octobers and years from now.

     5

This year the poems came back, when the leaves fell.
Kicking the leaves, I heard the leaves tell stories,
remembering, and therefore looking ahead, and building
the house of dying. I looked up into the maples
and found them, the vowels of bright desire.
I thought they had gone forever
while the bird sang *I love you, I love you*
and shook its black head
from side to side, and its red eye with no lid,
through years of winter, cold
as the taste of chickenwire, the music of cinderblock.

     6

Kicking the leaves, I uncover the lids of graves.
My grandfather died at seventy-seven, in March
when the sap was running; and I remember my father
twenty years ago,
coughing himself to death at fifty-two in the house
in the suburbs. Oh, how we flung

leaves in the air! How they tumbled and fluttered around us,
like slowly cascading water, when we walked together
in Hamden, before the war, when Johnson's Pond
had not surrendered to houses, the two of us
hand in hand, and in the wet air the smell of leaves
burning;
and in six years I will be fifty-two.

7

Now I fall, now I leap and fall
to feel the leaves crush under my body, to feel my body
buoyant in the ocean of leaves, the night of them,
night heaving with death and leaves, rocking like the ocean.
Oh, this delicious falling into the arms of leaves,
into the soft laps of leaves!
Face down, I swim into the leaves, feathery,
breathing the acrid odor of maple, swooping
in long glides to the bottom of October—
where the farm lies curled against winter, and soup steams
its breath of onion and carrot
onto damp curtains and windows; and past the windows
I see the tall bare maple trunks and branches, the oak
with its few brown weathery remnant leaves,
and the spruce trees, holding their green.
Now I leap and fall, exultant, recovering
from death, on account of death, in accord with the dead,
the smell and taste of leaves again,
and the pleasure, the only long pleasure, of taking a place
in the story of leaves.

EATING THE PIG

Twelve people, most of us strangers, stand in a room
in Ann Arbor, drinking Cribari from jars.

Then two young men, who cooked him,
carry him to the table
on a large square of plywood: his body
striped, like a tiger cat's, from the basting,
his legs long, much longer than a cat's,
and the striped hide as shiny as vinyl.

Now I see his head, as he takes his place
at the center of the table,
his wide pig's head; and he looks like the javelina
that ran in front of the car, in the desert outside Tucson,
and I am drawn to him, my brother the pig,
with his large ears cocked forward,
with his tight snout, with his small ferocious teeth
in a jaw propped open
by an apple. How bizarre, this raw apple clenched
in a cooked face! Then I see his eyes,
his eyes cramped shut, his no-eyes, his eyes like X's
in a comic strip, when the character gets knocked out.

This afternoon they read directions
from a book: *The eyeballs must be removed*
or they will burst during roasting. So they hacked them out.
"I nearly fainted," says someone.
"I never fainted before, in my whole life."
Then they gutted the pig and stuffed him,
and roasted him five hours, basting the long body.

           ∾

Now we examine him, exclaiming, and we marvel at him—
but no one picks up a knife.

Then a young woman cuts off his head.
It comes off so easily, like a detachable part.
With sudden enthusiasm we dismantle the pig,

we wrench his trotters off, we twist them
at shoulder and hip, and they come off so easily.
Then we cut open his belly and pull the skin back.

For myself, I scoop a portion of left thigh,
moist, tender, falling apart, fat, sweet.
We forage like an army starving in winter
that crosses a pass in the hills and discovers
a valley of full barns—
cattle fat and lowing in their stalls,
bins of potatoes in root cellars under white farmhouses,
barrels of cider, onions, hens squawking over eggs—
and the people nowhere, with bread still warm in the oven.

Maybe, south of the valley, refugees pull their carts
listening for Stukas or elephants, carrying
bedding, pans, and silk dresses,
old men and women, children, deserters, young wives.

No, we are here, eating the pig together.

∾

In ten minutes, the destruction is total.

His tiny ribs, delicate as birds' feet, lie crisscrossed.
Or they are like crosshatching in a drawing,
lines doubling and redoubling on each other.

Bits of fat and muscle
mix with stuffing alien to the body,
walnuts and plums. His skin, like a parchment bag
soaked in oil, is pulled back and flattened,
with ridges and humps remaining, like a contour map,
like the map of a defeated country.

The army consumes every blade of grass in the valley,
every tree, every stream, every village,
every crossroad, every shack, every book, every graveyard.

His intact head
swivels around, to view the landscape of body
as if in dismay.

"For sixteen weeks I lived. For sixteen weeks
I took into myself nothing but the milk of my mother
who rolled on her side for me,
for my brothers and sisters. Only five hours roasting,
and this body so quickly dwindles away to nothing."

              ~

By itself, isolated on this plywood,
among this puzzle of forgone possibilities,
his intact head seems to want affection.
Without knowing that I will do it,
I reach out and scratch his jaw,
and I stroke him behind his ears,
as if he might suddenly purr from his cooked head.

"When I stroke your pig's ears,
and scratch the striped leather of your jowls,
the furrow between the sockets of your eyes,
I take into myself, and digest,
wheat that grew between
the Tigris and the Euphrates rivers.

"And I take into myself the flint carving tool,
and the savannah, and hairs in the tail
of Eohippus, and fingers of bamboo,
and Hannibal's elephant, and Hannibal,
and everything that lived before us, everything born,

exalted, and dead, and historians
who carved in the Old Kingdom
when the wall had not heard about China."

I speak these words
into the ear of the Stone Age pig, the Abraham
pig, the ocean pig, the Achilles pig,
and into the ears
of the fire pig that will eat our bodies up.

"Fire, brother and father,
twelve of us, in our different skins, older and younger,
opened your skin together
and tore your body apart, and took it
into our bodies."

WOLF KNIFE

from The Journals of C. F. Hoyt, USN, 1826–1889

"In mid-August, in the second year
of my First Polar Expedition, the snows and ice of winter
almost upon us, Kantiuk and I
attempted to dash by sledge
along Crispin Bay, searching again for relics
of the Franklin Expedition. Now a storm blew,
and we turned back, and we struggled slowly
in snow, lest we depart land and venture onto ice
from which a sudden fog and thaw
would abandon us to the Providence
of the sea.

        "Near nightfall
I thought I heard snarling behind us.
Kantiuk told me

that two wolves, lean as the bones
of a wrecked ship,
had followed us the last hour, and snapped their teeth
as if already feasting.
I carried but the one charge
in my rifle, since, approaching the second winter,
we rationed stores.

         "As it turned dark,
we could push no farther, and made
camp in a corner
of ice-hummocks,
and the wolves stopped also, growling
just past the limits of vision,
coming closer, until I could hear
the click of their feet on ice. Kantiuk laughed
and remarked that the wolves appeared to be most hungry.
I raised my rifle, prepared to shoot the first
that ventured close, hoping
to frighten the other.

         "Kantiuk struck my rifle
down, and said again
that the wolves were hungry, and laughed.
I feared that my old companion
was mad, here in the storm, among ice-hummocks,
stalked by wolves. Now Kantiuk searched
in his pack, and extricated
two knives—*turnoks*, the Inuit called them—
which by great labor were sharpened, on both sides,
to a sharpness like the edge of a barber's razor,
and approached our dogs
and plunged both knives
into the body of our youngest dog
who had limped all day.

                    "I remember
that I considered turning my rifle on Kantiuk
as he approached, then passed me,
carrying knives red with the gore of our dog—
who had yowled, moaned, and now lay
expiring, surrounded
by curious cousins and uncles,
possibly hungry—and thrust the knives
handle-down in the snow.

                    "Immediately
he left the knives, the vague, gray
shapes of the wolves
turned solid, out of the darkness and the snow,
and set ravenously
to licking blood from the honed steel.
The double edge of the knives
so lacerated the tongues of the starved beasts
that their own blood poured
copiously forth
to replenish the dog's blood, and they ate
more furiously than before, while Kantiuk laughed,
and held his sides
laughing.

          And I laughed also,
perhaps in relief that Providence had delivered us
yet again, or perhaps—under conditions of extremity,
far from Connecticut—finding these creatures
acutely ridiculous, so avid
to swallow their own blood. First one, and then the other
collapsed, dying,
bloodless in the snow black with their own blood,
and Kantiuk retrieved
his *turnoks*, and hacked lean meat

from the thigh of the larger wolf,
which we ate
gratefully, blessing the Creator, for we were hungry."

On Reaching the Age of Two Hundred

When I awoke on the morning
of my two hundredth birthday,
I expected to be consulted
by supplicants
like the Sibyl at Cumae.
I could tell them something.

Instead, it was the usual thing:
dried grapefruit for breakfast,
Mozart all morning, interrupted
by bees' wings,
and making love with a woman
one hundred and eighty-one years old.

At my birthday party
I blew out two hundred candles
one at a time, taking
naps after each twenty-five.
Then I went to bed, at five-thirty,
on the day of my two hundredth birthday,

and slept and dreamed
of a house no bigger than a flea's house
with two hundred rooms in it,
and in each of the rooms a bed,
and in each of the two hundred beds
me sleeping.

The Flies

A fly slept on the field of a green curtain.
I sat by my grandmother's side, and rubbed her head
as if I could comfort her. Ninety-seven years.
Her eyes stayed closed, her mouth open,
and she gasped in her blue nightgown—pale blue,
washed a thousand times. Now her face went white,
and her breath slowed until it seemed to stop.
Then she gasped again, and pink returned to her face.
Between the roof of her mouth and her tongue,
strands of spittle wavered as she breathed. A nurse
shook her head over my grandmother's sore mouth
and fetched a glass of water, a spoon, and a flyswatter.
My grandmother choked on a spoonful of water
and the nurse swatted the fly.

                 In Connecticut suburbs
where I grew up, and in Ann Arbor, there were houses
with small leaded panes, where Formica shone
in the kitchens, and hardwood in closets under paired
leather boots. Carpets lay thick underfoot in bedrooms,
bright, clean, with no dust or hair in them.
Florist's flowers leaned from Waterford vases
for the Saturday dinner party. Even in houses like these,
the housefly wandered and paused—and I listened
for the buzz of its wings and its tiny feet, as it struggled
among cut flowers and bumped into leaded panes.

In the afternoon my mother took over
at my grandmother's side in the Peabody Home,
while I went back to the farm. I napped in the room
my mother and grandmother were born in.

At night we assembled beside her. Her shallow, rapid
breath rasped, and her eyes jerked, and the nurse
found no pulse, as her strength concentrated wholly
on half an inch of lung space, and she coughed faintly,
quick coughs, like fingertips on a ledge. Her daughters
stood by the bed—solemn in the slow evening,
in the shallows of after-supper—Caroline, Nan, and Lucy,
her eldest daughter, seventy-two, who held
her hand to help her die, as twenty years ago
she did the same for my father. Then her breath slowed
again, as it did all day. Pink vanished from cheeks
we had kissed so often, nostrils quivered,
and she breathed one more quick breath.
Her mouth twitched sharply, as if she spoke
a word we couldn't hear.

                    She lay in a casket of gray linen
at Chadwick's Funeral Parlor in New London,
on the ground floor under the I.O.O.F. Her fine hair
lay combed on the pillow. Her teeth in, her mouth
closed, she looked the way she used to look,
except that her face was tinted, tanned
as if she worked in the fields. The air was so still
it had bars. I imagined a fly wandering in,
through these dark-curtained windows, to land
on my grandmother's nose.

                    At the Andover graveyard,
Astroturf covered the dirt next to the dug shaft.
By the hole, Mr. Jones said a prayer,
who preached at the South Danbury Church
when my grandmother still played the organ.
He raised his narrow voice, which gave itself over
to August and blue air, and told us that Kate
in heaven "will keep on growing . . . and growing . . .

and growing..." and he stopped abruptly
as if the sky abandoned him.

                    I walked by myself
in the barn where I spent summers
next to my grandfather. In the tie-up a chaff
of flies roiled in the leather air, as he milked
his Holsteins morning and night, his bald head
pressed sweating into their sides, fat female
Harlequins. Their black-and-white tails
swept back and forth, stirring the flies up. His voice
spoke pieces he learned for the Lyceum,
and I listened crouched on a three-legged stool
as his hands kept time *strp strp* with alternate streams
of hot milk, the sound softer as milk foamed
to the pail's top. In the tie-up the spiders
feasted like Nero. Each April he broomed the webs out
and whitewashed the wood, but spiders and flies
came back, generation on generation—like the cattle,
mothers and daughters, for a hundred and fifty years,
until my grandfather's heart flapped in his chest.
One by one the slow Holsteins climbed the ramp
into a cattle truck.

                    In the kitchen with its bare
hardwood floor, my grandmother stood
by the clock's mirror to braid her hair every morning.
She looked out the window toward Kearsarge,
and said, "Mountain's pretty today,"
or, "Can't see the mountain too good today."
She fought the flies all summer. She shut
the screen door quickly, but flies gathered
on canisters, on the clockface, on the range
when the fire was out, on set-tubs, tables, chairs.
Flies buzzed on cooling lard, when my grandmother
made doughnuts. Flies lit on a drip of jam

before she could wipe it up. Flies whirled
over simmering beans, in the steam
of maple syrup. My grandmother fretted,
and took good aim with a flyswatter,
and hung strips of sticky paper behind the range,
where nobody would tangle her hair.
She gave me a penny for every ten I killed.
All day with my mesh flyswatter I patrolled
kitchen and dining room, living room,
even the dead air of the parlor. Though I killed
every fly in the house by bedtime,
when my grandmother washed the hardwood floor,
by morning their sons and cousins
assembled in the kitchen, like the woodchucks
my grandfather shot in the vegetable garden,
that doubled and returned; like the deer
that watched for a hundred and fifty years
from the brush on Ragged Mountain,
and when my grandfather died,
stalked down the mountainside to graze
among peas and beans.

                We live in their house
with our books and pictures, gazing each morning
at blue Kearsarge. We live in the house left behind.
We sleep in the bed where they whispered together
at night. One morning I woke hearing a voice from sleep:
"The blow of the axe resides in the acorn."
I got out of bed and drank cold water in the dark
morning from the sink's dipper
at the window under the leaning maple,
and a fly woke buzzing beside me,
and swept over set-tubs and range,
one of the hundred-thousandth generation. I planned
long ago I would live here, somebody's grandfather.

Ox Cart Man

In October of the year,
he counts potatoes dug from the brown field,
counting the seed, counting
the cellar's portion out,
and bags the rest on the cart's floor.

He packs wool sheared in April, honey
in combs, linen, leather
tanned from deerhide,
and vinegar in a barrel
hooped by hand at the forge's fire.

He walks by his ox's head, ten days
to Portsmouth Market, and sells potatoes,
and the bag that carried potatoes,
flaxseed, birch brooms, maple sugar, goose
feathers, yarn.

When the cart is empty he sells the cart.
When the cart is sold he sells the ox,
harness and yoke, and walks
home, his pockets heavy
with the year's coin for salt and taxes,

and at home by fire's light in November cold
stitches new harness
for next year's ox in the barn,
and carves the yoke, and saws planks
building the cart again.

Stone Walls

1

Stone walls emerge from leafy ground
and show their bones. In September a leaf
falls singly down, then a thousand leaves whirl
in frosty air. I am wild
with joy of leaves falling, of stone walls
emerging, of return to the countryside
where I lay as a boy
in the valley of noon heat, in the village
of little sounds; where I floated
out of myself, into the world that lives in the air.

In October the leaves turn
on low hills in middle distance, like heather, like tweed,
like tweed woven from heather and gorse,
purples, greens, reds, grays, oranges, weaving together
this joyful fabric,
and I walk in the afternoon sun, kicking the leaves.

In November the brightness washes from the hills
and I love the land most, leaves down, color drained out
in November rain,
everything gray and brown, against the dark evergreen,
everything rock and silver, lichen and moss on stone,
strong bones of stone walls showing at last
in November cold,
making wavy rectangles on the unperishing hills.

2

Wesley Wells was my grandfather's name.
He had high cheekbones, and laughed as he hoed,
practicing his stories.

The first time I remember him, it was summer at twilight.
He was weak from flu, and couldn't hike for his cows
on Ragged Mountain; he carried the old chair with no back
that he used for milking
to the hillside over the house and called up-mountain:
"Ke-bosh, ke-bosh, ke-bo-o-o-o-sh, ke-bosh . . ."

          ~

While he milked he told about drummers and baseball;
he recited Lyceum poems about drunk deacons,
or about Lawyer Green, whose skin was the color green,
ridiculed as a schoolboy, who left town and returned triumphant;
and riding home from the hayfields, he handed me the past:
how he walked on a row of fenceposts
in the blizzard of 'eighty-eight; or sawed oblongs
of ice from Eagle Pond; or in summer
drove the hayrack into shallow water, swelling wooden
wheels tight inside iron rims;
or chatted and teased outside Amos Johnson's with Buffalo Billy
Fiske who dressed like a cowboy.

While I daydreamed my schoolyear life
at Spring Glen Grammar School, or Hamden High,
I longed to return to him, in his awkward coat and cap,
in his sweater with many holes.

    3
A century ago these hills were bare;
you could see past Eagle Pond to sheep in the far pasture,
walls crossing cleared land, keeping Keneston
lambs from Peasly potatoes.

Today I walk in fields grown over—among
bare birches, oak saplings, enormous
sugarmaples gone into themselves for winter—

beside granite that men stacked
"for twenty-five cents a rod, and forage
for oxen," boulders sledded into place,
smaller stones
fitted by clever hands to lock together, like the arched
ramparts at Mycenae.

I come to the foundations of an abandoned mill;
at the two sides of a trout stream, fieldstone walls emerging
uncut and unmortared
rear like a lion gate,
                  emptiness over
the still-rushing waters.

    4
Allende's murderers follow Orlando Letelier
to Washington; they blow up his car by remote control.
His scream is distant, like the grocer's scream
stabbed in the holdup. These howls—
and Tsvetayeva's in Yelabuga,
who hangs herself in her cottage—
                            pulse, reverberate, and die
in the scrub pine that grows from granite ledges
visible against snow at the top of Kearsarge,
because jamming plates drove
the Appalachian range through the earth crust
before men and women, before squirrels, before spruce and
    daisies,
when only amoebas wept
to divide from themselves. Stone dwindled
under millennial rain
like snowbanks in March, and diminished under glaciers,
under the eyes of mice and reindeer, under the eyes of foxes,
under Siberian eyes
tracking bear ten thousand years ago

on Kearsarge;

         and the Shah of Iran's opponents
wake to discover nails
driven through their kneecaps. When Pinochet frowns
in Chile, hearing these howls,
the corners of his mouth twitch with an uncontrollable grin;
Tiberius listening grins.

            Each morning we watch stone walls
emerge on Kearsarge and on Ragged Mountain;
I love these mountains which do not change.
The screams persist. I continue my life.

    5
At Thornley's Store,
the dead mingle with the living; Benjamin Keneston hovers
with Wesley among hardware; Kate looks over spools of thread
with Nanny; and old shadows stand among dowels and raisins,
woolen socks and axes. Now Ansel stops to buy salt
and tells Bob Thornley it got so cold he saw
two hounddogs put jumper cables on a jackrabbit.
Skiers stop for gas; summer people join us, hitchhikers,
roadworkers, machinists, farmers, saw-sharpeners;
our cries and hungers, stories and music, reverberate
on the hills and stone walls, on the Exxon sign and clapboard
of Thornley's Store.

    6
At church we eat squares of bread, we commune with mothers
and cousins, with mothering-fathering hills, with dead and
    living,
and go home in gray November, in Advent waiting,
among generations unborn
who will look at the same hills, as the leaves fall and turn gray,
and watch stone walls ascending Ragged Mountain.

     〜

These walls are the bones of presidents, men and women
who were never born
and will never lead the Republic into the valley of cattle.

∽

When gangs fight with dogs for the moose's body,
and poems for Letelier are scattered like the molecules of his
    body,
and the books are burnt, and this room wet ashes, and language
burnt out, and the dead departed along with the living,
wavering stone lines
will emerge from leaves in November, on mountains without
    names.

∽

Pole beans raise their green flags in the summer garden.
I grow old, in the house I wanted to grow old in.
When I am sleepy at night, I daydream only
of waking the next morning—to walk on the earth of the present
past noons of birch and sugarbush, past cellarholes,
many miles to the village of nightfall.

OLD ROSES

White roses, tiny and old, flare among thorns
by the barn door.
                    For a hundred years
under the June elm, under the gaze
of seven generations,
                    they lived briefly
like this, in the month of roses,
                        by the fields
stout with corn, or with clover and timothy
making thick hay,
                    grown over, now,

with milkweed, sumac, paintbrush.

Old

roses survive
winter drifts, the melt in April, August
parch,
      and men and women
who sniffed roses in spring and called them pretty
as we call them now,
           walking beside the barn
on a day that perishes.

TRAFFIC

Trucks and station wagons, VWs, old Chevys, Pintos,
drive stop-and-go down Whitney Avenue this hot
May day, bluing the coarse air, past graveyard and florist,
past this empty brick building covered
with ivy like a Mayan temple,
like a pyramid grown over with jungle vines,
                I walk around
the building as if I were dreaming it; as if
I had left my planet at twenty
and wandered a lifetime among galaxies and come home
to find my planet aged ten thousand years,
ruined, grown over,
the people gone, ruin taking their places.
            They
have gone into graveyards, who worked at this loading dock
wearing brown uniforms with the pink and blue lettering
of the Brock-Hall Dairy:
Freddie Bauer is dead, who watched over the stockroom;
Agnes McSparren is dead, who wrote figures in books
at a yellow wooden desk; Harry Bailey is dead,
who tested for bacteria

wearing a white coat; Karl Kapp is dead,
who loaded his van at dawn,
conveyor belt supplying butter, cottage cheese, heavy cream,
B, buttermilk, A with its creamline—
and left white bottles at backdoors in North Haven and Hamden
for thirty years; my father is dead
and my grandfather.
    I stand by the fence at lot's end
where the long stable stood—
fifty workhorses alive
in the suburbs, chestnuts with thick manes, their hooves
the size of oak stumps, that pulled forty thousand quarts
through mists in the early morning to sleeping doorsteps,
until new trucks jammed the assembly lines
when the war ended.
    I separate ivy
like long hair over a face
to gaze into the room where the bottlewasher
stretched its aluminum length like an Airstream trailer.
When our teacher brought the first grade to the dairy,
men in white caps stacked dirty bottles
at the machine's end, and we heard them clink
forty feet to where they rode out shining
on a belt to another machine
that turned them instantly white, as if someone said a word
that turned them white. I was proud
of my father and grandfather,
of my last name.
    Here is the place
that was lettered with my father's name,
where he parked his Oldsmobile in the fifties.
I came to the plant with him one summer
when I was at college, and we walked across blacktop
where people my age washed trucks;
both of us smiled and looked downwards. That year

the business grossed sixteen million dollars
with four hundred people bottling and delivering milk
and Agnes McSparren was boss
over thirty women.
                              At the roof's edge,
imperial Roman cement urns
flourish and decorate exhausted air.
Now suburbs have migrated north
leaving Whitneyville behind, with its dead factory
beside a dead movie. They lived in Whitneyville
mostly—Freddie Bauer, Agnes McSparren, Karl Kapp,
Harry Bailey—who walked their lives
into brick, whose hours turned into milk,
who left their lives inside pitted brick
that disappears beneath ivy
for a thousand years, until the archeologist from a far galaxy
chops with his machete . . .
                              No, no, no.
In a week or a year
the wrecker's derrick with fifteen-ton cement ball
on a flatbed trailer
will stop traffic as it squeezes up Whitney Avenue,
and brick will collapse, and dump trucks take clean fill
for construction rising from a meadow
ten miles in the country.
                              I wait
for the traffic to pause, shift, and enter the traffic.

5 *Lady Ghost*

THE BLACK-FACED SHEEP

Ruminant pillows! Gregarious soft boulders!

If one of you found a gap in a stone wall,
the rest of you—rams, ewes, bucks, wethers, lambs;
mothers and daughters, old grandfather-father,
cousins and aunts, small bleating sons—
followed onward, stupid
as sheep, wherever
your leader's sheep-brain wandered to.

My grandfather spent all day searching the valley
and edges of Ragged Mountain,
calling "Ke-*day!*" as if he brought you salt,
"Ke-*day!* Ke-*day!*"

      ∾

When the shirt wore out, and darns in the woolen
shirt needed darning,
a woman in a white collar
cut the shirt into strips and braided it,
as she braided her hair every morning.

In a hundred years
the knees of her great-granddaughter
crawled on a rug made from the wool of sheep
whose bones were mud,
like the bones of the woman who stares
from an oval in the parlor.

      ∾

I forked the brambly hay down to you
in nineteen fifty. I delved my hands deep
in the winter grass of your hair.

When the shearer cut to your nakedness in April
and you dropped black eyes in shame,
hiding in barnyard corners, unable to hide,
I brought grain to raise your spirits,
and ten thousand years
wound us through pasture and hayfield together,
threads of us woven
together, three hundred generations
from Africa's hills to New Hampshire's.

∾

You were not shrewd like the pig.
You were not strong like the horse.
You were not brave like the rooster.

Yet none of the others looked like a lump of granite
that grew hair,
and none of the others
carried white fleece as soft as dandelion seed
around a black face,
and none of them sang such a flat and sociable song.

∾

Now the black-faced sheep have wandered and will not return,
even if I should search the valleys
and call "Ke-*day*," as if I brought them salt.

Now the railroad draws
a line of rust through the valley. Birch, pine, and maple
lean from cellarholes
and cover the dead pastures of Ragged Mountain

except where machines make snow
and cables pull money up hill, to slide back down.

          ∾

At South Danbury Church twelve of us sit—
cousins and aunts, sons—
where the great-grandfathers of the forty-acre farms
filled every pew.
I look out the window at summer places,
at Boston lawyers' houses
with swimming pools cunningly added to cowsheds,
and we read an old poem aloud, about Israel's sheep,
old lumps of wool, and we read

that the rich farmer, though he names his farm for himself,
takes nothing into his grave;
that even if people praise us, because we are successful,
we will go under the ground
to meet our ancestors collected there in the darkness;
that we are all of us sheep, and death is our shepherd,
and we die as the animals die.

Names of Horses

All winter your brute shoulders strained against collars, padding
and steerhide over the ash hames, to haul
sledges of cordwood for drying through spring and summer,
for the Glenwood stove next winter, and for the simmering range.

In April you pulled cartloads of manure to spread on the fields,
dark manure of Holsteins, and knobs of your own clustered with
          oats.
All summer you mowed the grass in meadow and hayfield, the
          mowing machine
clacketing beside you, while the sun walked high in the morning;

and after noon's heat, you pulled a clawed rake through the same
    acres,
gathering stacks, and dragged the wagon from stack to stack,
and the built hayrack back, up hill to the chaffy barn,
three loads of hay a day, hanging wide from the hayrack.

Sundays you trotted the two miles to church with the light load
of a leather quartertop buggy, and grazed in the sound of hymns.
Generation on generation, your neck rubbed the window sill
of the stall, smoothing the wood as the sea smooths glass.

When you were old and lame, when your shoulders hurt bending
    to graze,
one October the man who fed you and kept you, and harnessed
    you every morning,
led you through corn stubble to sandy ground above Eagle Pond,
and dug a hole beside you where you stood shuddering in your
    skin,

and laid the shotgun's muzzle in the boneless hollow behind your
    ear,
and fired the slug into your brain, and felled you into your grave,
shoveling sand to cover you, setting goldenrod upright above
    you,
where by next summer a dent in the ground made your
    monument.

For a hundred and fifty years, in the pasture of dead horses,
roots of pine trees pushed through the pale curves of your ribs,
yellow blossoms flourished above you in autumn, and in winter
frost heaved your bones in the ground—old toilers, soil makers:

O Roger, Mackerel, Riley, Ned, Nellie, Chester, Lady Ghost.

In the dark tie-up seven huge Holsteins
lower their heads to feed, chained loosely to old saplings
with whitewashed bark still on them.
They are long dead; they survive, in the great day
that cancels the successiveness of creatures.
Now she stretches her wrinkly neck, her turnip eye
rolls in her skull, she sucks up breath,
and stretching her long mouth mid-chew she expels:
mm-mmm-mmmmm-mmmmmmmm-ugghwanchhh.
—Sweet bellowers enormous and interchangeable,
your dolorous ululations
swell out barnsides, fill spaces inside haymows,
resound down valleys. Moos of revenant cattle
shake ancient timbers and timbers still damp with sap.

      ∽

Now it is warm, late June. The old man strokes
white braids of milk, *strp strp*, from ruminant beasts
with hipbones like tentpoles, the rough
black-and-white hanging crudely upon them.
Now he tilts back his head to recite a poem
about an old bachelor who loves a chicken named Susan.
His voice grows loud with laughter and emphasis
in the silent tie-up where old noises gather.

      ∽

Now a tail lifts to waterfall huge and yellow
or an enormous flop presses out. Done milking, he lifts
with his hoe a leather-hinged board
to scrape manure onto the pile underneath, in April
carted for garden and fieldcorn.
                           The cows in their house
decree the seasons; spring seeds corn,
summer hays, autumn fences, and winter saws ice
from Eagle Pond, sledging it up hill to pack it away

in sawdust; through August's parch and Indian summer
great chunks of the pond float in the milkshed tank.

      ∾

Pull down the spiderwebs! Whitewash the tie-up!
In the great day there is also the odor of poverty
and anxiety over the Agricultural Inspector's visit.

      ∾

They are long dead; they survive, in the great day
of August, to convene afternoon and morning
for milking. Now they graze Ragged Mountain:—
steep sugarbush, little mountain valleys and brooks,
high clovery meadows, slate-colored lowbush blueberries.
When grass is sweetest they are slow to leave it;
late afternoons he spends hours searching.
He knows their secret places; he listens for one peal
of a cowbell carried on a breeze; he calls:
"Ke-bosh, ke-bo-o-sh, ke-bosh, ke-bosh..."
He climbs dry creekbeds and old logging roads
or struggles up needle-banks pulling on fir branches.
He hacks with his jackknife a chunk of sprucegum
oozing from bark and softens it in his cheek-pouch
for chewing.
           Then he pushes through hemlock's gate
to join the society of Holsteins; they look up from grass
as if mildly surprised, and file immediately downwards.

      ∾

Late in October after the grass freezes
the cattle remain in their stalls, twice a day loosed
to walk stiff-legged to the watering trough
from which the old man lifts a white lid of ice.
Twice a day he shovels ensilage into their stalls
and shakes hay down from the loft, stuffing a forkful
under each steaming nose.
            In late winter,
one after one, the pink-white udders

dry out as new calves swell their mothers' bellies.
Now these vessels of hugeness bear, one after one,
skinny-limbed small Holsteins eager to suck
the bounty of freshening. Now he climbs to the barn
in boots and overalls, two sweaters,
a cloth cap, and somebody's old woolen coat;
now he parts the calf from its mother after feeding,
and strips the udder clean,
to rejoice in the sweet frothing tonnage of milk.

∾

Now in April, when snow remains on the north side
of boulders and sugarmaples, and green
starts from wet earth in open places the sun touches,
he unchains the cows one morning after milking
and lopes past them to open the pasture gate.
Now he returns whooping and slapping their buttocks
to set them to pasture again, and they are free
to wander eating all day long. Now these wallowing
big-eyed calf-makers, bone-rafters for leather,
awkward arks, cud-chewing lethargic mooers,
roll their enormous heads, trot, gallop, bounce,
cavort, stretch, leap, and bellow—
as if everything heavy and cold vanished at once
and cow spirits floated
weightless as clouds in the great day's windy April.

∾

When his neighbor discovers him at eighty-seven, his head
leans into the side of his last Holstein;
she has kicked the milkpail over, and blue milk drains
through floorboards onto the manure pile in the great day.

1

From the dark yard by the sheepbarn the cock crowed
to the sun's pale
spectral foreblossoming eastward in June,
crowed,
      and crowed,
later each day through fall and winter, conquistador
of January drifts, almost useless vain strutter
with wild monomaniac eye, burnished swollen chest,
yellow feet serpent-scaled, and bloodred comb,
who mounted with a mighty flutter
his busy hens: Generalissimo Rooster
of nobody's army.
         When he was old we cut his head off
on the sheepyard choppingblock, watching his drummajor
prance, his last resplendent march.
As I saw him diminish, as we plucked each feathery badge,
cut off his legs, gutted him,
and boiled him three hours for our fricassee Sunday
dinner, I understood
How the Mighty Are Fallen, and my great-uncle Luther,
who remembered the Civil War,
risen from rest after his morning's sermon, asked
God's blessing on our food.

2

At the depot in April, parcel post went cheep-cheep
in rectangular cardboard boxes, each
trembling with fifty chicks. When we opened
the carton in the cool toolshed
fifty downed fluffers cheep-cheeping
rolled and teetered.
         All summer it was my chore

to feed them, to water them.
Twice a day I emptied a fouled pan
and freshened it from the trough; twice a day
I trudged up hill to the grainshed, filled
sapbuckets at wooden tubs and poured
grain into V-shaped feeders, watching the greedy
fluster and shove.
                              One summer
I nursed a blind chick six weeks—pale yellow,
frail, tentative, meek,
who never ate except when I gapped space for her.
I watched her grow little by little,
but every day outpaced
by the healthy beaks that seized feed
to grow monstrous—and one morning
discovered her dead: meatless, incorrigible.

        3
At summer's end the small roosters departed
by truck, squawking. Pullets
moved to the henhouse and extruded each day
new eggs, harvested morning and night. Hens roosted
in darkness locked from skunk and fox,
and let out at dawn footed the brittle yard,
tilting on stiff legs to peck the corncobs
clean; to gobble turnip peels, carrot tops, even
the shells of yesterday's eggs. Hens labored
to fill eggboxes the eggman shipped
to Boston, and to provide our breakfast, gathered
at the square table.
                              When the eggmaking frenzy
ceased, when each in her own time set
for weeks as if setting itself made eggs,
each used-up, diligent hen
danced on the packed soil of the henyard her final

headless jig, and boiled
in her pale shape
                    featherless as an egg, consumed
like the blind chick, like Nannie,
who died one summer at seventy-seven, childish,
deaf, unable to feed herself, demented...

New Animals

Waking one morning
we cannot find
Kate or Wesley,
or his cows and sheep,
or the hens she looks
after. In my dream
we spend all morning
looking for their old
bodies in tall grass
beside barn
and henyard. Finally
we discover them,
marching up the dirt
road from Andover—
excited, laughing, waving
to catch our attention
as they shepherd
new animals
home to the farm.
They traded Holsteins
and Rhode Island Reds
for zebras, giraffes,
apes, and tigers. They lead
their parade back
to the barn, and the sheep-

dog ostrich
nips at the errant
elephant's heels
and goads the gaudy
heroic lions
and peacocks that keen
AIEE AIEE.

Scenic View

Every year the mountains
get paler and more distant—
trees less green, rock piles
disappearing—as emulsion
from a billion Kodaks
sucks color out.
In fifteen years
Monadnock and Kearsarge,
the Green Mountains
and the White, will turn
invisible, all
tint removed
atom by atom to albums
in Medford and Greenwich,
while over the valleys
the still intractable granite
rears with unseeable peaks
fatal to airplanes.

Old Timers' Day

When the tall puffy
figure wearing number

nine starts
late for the fly ball,
laboring forward
like a lame truckhorse
startled by a gartersnake,
—this old fellow
whose body we remember
as sleek and nervous
as a filly's—

and barely catches it
in his glove's
tip, we rise
and applaud weeping:
On a green field
we observe the ruin
of even the bravest
body, as Odysseus
wept to glimpse
among shades the shadow
of Achilles.

The Baseball Players

Against the bright
grass the white-knickered
players tense, seize,
and attend. A moment
ago, outfielders
and infielders adjusted
their clothing, glanced
at the sun and settled
forward, hands on knees;
the pitcher walked back

of the hill, established
his cap and returned;
the catcher twitched
a forefinger; the batter
rotated his bat
in a slow circle. But now
they pause: wary,
exact, suspended—
     while
abiding moonrise
lightens the angel
of the overgrown
garden, and Walter Blake
Adams, who died
at fourteen, waits
under the footbridge.

GRANITE AND GRASS

1

On Ragged Mountain birches twist from rifts in granite.
Great ledges show gray through sugarbush. Brown bears
doze all winter under granite outcroppings or in cellarholes
the first settlers walled with fieldstone.
Granite markers recline in high abandoned graveyards.

Although split by frost or dynamite, granite is unaltered;
earthquakes tumble boulders across meadows; glaciers
carry pebbles with them as they grind south
and melt north, scooping lakes for the Penacook's trout.
Stone bulks, reflects sunlight, bears snow, and persists.

When highway-makers cut through a granite hill, scoring
deep trench-sides with vertical drillings, they leave behind

glittering sculptures, monuments to the granite state
of nature, emblems of permanence
that we worship in daily disease, and discover in stone.

2

But when we climb Ragged Mountain past cordwood stumpage,
over rocks of a dry creekbed, in company of young hemlock,
only granite remains unkind. Uprising in summer, in woods
and high pastures, our sister the fern breathes, trembles,
and alters, delicate fronds outspread and separate.

The fox pausing for scent cuts holes in hoarfrost.
Quail scream in the fisher's jaw; then the fisher dotes.
The coy-dog howls, raising puppies that breed more puppies
to rip the throats of rickety deer in March.
The moose's antlers extend, defending his wife for a season.

Mother-and-father grass lifts in the forsaken meadow,
grows tall under sun and rain, uncut, turns yellow,
sheds seeds, and under assault of snow relents; in May
green generates again. When the bear dies, bees construct
honey from nectar of cinquefoil growing through rib bones.

3

Ragged Mountain was granite before Adam divided.
Grass lives because it dies. If weary of discord
we gaze heavenward through the same eye that looks at us,
vision makes light of contradiction:
Granite is grass in the holy meadow of the soul's repose.

A SISTER ON THE TRACKS

Between pond and sheepbarn, by maples and watery birches,
Rebecca paces a double line of rust

in a sandy trench, striding on black
creosoted eight-by-eights.
                              In nineteen forty-three,
wartrains skidded tanks,
airframes, dynamos, searchlights, and troops
to Montreal. She counted cars
from the stopped hayrack at the endless crossing:
ninety-nine, one hundred; and her grandfather Ben's
voice shaking with rage and oratory told
how the mighty Boston and Maine
kept the Statehouse in its pocket.
                              Today Rebecca walks
a line that vanishes, in solitude
bypassed by wars and commerce. She remembers the story
of the bunting'd day her great-great-great-
grandmother watched the first train roll and smoke
from Potter Place to Gale
with fireworks, cider, and speeches. Then the long rail
drove west, buzzing and humming; the hive of rolling stock
extended a thousand-car'd perspective
from Ohio to Oregon, where men who left stone farms
rode rails toward gold.
                              On this blue day she walks
under a high jet's glint of swooped aluminum pulling
its feathery contrail westward. She sees ahead
how the jet dies into junk, and highway wastes
like railroad. Beside her the old creation retires,
hayrack sunk like a rowboat
under its fields of hay. She closes her eyes
to glimpse the vertical track that rises
from the underworld of graves,
soul's ascension connecting dead to unborn, rails
that hum with a hymn of continual vanishing
where tracks cross.
                              For she opens her eyes to read

on a solitary gravestone next to the rails
the familiar names of Ruth and Matthew Bott, born
in a Norfolk parish, who ventured
the immigrant's passionate exodus westward to labor
on their own land. Here love builds
its mortal house, where today's wind carries
a double scent of heaven and cut hay.

A Sister by the Pond

1

An old *Life* photograph
prints itself on Rebecca's mind: The German
regular army hangs
partisans on the Russian front.
Grandfather Wehrmacht in his tight-
collared greatcoat adjusts
the boy's noose as his elderly
adjutant watches. Beside the boy,
his girl companion has already
strangled, her gullet cinched when a soldier
kicked the box from her feet.
In the photograph, taken
near Minsk, gray sky behind him
the summer of nineteen forty-one,
the boy smiles—
as if he understands that being hanged
is no great matter.

2

At this open winter's end, in the wrack
and melt of April,
Rebecca walks on the shore by her summer
swimming place, by Eagle Pond
where the ice rots. Over

the pocked glaze, puddles of gray stain
spread at midday. Every year
an ice-fisherman waits one weekend
too many, and his shack drowns
among reeds and rowboats. She counts
the season's other
waste: mostly the beaver's work—stout
trees chewed through, stripped
of bark, trailing
twigs in the water. Come summer,
she will drag away the trash, and loll on red
blossoms of moss.

    3

She walks on the shore today
by "Sabine," the beach her young
aunts made, where they loafed together,
hot afternoons of the war. She arranged
freshwater mussels on moss;
watched a mother duck
lead her column; studied the quick
repose of minnows; lying on pine needles loosened
out of her body. Forty years
later Rebecca walks
by the same water: When July's lilies
open in the cove
by the boggy place where bullfrogs
bellow, they gather the sun
as they did when she picked a bunch
for her grandfather Ben
in his vigorous middle age.

    4

In October she came here last,
strolling by pondside with her daughter,
whose red hair brightened

against black-green fir.
Rebecca gazed at her daughter's pale
watery profile, admiring the forehead broad
and clear like Ben's, without guile,
and took pleasure in the affection
of her silent company. By the shore
a maple stood upright,
casting red leaves, its trunk gnawed
to a three-inch waist
of centerwood that bore the branches'
weight. Today when she looks for it, it
is eaten all the way down; blond splinters
show within the gray
surface of the old chewing.

        5
Two weeks ago she drove her daughter
to the Hematology Clinic
of the Peter Bent Brigham Hospital
and paced three hours
among bald young women and skeletal boys
until a resident spoke
the jargon of reassurance. By the felled
maple Rebecca's heart
sinks like the fisherman's shack. She sees again
her son's long body twist
in the crushed Fiesta: A blue light revolves
at three in the morning; white-coated helpers
lift him onto a stretcher;
the pulverized windshield glitters
on black macadam
and in the abrasions of his face.

        6
In the smile of the boy hanged
near Minsk, and in the familiar entropy

of April at Eagle Pond,
she glimpses ahead a winter
of skeleton horses in electric snow.
That April, only the deep burrow-hiders
will emerge who slept
below breath and nightmare: Blacksnake,
frog, and woodchuck
take up their customs among milkweed
that rises through bones
of combines. That summer, when blackberries
twist from the cinders
of white houses, the bear
will pick at the unripe fruit
as he wastes and grows thin, fur
dropping off in patches from his gray skin.

7

Today, at the pond's edge, old
life warms from the suspense of winter.
Pickerel hover under the pitted, corrupt
surface of April ice
that erodes at the muddy shoreline
where peepers will sing
and snapping turtles bury their eggs.
She sways in the moment's trembling
skin and surge: She desires only
repose, wishing to rise
as the fire wishes or to sink
with the wish and nature of stones.
She wants her soul to loosen
from its body, to lift into sky
as a bird or withdraw as a fish into water
or into water itself
or into weeds that waver in water.

THE DAY I WAS OLDER

The Clock
The clock on the parlor wall, stout as a mariner's clock,
disperses the day. All night it tolls the half-hour
and the hour's number with resolute measure,
approaching the poles and crossing the equator
over fathoms of sleep. Warm
in the dark next to your breathing,
below the thousand favored stars, I feel
horns of gray water heave
underneath us, and the ship's pistons
pound as the voyage continues over the limited sea.

The News
After tending the fire, making coffee, and pouring milk
for cats, I sit in a blue chair each morning,
reading obituaries in the Boston *Globe*
for the mean age; today there is MANUFACTURER CONCORD 53,
EX-CONGRESSMAN SAUGUS 80—and I read
that Emily Farr is dead, after a long illness in Oregon.
Once in an old house we talked for an hour, while a coal fire
brightened in November twilight and wavered
our shadows high on the wall
until our eyes fixed on each other. Thirty years ago.

The Pond
We lie by the pond on a late August afternoon
as a breeze from low hills in the west stiffens water
and agitates birch leaves yellowing above us.
You set down your book
and lift your eyes to white trunks tilting from shore.
A mink scuds through ferns; an acorn tumbles.
Soon we will turn to our daily business.
You do not know that I am watching, taking pleasure

in your breasts that rise and fall as you breathe.
Then I see mourners gathered by an open grave.

The Day
Last night at suppertime I outlived my father, enduring
the year, month, day, hour, and moment
when he lay back on a hospital bed in the guest room
among cylinders of oxygen—mouth open, nostrils and pale
blue lips fixed unquivering. Father of my name,
father of long fingers, I remember your dark hair
and your face almost unwrinkled. Now I have waked
more mornings to frost whitening the grass,
read the newspaper more times, and stood more times,
my hand on a doorknob without opening the door.

The Cup
From the Studebaker's back seat, on our Sunday drives,
I watched her earrings sway. Then I walked uphill
beside an old man carrying buckets
under birches on an August day. Striding at noontime,
I looked at wheat and at river cities. In the crib
my daughter sighed opening her eyes. I kissed the cheek
of my father dying. By the pond an acorn fell.
You listening here, you reading these words as I write them,
I offer this cup to you: Though we drink
from this cup every day, we will never drink it dry.

FOR AN EXCHANGE OF RINGS

They rise into mind,
the young lovers
of eighteen nineteen:
As they walk together
in a walled garden

of Hampstead, tremulous,
their breathing quick,
color high, eyes lucent,
he places the floral
ring with its almondine
stone on her finger.
Although in two winters,
hopeless in Rome,
her letters unopened
beside him, he will
sweat, cough, and die;
although forty years
later a small old
woman will wear
his ring and locket
of hair as she stops
breathing—now, in
Hampstead, in eighteen
nineteen, they are
wholly indifferent
to other days as they
moisten and swell.

THE IMPOSSIBLE MARRIAGE

The bride disappears. After twenty minutes of searching
we discover her in the cellar, vanishing against a pillar
in her white gown and her skin's original pallor.
When we guide her back to the altar, we find the groom
in his slouch hat, open shirt, and untended beard
withdrawn to the belltower with the healthy young sexton
from whose comradeship we detach him with difficulty.
O never in all the meetinghouses and academies
of compulsory Democracy and free-thinking Calvinism

will these poets marry!—O pale, passionate
anchoret of Amherst! O reticent kosmos of Brooklyn!

Mr. Wakeville on Interstate 90

"Now I will abandon the route of my life
as my shadowy wives abandon me, taking my children.
I will stop somewhere. I will park in a summer street
where the days tick like metal in the stillness.
I will rent the room over Bert's Modern Barbershop
where the TO LET sign leans in the plateglass window;
or I will buy the brown BUNGALOW FOR SALE.

"I will work forty hours a week clerking at the paintstore.
On Fridays I will cash my paycheck at Six Rivers Bank
and stop at Harvey's Market and talk with Harvey.
Walking on Maple Street I will speak to everyone.
At basketball games I will cheer for my neighbors' sons.
I will watch my neighbors' daughters grow up, marry,
raise children. The joints of my fingers will stiffen.

"There will be no room inside me for other places.
I will attend funerals regularly and weddings.
I will chat with the mailman when he comes on Saturdays.
I will shake my head when I hear of the florist
who drops dead in the greenhouse over a flat of pansies;
I spoke with her only yesterday.
When lawyer elopes with babysitter I will shake my head.

"When Harvey's boy enlists in the Navy
I will wave goodbye at the Trailways depot with the others.
I will vote Democratic; I will vote Republican.
I will applaud the valedictorian at graduation
and wish her well as she goes away to the university

and weep as she goes away. I will live in a steady joy;
I will exult in the ecstasy of my concealment."

My Friend Felix

"Beginning at five o'clock, just before dawn rises
in the rearview mirror, I drive at eighty, alone,
all day through Texas. I am a pencil extending
a ruler's line to the unchangeable horizon
west as I repeat a thousand quarrels with my wives.
My grip on the steering wheel slackens; my mind's voice turns
mild and persuasive, quietly addressing the young
doctor at the detox center . . . but I cannot stop
hearing again, word-for-word, last winter's two o'clock
call from a motel in Albany—she would not say
where she was—as my daughter wept, sighed, begged forgiveness,
and allowed the telephone to drop from her fingers.
When I have driven straight through daylight, five-foot neon
letters rise crimson in the pale west: BAR. Thirty years
drown: I am a young man again driving with Felix
from New Haven to San Diego where he will join
his Crusader and his carrier, and in two months
overshoot the runway and slide to the Pacific's
silt bottom without jettisoning his canopy,
while a helicopter hovers an hour above him.
For a moment Felix sits alongside me again,
a young man forever, with his skin wrinkled and puffed
from thirty years of soaking in his watery chair:
All day we drove west on a ruled highway: At a BAR
we swallowed two pitchers, and back on the road again
I pulled out to pass a tractor-trailer. Another
approached and neither truck would give way; I labored past
the semi inch-by-inch and at the last half-second
sideslipped in front. As our pulses slowed we stared ahead,

and from the slipcovered seat beside me Felix spoke:
'The time that we lose, by stopping to drink, we make up
by drunken driving.' Continuing straight west I dream
of my lucky friend Felix the singlewing halfback."

MERLE BASCOM'S .22

"I was twelve when my father gave me this .22
Mossberg carbine—hand-made, with a short octagonal
barrel, stylish as an Indianfighter posing
for a photograph. We ripped up Bokar coffeecans
set into the sandbank by the track—competitive
and companionable. He was a good shot, although
his hands already trembled. Or I walked with my friend
Paul who loved airplanes and wanted to be a pilot,
and carried my rifle loosely, pointing it downward;
I aimed at squirrels and missed. Later I shot woodchucks
that ate my widowed mother's peas and Kentucky
Wonders when I visited on weekends from college,
or drove up from my Boston suburb, finding the gun
in its closet behind the woodstove. Ten years ago
my mother died; I sold up, and moved here with my work
and my second wife, gladly taking my tenancy
in the farmhouse where I intended to live and die.
I used my rifle on another generation
of woodchucks that ate our beans. One autumn an old friend
from college stayed with us after a nervous breakdown:
trembling from electroshock, depressed, suicidal.
I wrapped the octagonal Mossberg in a burlap
bag and concealed it under boards in the old grainshed.
In our quiet house he strengthened and stopped shaking.
When he went home I neglected to retrieve my gun,
and the next summer woodchucks took over the garden.
I let them. Our lives fitted mountain, creek, and hayfield.

Long days like minnows in the pond quickened and were still.
When I looked up from Plutarch another year had passed.
One Sunday the choir at our church sang Whittier's hymn
ending with 'the still small voice of calm.' Idly I thought,
'I must ask them to sing that hymn at my funeral.'
Soon after, I looked for the .22 in the shed,
half expecting it to have vanished, but finding it
wrapped intact where I left it, hardly rusted. I spent
a long evening taking it apart and cleaning it;
I thought of my father's hands shaking as he aimed it.
Then I restored the Mossberg to its accustomed place
in the closet behind the stove. At about this time
I learned that my daughter-in-law was two months pregnant:
It would be the first grandchild. One day I was walking
alone and imagined a granddaughter visiting:
She loved the old place; she swam in the summer pond with us;
she walked with us in red October; she grew older, she fell
in love with a neighbor, she married. As I daydreamed,
suddenly I was seized by a fit of revulsion:
I thought: 'Must I go through all that again? Must I live
another twenty years?' It was as if a body
rose from a hole where I had buried it years ago
while my first marriage was twisting and thrashing to death.
One night I was drunk and lost control of my Beetle
off 128 near my ranchhouse. I missed a curve
at seventy miles an hour and careered toward a stone wall.
In a hundredth of a second I knew I would die;
and, as joy fired through my body, I knew something else.
But the car slowed itself on rocks and settled to rest
between an elm and a maple; I sat breathing,
feeling the joy leach out, leaving behind the torment
and terror of my desire. Now I felt this affliction
descend again and metastasize through my body.
Today I drove ninety miles, slowly, seatbelt fastened
to North Andover and Paul's house, where he lives flying

out of Logan for United. I asked him to hide
the firing pin of an octagonal .22.
He nodded and took it from my hands without speaking.
I cannot throw it away; it was my father's gift."

Cider 5¢ a Glass

"When I heard Monica's
    voice on the telephone, I
knew what had happened. She
    spoke almost coldly, holding
the tears or hysteria back.
    Sam had pecked her goodbye
in bed that morning the way
    he usually did;
when she got up, she assumed
    he'd left for the office
on schedule until she
    looked out and saw the Buick
parked in the carport. Sam sat
    upright in the driver's
seat with his eyes open.

    "Because I am sixty, I have
lost many friends (my mother
    who lived to be eighty-
seven looked at newspapers
    in her last years only
to read the obituaries)
    —but not friends like Sam:
We met at boarding school, roomed
    together in college,
and were best man at each
    other's wedding. It started

when we were new at Holderness,
     homesick and lonesome
as we watched the returning
     boys greeting each other
after their summers on the Cape.
     We took walks, we talked.
Our friendship endured college,
     political quarrels,
one drunken fistfight, dating
     each other's ex-girlfriends,
hitchhiking, graduation,
     and marriage; and survived
although Sam left the East
     to settle in Chicago
and drudge for a conglomerate's
     legal department,
pleading in court to deny
     workmen's compensation.
I write for the Boston *Globe*,
     considered liberal,
and whenever we met Sam
     started right in on me
for the naiveté
     of my politics. Sometimes
we argued all night long . . .
     but I learned: If I refused
to fight, one night at the end
     of our visit, after
our wives had gone to bed
     and we drank one last bourbon
together, Sammy
     would confess that he hated what
he did—work, boss, and company.
     He wanted to quit;
and he *would*, too, as soon

as he found another job.
One night he wept
    as he told a confusing story
about a man in Florida,
    paralyzed for life
when a fork-lift crushed
    his spinal cord, who was accused
of being drunk on the job,
    which he wasn't. When Sam's
department won its case,
    Sam got a bonus. Of course
he never quit his job
    and his salary to work
for César Chávez or sail
    his boat around the world.
He spent ten years planning
    early retirement and died
six weeks before retiring.

    "Sam was a good father
and loyal husband most
    of the time; in private life
he was affectionate
    and loyal; many people
virtuous in public
    privately abuse their wives
and children. Then I think:
    'What about the night-watchman,
paralyzed and cheated?
    What about *his* family?'
Then I stop thinking.

    "Sam wrote letters rarely. We met
every couple of years, here
    or there, and he called up

impulsively. Last August
  Sam and Monica drove
to our place. He looked good
  although he wheezed a little.
He referred to someone
  by name, as if I should know
who she was, and shook his head
  sharply, two or three times,
insisting: 'It was only
  an infatuation.'
One night after dinner,
  neither of us drinking much
these days, he took his guitar
  from the trunk of the car
so that we could sing old
  songs and reminisce. On Labor
Day they headed back.

  "After Monica's call I dreamed
about Sam all night. Today
  I am ten thousand times
more alive in the rearward
  vision of memory
than I am editing stories
  by recent college
graduates or typing
  'graphs on a green terminal.
I lean back, closing my eyes,
  and my sore mind repeats
home movies of one day:

  "It's October, a Sunday
in nineteen forty-four,
  Indian summer bright with
New Hampshire leaves: Sammy

and I walk (happy in our
new friendship, sixteen and
    seventeen years old) under
tall sugarmaples
    extravagantly Chinese red,
and russet elms still thriving,
    enormous and noble
in the blue air.
    We talk about the war going on
overseas and whether we
    will fight in it; we talk
about what we will do
    after the war and college.
I admit: I want to write novels.
    Sam thinks maybe
he could be a musician
    (he plays guitar and sings
Josh White songs) 'but maybe
    it would be better to do
something that *helps* people . . .'
    Maybe he should think about
law school? (I understand:
    He feels that his rich father
leads a fatuous life
    with his Scotch and his girlfriends.)
Although we talk excitedly,
    although we mean what
we say and listen closely
    to each other, the real
burden of our talk
    is the affection that contains
and exalts us. As it turns dark,
    we head back toward school
on a shadowy gravel road;
    we are astonished

to see ahead (on a lane
      without cars in nineteen
forty-four, as if an apparition
      conjured there
to conclude this day that fixed
      our friendship forever)
a small table with a pitcher
      on it, three glasses,
and a sign: CIDER 5¢
      A GLASS. A screendoor swings
open on the gray unpainted
      porch of a farmhouse,
and a woman (old, fat,
      and strong) walks down the dirt path
to pour us our cider.
      She takes our nickels and sells
us a second glass and then
      gives us a third. All day
today I keep tasting
      that Sunday's almost painful
detonation of cider sweet
      and harsh in my mouth."

OLIVER AT THIRTEEN

"While I perform the procedures
      expected of me
(pouring milk on cornflakes,
      complaining about homework,
playing a game of catch
      with my father), I observe
and collect evidence until
      I become certain:
They are all actors—mother,
      students at school, busdrivers,

saleswomen, father.
    Even the crowds on the Green
and sunbathers at Hammonasset
    are bit players or extras,
rehearsed to behave
    as crowds are supposed to behave,
who watch the subject
    of the experiment: Will he,
would *anyone,* even with a script
    as ingenious as it is
preposterous, believe:
    house, West Rock, television,
teacher, thirteen, Connecticut,
    Oliver, hospital."

EDWARD'S ANECDOTE

"Late one night she told me.
    We'd come home from a party
where she drank more wine
    than usual, from nervousness

"I suppose. I was astonished,
    which is typical,
and her lover of course
    was my friend. My naiveté

"served their purposes: What
    you don't know beats your head in.
After weeping for an hour or so
    I tried screaming.

"Then I quieted down;
    then I broke her grandmother's

teapot against the pantry brickwork,
    which helped a bit.

"She kept apologizing
    as she walked back and forth,
chainsmoking. I hated her,
    and thought how beautiful

"she looked as she paced,
    which started me weeping again.
Old puzzlements began to solve
    themselves: the errand

"that took all afternoon;
    the much-explained excursion
to stay with a college roommate
    at a hunting lodge

"without a telephone;
    and of course the wrong numbers.
Then my masochistic mind
    printed Kodacolors

"of my friend and my wife
    arranged in bed together.
When I looked out the window,
    I saw the sky going

"pale with dawn; soon the children
    would wake: Thinking of them
started me weeping again.
    I felt exhausted, and

"I wanted to sleep neither
    with her nor without her,

which made me remember:
   When I was a child we knew

"a neighbor named Mr. Jaspers—
   an ordinary
gray and agreeable
   middle-aged businessman who

"joked with the neighborhood
   children when he met us on
the street, giving us pennies,
   except for once a year

"when he got insanely drunk
   and the police took him.
One time he beat his year-old
   daughter with a broomstick,

"breaking a rib bone, and as
   she screamed she kept crawling
back to her father: Where else
   should she look for comfort?"

6 The One Day

Each man bears the entire form of man's estate.

—Michel de Montaigne

Every human being is a colony.

—Pablo Picasso

When the coach clattered into the inn-yard, the old gen-
tleman hastened to finish his story: "It remained silent
thereafter." Gathering his luggage he prepared to depart...
adding, "There are other voices, within my own skull I
daresay. A woman speaks clearly from time to time; I do
not know her name. Especially there speaks a man who re-
sembles me overmuch yet is distinctly not me." So saying he
departed...

—Abbé Michel de Bourdeille
from *Historia Mei Temporis*

I

Shrubs Burnt Away

What then are the situations, from the representation of
which, though accurate, no poetical enjoyment can be de-
rived? They are those in which the suffering finds no vent in
action; in which a continuous state of mental distress is pro-
longed, unrelieved by incident, hope, or resistance; in which
there is everything to be endured, nothing to be done.

—Matthew Arnold

Mi-t'o Temple after thirty li. A most desolate spot ... For fear
of them hiding tigers, all trees and shrubs have been burnt.

—Hsu Hsia-k'o

"Once a little boy and his sister"—my mother lay
on top of the quilt, narrow and tense, whispering—
"found boards piled up, deep in the woods, and nails,
and built a house for themselves, and nobody knew
how they built their house each day in the woods . . ."
I listened and fell asleep, like a baby full of milk,
and carried the house into sleep where I built it
board by board all night, each night
from the beginning; from a pile of boards I built it,
painted it, put doorknobs on it . . .

As I sit by myself, middle-aged in my yellow chair,
staring at the vacant book of the ceiling, unfit
to work or love, aureoled with cigarette smoke
in the unstoried room, I daydream to build
the house of dying: The old man alone in the farmhouse
makes coffee, whittles, walks, and cuts an onion
to eat between slices of bread. But the white loaf
on the kitchen table comes undone:—
Milk leaks; flour and yeast draw apart;
sugar and water puddle the table's top.

Bullied, found wanting, my father drove home
from his work at the lumberyard weeping,
and shook his fist over my cradle: "He'll do
what he wants to do!"—and kept to it twenty
years later, still home from his job hopeless
in outrage, smoking Luckies, unable to sleep
for coughing. Forty years I have waked
to the shallow light, forty years of the day's
aging; today I observe for the first time
white hair that grows from my wrist's knuckle.

I lay in my dark bedroom hearing trees scrape
like Hauptmann's ladder on the gray clapboard.
Downstairs the radio diminished, Bing Crosby,
and I heard voices like logs burning, flames
rising and falling, one high and steady, one
urgent and quick. If I cried, if I called . . . I called
softly, sore in the wrapped dark, but there was nothing,
I was nothing, the light's line at the closed door faint.
I called again; I heard her steps:—
Light swept in like a broom from the opening door

and my head lay warm on her shoulder, and her breath
sang in my ear:—"A Long Long Trail A-winding";
"Backward Turn Backward O Time in Thy Flight . . ."
In the next room a drawer banged shut. When my father
lay dying at fifty-one, he could not deliver
the graduation speech at Adams Avenue School
near the house he was born in. As I took my father's
place, my head shook like a plucked wire.
I told the fourteen-year-olds:
"Never do anything except what you want to do."

I could not keep from staring out the window.
Teachers told my mother I was an intelligent girl,
if I would only apply myself. But I continued
to gaze at hills pushing upward, or to draw with my crayons.
In the third grade Mr. Blake came on Wednesdays;
he said I was the best young artist in the township.
At home when my mother made Parker House rolls
she let me mold scraps of dough on the oilcloth
of the kitchen table, and I shaped my first soft
rising edible sculptures: So my life started.

The year after my father burned in the wrecked car,
my mother came home early from the job she hated,
teaching bookkeeping at the secretarial college.
Sometimes she wept because she had flunked someone
she caught cheating. Each day I comforted her;
I was fifteen years old. I cooked supper for her—
hamburgers and hot dogs, baked beans, corn niblets.
Once I took a recipe from "Confidential Chat,"
using Ritz crackers, asparagus soup, and waterchestnuts.
She said I would make some man happy.

That was the year I stopped drawing. Sometimes at night
when she fell asleep I would look at my old portfolio
and cry, and pick up a pencil, and set it down.
Every night before supper we played Chinese checkers
and I beat her; she trembled lifting the marbles, only forty
years old. She came home exhausted, not wanting to play.
After a while we played no more checkers
and she collapsed early listening to her radio mysteries
in the blue leather lounger, with the vodka that ruptured
her liver through her abdomen ten years later.

Closing my eyes I recognize other citizens
and colonists: One is an actor, homosexual, in a rent-
controlled apartment near Sullivan Square; he waits
for the telephone—two weeks in *General Hospital*
as a kindly thoracic surgeon. In Woodbridge outside
New Haven another lives—ironic, uxorious, the five
children grown and gone; he waters his lawn with irony;
he works forty hours of irony a week and lives
to retire. Another died dropping from a parking structure
last April, climbing the parapet drunk with purpose.

When I was twelve I spent the summer on the farm,
painting watercolors all morning, all afternoon hoeing
the garden with my grandmother who told stories.
We fed the hens; we gathered eggs. Once we discovered
four hen-husks drained dry by a weasel.
That summer I painted One Hundred Views
of house, hill, and covered bridge. When my grandmother
woke me at six o'clock with black coffee
the day lay before me like a green alley of grass
through a meadow I invented by setting my foot to it.

When my mother came home from the drying-out hospital,
still convulsive, she took pills and talked without stopping.
She told me about her first breakdown
when she was nine years old. She had a nightmare
over and over again: Bearded men—who looked like the tramps
asking for bread and butter at the porch door
or like the gypsies camping in their wagons every summer—
made a circle around her, and the circle grew smaller
as the bearded men shuffled close. Every night
she woke up screaming, unable to stop. She knew

they wanted to cut her up for a patchwork quilt. Her mother
and father set a small cot beside their bed; when she woke
screaming they comforted her. The circle of men
came closer; even when she was awake in her mother's arms
the circle tightened; she heard her grandfather
tell somebody on the porch, "We're going to lose
our little girl." When she stopped crying her mother
pumped a cup of water. She remembered once
her mother brought water in an unwashed coffee cup
and there was sugar stuck in the bottom of the cup.

The Bee Gee, huge engine and tiny stub wings,
snapped around pylons in the Nationals; each year
they clipped more wing off. *On the Fourth of July*
I turned nine years old, I was playing in the woods
with Bingo and Harold Johnson; Bingo had a crush on me.
We were chasing each other and ran into a clearing
and found Bingo and Harold's father and my mother
drunk, rolling in the grass with their clothes off.
Douglas Corrigan took off from Long Island, flight plan
filed for California, plane heavy with gasoline,

and flew to Ireland—Wrong-Way Corrigan:
a mistake, he claimed; no sense of direction . . .
Later we returned to the house with the grown-ups
and my father threw his old-fashioned in my mother's face.
When I tried to run outside my uncle caught me
and set me on his lap; I kept on watching in my blue
shirt over my lace birthday blouse. For three years
a Pomona fireman worked weekends in his garage building
an airplane that used the motors from six lawnmowers.
The CAB refused a license; a strut washed up on Catalina.

My father ran from the house carrying a winebottle.
When he backed out of the driveway
he knocked the mailbox over. My mother got my uncle
to chase him along dirt roads at midnight
very fast;—I sat in the back seat, frightened.
He lost us but we knew where he was going. Wiley Post
and Will Rogers flew from the Walaka Lagoon; Inuit
found their bodies. In the Pacific, Navy patrol-planes
searched for Amelia Earhart while her Lockheed foundered
through fathoms with its cargo of helmeted corpses.

Now an old man walks on blacktop, farmhouse
to postoffice, by a ditch gray with late August grass.
Now he is a boy carrying his scythe to join
his grandfather mowing on the machine in the hayfield,
where he will trim around rocks. He tilts his blade
toward German prisoners, sleeping by day in ditches,
who escaped last week from the Canadian prison camp.
When he returns, old man again, to the farmhouse
by the strong cowbarn, past Aunt Bertha's cottage,
blond prisoners drink schnapps in the livingroom.

Now I told my wife: Consider me a wind that lifts
the square white houses up and spins them
into each other; or as a flood loosening houses
from their cellarholes; or as a fire that burns
white wooden houses down. I was content in the dark
livingroom, fixed in the chair with whiskey.
I claimed that the wind was out of control
while I looked through a window where the June trees
blew in the streetlight at two o'clock; leaves broke
from their stems but the trunk did not split open.

Now I declared that everywhere at two in the morning
men sat awake in yellow chairs, doing nothing,
while their wives lay upstairs in bed with open eyes.
Last night at the reception I glimpsed the made-up faces
of women I knew elsewhere—pale, shaking,
passionate, weeping. We understood together:
The world is a bed. In discontented peace,
in boredom and tolerance, only adultery proves
devotion by risk; only the pulse of betrayal
makes blood pelt in the chest as if with joy.

(Who is it that sets these words on blue-lined paper?
It is the old man in the room of bumpy wallpaper.
It is the girl who sits on her drunken mother's lap
or carries her grandmother's eggs. It is the boy who reads
the complete works of Edgar Allan Poe. It is the middle-
aged man motionless in a yellow chair, unable to read,
daydreaming the house of dying: The colony takes comfort
in building this house which does not exist, because
it does not exist—as I stare at the wrist's knuckle,
idle, without purpose, fixed in a yellow chair.)

At the exact millisecond when two cells fused
and multiplied, I started this house. Through years of milk
and potty I constructed foundations; *in Mr. Blake's
classroom I built it;* in vacant lots hopeless at football,
at Walter's Creek hunting for frogs and turtles,
under leaf's breath, in rotted leaves I built it;
in months at the worktable assembling model airplanes,
at the blackboard doing sums, *in blue summer painting
watercolors at my grandmother's I built this house.*
I build it over again, stiff in the permanent chair.

There was the dream of the party: a French farce,
frolic behind curtains, exits and entrances—
like a child fooling parents. I departed
alone on a bus that bumped down the white staircase
of the mansion over the bodies of three women
who stood complacent and pretty in the bus's way,
their faces familiar as photographs. When I looked
back from the bus's rear window at their bodies,
they waved to me although they were dead:—
They forgave me because no one was driving the bus.

*My daughter curled in my lap, wailing and red,
six years old. My fifteen-year-old son's long legs
writhed from a chair as tears fell on his spectacles.
Their mother was leaving them . . . I
was leaving them. Their muscles contracted
knees to chin, as I watched from my distance,
and their limbs twitched and jerked in the velvet room.
My daughter wanted to see the place I had rented
to move to. She whirled among cheap furniture,
over bare linoleum, saying, "Cozy, cozy . . ."*

It rains on Sunset Boulevard. I walk with the collar
of my jacket turned up. Topless go-go dancers twist
at the back of a bar, while men on the wet sidewalk
peer into the doorway at the young women's bodies,
their smooth skin intolerably altered by ointments
and by revolving orange and purple lights.
Lights bruise their thighs:—for three thousand years
these lights and ointments . . . I rejected
the comforts I had contrived for myself; I exchanged them
for a rain of small faces on the abandoned street.

I am a dog among dogs, and I whine about waking
to the six o'clock sun of summer, or brag
about Sinbad's adventures, for which I left houses
excessive with shrubbery, carpets, and mirrors.
Justifying myself I claim: After the breathless blue
of my father's face, I chose the incendiary flower:
Yellow flame budded from clapboard; therefore,
rain on the Boulevard. Now in the gray
continuous morning, water drips from the cindery houses
that wanted to bloom in the night, I stay up all night

at the Hollywood–La Brea Motel looking at television,
black-and-white war movies, Marines at Iwo,
sailors and blondes, B-24s; I do not understand
what happens. I listen to shills in blazers
with sixpenny London accents pitch acrylic while I drink
Scotch from the bottle. Studying a bikini'd
photograph on a matchbox, I dial BONNIE FASHION
MODEL AVAILABLE at four in the morning
from my vinyl room, and the answering service tells me
that Bonnie is out to lunch . . .

I take out my sketchbook as I wait for the plane
in a blockhouse at the airport's edge; then the cement
walls vibrate as if an earthquake shook them.
I understand: The plane from Chicago has crashed
trying to land. Immediately I watch a conveyor belt
remove bodies covered with brown army blankets
from the broken snake of the fuselage. One of the dead
sits up abruptly, points a finger at me,
and stares accusingly. It is an old man with an erection:
Then I notice that all of the dead are men.

Another self sits all day in a watchpocket
of cigarette smoke, staring at the wrist-knuckle,
in repetitious vacancy examining the ceiling, its cracks
and yellowed paint, unprinted emptiness rolling
as continuous as the ocean, no ship or landfall anywhere,
no bird or airplane. I climb from the yellow chair
to the bare bedroom and lie on my back smoking
and staring . . . until ice in a glass, golden whiskey,
euphoria, falling down, and sleep with two yellowjacketed
Nembutals pave the undreaming gilt road to nothing.

Therefore I envy an old man hedging and ditching
three hundred years ago in Devon. I envy the hedge
and the ditch. When my father came home
from the lumberyard, head shaking, fingers
yellow with Luckies, I begged him to play catch
with me. He smacked the pocket
of a catcher's mitt: "Put her there!"—and I threw
a fastball ten feet over his head. As he trotted
after the ball I waited, ashamed of being
wild:—enraged, apologetic, unforgiving.

When I was in my thirties, in love with the fires
that burned white houses down, desires and treacheries
passed the time. My children receded, waving. Janis
Joplin said, "It's always the same fucking day."
I counted divorces; I slept drugged sleep through years
of continual winter, frost in July and August, as in 1816,
the Poverty Year my grandmother's grandmother told of:—
The cornfield, frozen and planted again, froze yet again,
tomatoes pustulent on vines of August, hard frost
twelve months out of twelve, and "We ate the seedcorn."

During the gelid midsummers of middle-life, I saw
dream hayfields scattered with boxes long and narrow
like haybales; I stumbled in a darkness of waking dream
against these oblongs; under the full moon I gazed
at their luminous shapes, rounded on top with snow
like enormous loaves. Sitting in my chair I walked
in the corpsefield: babies among them,
old women, young men, mothers and fathers, corpses
of men and women. My stub-winged airplanes crashed.
When I slept without drugs, cannibal dreams awoke me.

Now in my mind a solitary old man walks back and forth
from linoleum to carpet to linoleum again.
In Laurel Canyon I stand smiling, shifting my weight,
among middle-aged rich who eat shrimp curled on ice,
who wear tartan jackets or earrings coded to their shoes.
They do not notice how I descend to the root cellar
with its dirt floor where a mirror hangs in the gloom;
I make out a white beard and glasses that reflect
nothing. But when I touch my chin my face is smooth;
I rejoin the party; I smile; I am careful drinking.

Nothing remains except a doll strangled on fencewire.
Night after night I sleep on pills and wake exhausted:
Rage weighs its iron on my chest. I cannot enter
the orchard's farmhouse on the hill, or find the road
vanished under burdock. I burn another house
and self-pity exhausts me. Bonnie orders a burger.
I pour the first tumbler over icecubes that dull the taste:
Roots of my hair go numb; numbness spreads downward
over the forehead's wrinkles past bloody eyes
to stomach, to wrist's white hair, to dead penis.

The world is a bed, I announced; my love agreed.
A hundred or a thousand times our eyes encountered:
Each time the clothes sloughed off, anatomies
of slippery flesh connected again on the world's bed
and the crescent of nerves described itself
in the ordinary curve of bliss. We were never alone;
we were always alone. If we were each the same
on the world's bed, if we were each a manikin of the other,
then the multitude was one and one was the multitude;
many and one we performed procedures of comfort.

I am very happy. I dance supine on my bed laughing
until four in the morning when the bottle is empty
and the liquor store closed on Hollywood and La Brea.
I must not drive the car for cigarettes;—
therefore I lurch a mile to the All-Nite Laundro-Mart
and falter back coughing. In the morning I lie
waking dozing twisted in the damp workclothes
of lethargy, loathing, and the desire to die.
My father's head shook like a plucked wire:
"Never do anything except what you want to do."

I am sad in the convenient white kitchen, dreaming
that I weep as I start making dinner, setting things out.
The children themselves weep, bringing their sentences
on small folded squares of paper.
They will take pills to die without disturbance.
I help them count the pills out, and arrange
pillows for their comfort as they become sleepy.
While I slice onions and peppers on the breadboard,
someone whose identity hovers just out of sight, the way
a beekeeper's mask darkens a face,

walks up the busy street and enters the kitchen
to instruct me in preparing the children.
The visitor picks up the long rag doll and with scissors
carefully cuts the doll's limbs at the joints,
teaching me expertly, with anatomical explanations
and a scientific vocabulary, while measuring and cutting
the model, then places the doll's parts
on a high shelf, arranged with the gaps of dismemberment
visible, so that I may consult it while cutting,
as I must do, as it appears that I want to do.

II

Four Classic Texts

> Of the opposites that which tends to birth or creation is called
> war or strife. That which tends to destruction by fire is called
> concord or peace.
>
> —Heraclitus

> Poetry is preparation for death.
>
> —Nadezhda Mandelstam

PROPHECY

I will strike down wooden houses; I will burn aluminum
clapboard skin; I will strike down garages
where crimson Toyotas sleep side by side; I will explode
palaces of gold, silver, and alabaster:—the summer
great house and its folly together. Where shopping malls
spread plywood and plaster out, and roadhouses
serve steak and potatoskins beside Alaska king crab;
where triangular flags proclaim tribes of identical campers;
where airplanes nose to tail exhale kerosene,
weeds and ashes will drowse in continual twilight.

I reject the old house and the new car; I reject
Tory and Whig together; I reject the argument
that modesty of ambition is sensible because the bigger
they are the harder they fall; I reject Waterford;
I reject the five-and-dime; I reject Romulus and Remus;
I reject Martha's Vineyard and the slamdunk contest;
I reject leaded panes; I reject the appointment made
at the tennis net or on the seventh green; I reject
the Professional Bowlers Tour; I reject matchboxes;
I reject purple bathrooms with purple soap in them.

Men who lie awake worrying about taxes, vomiting
at dawn, whose hands shake as they administer Valium, —
skin will peel from the meat of their thighs.
Armies that march all day with elephants past pyramids
and roll pulling missiles past generals weary of saluting
and past president-emperors splendid in cloth-of-gold, —
soft rumps of armies will dissipate in rain. Where square
miles of corn waver in Minnesota, where tobacco ripens
in Carolina and apples in New Hampshire, where wheat
turns Kansas green, where pulpmills stink in Oregon, —

dust will blow in the darkness and cactus die
before it flowers. Where skiers wait for chairlifts,
wearing money, low raspberries will part rib bones.
Where the drive-in church raises a chromium cross,
dandelions and milkweed will straggle through blacktop.
I will strike from the ocean with waves afire;
I will strike from the hill with rainclouds of lava;
I will strike from darkened air
with melanoma in the shape of decorative hexagonals.
I will strike down embezzlers and eaters of snails.

I reject Japanese smoked oysters, potted chrysanthemums
allowed to die, Tupperware parties, Ronald McDonald,
Kaposi's sarcoma, the Taj Mahal, Holsteins wearing
electronic necklaces, the Algonquin, Tunisian aqueducts,
Phi Beta Kappa keys, the Hyatt Embarcadero, carpenters
jogging on the median, and betrayal that engorges
the corrupt heart longing for criminal surrender.
I reject shadows in the corner of the atrium
where Phyllis or Phoebe speaks with Billy or Marc
who says that afternoons are best although not reliable.

Your children will wander looting the shopping malls
for forty years, suffering for your idleness,
until the last dwarf body rots in a parking lot.
I will strike down lobbies and restaurants in motels
carpeted with shaggy petrochemicals
from Maine to Hilton Head, from the Skagit to Tucson.
I will strike down hang gliders, wiry adventurous boys;
their thigh bones will snap, their brains
slide from their skulls. I will strike down
families cooking wildboar in New Mexico back yards.

Then landscape will clutter with incapable machinery,
acres of vacant airplanes and schoolbuses, ploughs
with seedlings sprouting and turning brown through colters.
Unlettered dwarves will burrow for warmth and shelter
in the caves of dynamos and Plymouths, dying
of old age at seventeen. Tribes wandering
in the wilderness of their ignorant desolation,
who suffer from your idleness, will burn your illuminated
missals to warm their rickety bodies.
Terrorists assemble plutonium because you are idle

and industrious. The whippoorwill shrivels
and the pickerel chokes under the government of self-love.
Vacancy burns air so that you strangle without oxygen
like rats in a biologist's bell jar. The living god sharpens
the scythe of my prophecy to strike down red poppies
and blue cornflowers. When priests and policemen
strike my body's match, Jehovah will flame out;
Jehovah will suck air from the vents of bombshelters.
Therefore let the Buick swell until it explodes;
therefore let anorexia starve and bulimia engorge.

When Elzira leaves the house wearing her tennis dress
and drives her black Porsche to meet Abraham,
quarrels, returns to husband and children, and sobs
asleep, drunk, unable to choose among them,—
lawns and carpets will turn into tar together
with lovers, husbands, and children.
Fat will boil in the sacs of children's clear skin.
I will strike down the nations, astronauts and judges;
I will strike down Babylon, I will strike acrobats,
I will strike algae and the white birches.

Because professors of law teach ethics in dumbshow,
let the colonel become president; because chief executive
officers and commissars collect down for pillows,
let the injustice of cities burn city and suburb;
let the countryside burn; let the pineforests of Maine
explode like a kitchenmatch and the Book of Kells turn
ash in a microsecond; let oxen and athletes
flash into grease:—I return to Appalachian rocks;
I shall eat bread; I shall prophesy through millennia
of Jehovah's day until the sky reddens over cities:

Then houses will burn, even houses of alabaster;
the sky will disappear like a scroll rolled up
and hidden in a cave from the industries of idleness.
Mountains will erupt and vanish, becoming deserts,
and the sea wash over the sea's lost islands
and the earth split open like a corpse's gassy
stomach and the sun turn as black as a widow's skirt
and the full moon grow red with blood swollen inside it
and stars fall from the sky like wind-blown apples,—
while Babylon's managers burn in the rage of the Lamb.

Pastoral

MARC: Shepherd and shepherdess, I with my pipe and song,
   you leaning on your crook, in the kitchen's
   hot valley among slaveboys and electric knives,
   now the young husband kisses the young wife
   he is not married to. As our tissues swell with blood,
   as lubricant juices collect, we admire
   important words: But the chiefest of these is love.
   We discover in twenty years of assignations and replicas—
   O Phyllis, O Phoebe, O Elzira—adventure or danger
   which we confuse with passion, gifts exchanged,

PHYLLIS: and exchanged again. As the blood pelts, we confer;
   and we pull off our clothes like opening junk mail.
   The world is a bed—O Abraham, O Marc, O Billy—
   where the multitude repeats itself for shepherd
   and shepherdess, you with your pipe, I leaning on my crook
   in the meadow; you leading your herd in summer
   from valley to mountain, in autumn to valley again;
   I kneeling to drink from the pool, hiding my face.
   Of course I never balanced food and clothing
   on my head as I led my children into stone hills,

MARC: away from airplanes. Of course my manager clearcuts
   the forest and paves the garden; your broker ploughs
   hillsides and destroys millennial loam for a crop
   of corn. Of course I couldn't kill a rat with my putter
   even if the rat shuddered in my daughter's crib.
   You never braided rope in your hut for the beaked ships.
   I never walked twenty miles through snow to hear
   my president speak from the train's observation platform.
   Now your green stationwagon, steady as a battering ram,
   enters the garage painted by college students,

PHYLLIS: and I carry, my dearest, the supermarket's paperbags
into my clean kitchen; I align the cans on shelves
just so. I set the oven for two hours and ten minutes
while I cross-country. Dryads with slim exact
hips and hair assemble in my livingroom for bridge.
I am cheerful in order to be approved of. We forget
every skill we acquired over ten thousand years of labor.
I practice smiling; I forget how to milk a goat.
You forget how to construct aqueduct, temple, and cloaca.
We vote for the candidate who vows to abolish caritas.

MARC: I live in an unfenced compound among swineherds
and milkmaids identical in age, income, and education.
I am unacquainted with anyone who lives in a trailer
or wears a tattoo, except for Joseph who mows
my grass, whom I fear and despise. O Phyllis, O Elzira,
you never sat by a cooling stove while the clock struck
to study the word by candlelight. I never doubted
that money excused anything done to acquire it.
I meet the church vestry or the faculty of engines
smiling and joshing, full of hate, resentment, and envy.

PHYLLIS: My Hermes, you sit with your pipes pocketed at committee
meetings and eat nonbiodegradable doughnuts and drink
whitened coffee without protest. You play sets of tennis
with the director you dislike, and laugh shaking your head
as your baseline shots continually fall past the baseline.
You make rules, piper, by which you cannot be fired.
I cheat my employer; I quit and take unemployment
because I deserve it. You exploit your employees.
My friend in the city attorney's office reduces the charges.
You weep, my love, chained to the trireme's oar.

MARC: I fly with my family to San Juan for a week attended
        by Moriscos. Drunk after the party, I fumble to embrace
        the babysitter, taking her home, who will not sit
        for my children again. I choose a girl from Records
        instead, who is twenty-three and thinks I am rich.
        Later when I am bored I disengage myself,
        sending her presents. Ingratiating to boss, insulting
        to employees, I endure my days without pleasure
        or purpose, finding distraction in Rodeo Drive, in
        duplicate bridge, in gladiators, and in my pastoral song.

HISTORY

When the knife slipped and cut deeply into the fingerpad
as he whittled a stick or trimmed ham from the bone,
at first he felt nothing, aware only of the nearly insensible
line on the skin. Always he imagined for one heartbeat
that he might undo the error and prevent the upsurge
of consequent blood: Such was the character of Juvenis,
who remembered always the doomed legions marching
as they left the city, their big arms swinging, or daydreamed
that the airplane halted inches from the rockface,
like the photograph of an airplane. In my only vision,

I Senex await calmly the formation rising rounded
from the finger's tip:—brilliant, certain, bountiful.
Now, pacing my battlements among sentries, I observe
how terrorists burn athletes; terrorists dynamite
the former ambassador of the executed prime minister;
terrorists sentence the kidnapped president for crimes
against the children they will never father or mother:
They shoot him through the head and stuff his body
into a Japanese sedan's trunk on a suburban street
where the regime's corrupt engines sniff him out.

In the trench there were several corpses. This was in France.
The heels of one stuck out from the dirt of the trenchwall,
the scalp of another. The most dreadful thing we saw
was an arm in field-gray with a hand, dead-white and wearing
a signet ring, that protruded from the wall of a saphead.
Wherever we dug for our safety, we dug into corpses,
more ours than the French. Whenever a mine exploded,
a chowder of flesh splashed through fog and gunsmoke to mark
our positions. Shreds of a Frenchman hung from the branch
of an apple tree. This was in May. This was in Vauquois.

For four hundred years and sixteen generations, I kept
my castle while vassals baked flatbread.
Hoplites protected the confluence of rivers. When plague
squatted in the streets, or when the brawn of Germany
crossed the river to cut soldiers and horses,
peasants and pigs turned wild in the hills. Drought starved,
flood drowned:—Then shires rose in the valleys again.
Bowmen and arquebusiers left bones in the Low Countries.
Seven generations built the wall. For a hundred years
redheaded barbarians walked through a gap in the wall;—

but Danegeld accumulated for bribes and fortifications.
Cabbages kept over winter. Grapes ripened into wine.
Boys gathered the eggs of birds in the June twilights.
Oaks cut for the cathedral roof left acorns behind
for pigs in the diocesan forest; then oaks grew
three centuries under the care of foresters, father and son,
to replace cathedral beams when the deathwatch beetle
chewed them hollow. And now when my managers fly
to Chicago on Tuesday and divorce in Santo Domingo
on Wednesday and cremate their stepchildren on Thursday

without learning on Friday the names their grandmothers
were born to—they weep, they drink a Manhattan straight up,
they tremble strapped to electrodes on a table.
When he assumed the throne Juvenis concentrated
on cost-effective methods for exterminating barbarians
under the boy's illusion that he might establish
permanent boundaries. When his Reichsmarschall Hanno
concluded the Rhine, Juvenis required him to find
a defensible durable allweather overland traderoute
from Cornwall to Cathay: Tin boxes preserved

aromas of Lapsang Souchong. John Ball and Spartacus
assemble plutonium for love, constructing a device
to reverse history's river. Titus Manlius scourged
and beheaded his own son for disobedient heroism.
We carried Bhutto to the gallows on a stretcher.
He weighed eighty-seven pounds, a sufficient weight;
he asked the hangman to expedite the matter.
Our imperial goal is simple and simple our mottoes:
PEACE FOR ETERNITY   NOT LIBERTY BUT ORDER.
Meantime as president-emperor I Senex employ

in the execution of governance the expedients
of postponement and triage:—These are the rules of rule.
What in our youth we considered solutions, what our public
relations officers with flourishing trumpets call
"Triumphs of Diplomacy," or "Our Leader's Military Genius,"
are stavings-off. When we stopped supplies for our camp
besieged on the Blue Nile, we gained petroleum and wheat
for the Manchurian campaign; Masada proved no obstacle,
nor the Wall. We strangled Vercingetorix
to purchase half a year. If a thousand decapitations

provide us a century of grain growing, water progressing
along aqueducts, and cattle freshening each spring,
who will not unbind the fasces and sharpen the axe?
Greek fire burnt Saracens at Byzantium's castle
and swamps over the same ages advanced and receded—
as now in the sour pond a pickerel chokes; as now
a whippoorwill dies unhatched in her frail shell.
Whenever mobs rise against torturers and murderers,
torturers and murderers rise to take their places
and Blues massacre Greens. Men enslave women

again and chop the beggar's hands off and tie
the homosexual's wrists to a killing post
and execute him with prostitutes and moneylenders.
Our former prime minister is dispatched by a single jurist
who empties a machine gun into his stomach.
Our Leader sends a note to the Arbiter, his obedient
counsellor, who opens his wrist in the bath while speaking
wittily with his entourage. But he dies too fast:
Slaves bandage his wrists. Remembering purpose at dawn,
he removes the gauze. Tiberius beheads six Jew doctors.

By Palmer Canyon the lemons in the irrigated groves
grow smaller each year. Here is the Republic's grave,
boneyard of Erasmus and Hume, Florentine gold
and azure, Donatello's bodily marble, graves of money
and liberty. Vertical barbarians ascend, the child armies
of passive ignorance. I Senex, president-emperor,
peering through cataracts, note that Greek fire has only
for the moment prevented Viking and Turk and Bolshevik
who scale my fortifications with devoted outrage
and howling for plunder break the small-paned windows.

ECLOGUE

Muses of Sicily, inspiration of father Theocritus
who muttered and meditated in Alexandria's pastures:—
Help me proclaim the child. Not everyone prays for fire
or adores the styrofoam cup and its trash compactor.
Equally we understand that the pinecone has its enemies,
that oxen and Rhode Island Reds resist affection
because they die. If we praise trees let us praise
the acorns of generation. While the Sibyl sings
the music of what happens, while Senex brags and grumbles
of millennia and legions, the jig of centuries

slows down, entropy's tune; and I sing before midnight,
before solstice, when the great year will regenerate
stone-heavy men and women from caves in oblivion's hills
to smelt iron again, to refine tools as fire discovers
the invented forge: iron, tin, bronze, silver.
New ages of metal will spiral with wars and prophets,
with heroes that poets sing of:—blind, scraping the bow
across the gusla. When the great year turns, the months
will lose their numbers, each hour outlasts a season,
spring and summer upthrust from new earth ten million

poppies, green flames of asparagus, and lilies
extravagant in breezes that waver corn and peonies;
and Holsteins dribble from abundant udders.
From the cradle daffodils and millet will spread
like water after blue rain in April, effluent
withdraw from air, the stream underground
with its eight-sided molecules purify itself,
and a fountain of clearness rise by its own pressure
into single light. Garlic will swell and deliver
garlic at the ninth month, Indian corn fly tassels,

swollen grapes turn purple and plump themselves
into wine, and the oak's acorns fatten for pigs of autumn.
By seed, by swelling and damp, the child will restore
bride to bridegroom and oldwife embrace her husband,
familiar skin rub against skin, ecstatic
adventure repeat itself, telling the flesh's circle
that coils into sleep, withdrawal and restoration,
to gather desire again. Work and love will increase
as grass enlarges in sun and downpour, emptying
itself to swell again: summer, autumn, winter, spring.

Meantime over the ages swamps advance and recede
and Phyllis stalls her Porsche at the intersection cursing
Marc who counts silver dollars into his piggy bank.
Senex turns senile, Juvenis in boyish furor studies
dialectics of the cattleprod; Amos rejects
history which ignores prophecy and camps armies
on the clearcut rainforest; Philip the Second sends
the Armada north again, Eric beaches among vines,
Caesar crosses the Channel, King John signs the paper under
baronial swords, Servetus escaping the inquisitor

burns in Zurich, Scott loses his way, Homer's agile fingers
draw the bow, and by his hexameters Grant besieges
Vicksburg again. But when the vector of greed withdraws
from the sea and the oak vessel sinks with its merchant,
and 727s disassemble on grownover airstrips,
out of the daily fields pomegranate trees and olives
will raise themselves, and without fertilizer or combines
Kansas and Dakota exalt perennial oats and barley;
sheep cropping the meadow will fleece themselves saffron
and green in bodily splendor for the splendor of looms.

Then will her born spirit enter the created tree
to uncreate the cracked bole and the black leaf; then
the universe will rest its domed head, and the spirited
seas of all worlds and lightyears in full arrest
with ghosts and molecules speak their exaltation
while the hour ends hours and the long soul lingers
in restitution of lost things and the return of fathers
and mothers from death's defensible castle:
Then will we worship creation in faithful skin;
then will we study the lamb careless in millet.

III

To Build a House

We consider that we have succeeded when hysterical misery turns into ordinary unhappiness.

—Sigmund Freud

A model! A model! What in hell would I do with a model? When I need to check something I go to my wife and lift her chemise.

—Aristide Maillol

Looking at May's blossoms, imagining bounty of McIntosh,
I praise old lilacs rising in woods beside cellarholes;
I praise toads. I predict the telephone call
that reports the friend from childhood cold on a staircase.
I praise children, grandchildren, and just-baked bread.
I praise fried Spam and onions on slices of Wonder Bread;
I praise your skin. I predict the next twenty years,
days of mourning, long walks growing slow and painful.
I reject twenty years of midlife; I reject rejections.
The one day stands unmoving in sun and shadow.

When I rise at eight o'clock my knuckles are stiff.
I sit for an hour wearing my nightgown in a sunny chair.
Hot water from the faucet, black coffee, and two aspirin
unstick my fingerjoints, and by these hands I join
the day that will never return. This is the single
day that extends itself, intent as an animal listening
for food, while I chisel at alabaster. All day I know
where the sun is. To seize the hour, I must cast myself
into work that I love, as the keeper hurls
horsemeat to the lion:—I am meat, lion, and keeper.

This afternoon the king and queen of Norway drove
downtown from their consulate to my studio. As we sat
drinking tea together, they were fastidious and democratic;
I had been told: It was not required to curtsy . . .
When the entourage disappeared into Third Avenue
I changed into jeans and climbed on my sore ankle
to the marble under the skylight. Matisse said, "Work
is paradise"; Rodin, "To work is to live without dying";
Flaubert, "It passes the time." For three hours
my mallet tapped while Donatello hovered above me.

There are ways to get rich: Find an old corporation,
self-insured, with capital reserves. Borrow
to buy: Then dehire managers; yellow-slip maintenance;
pay public relations to explain how winter is summer;
liquidate reserves and distribute cash in dividends:
Get out, sell stock for capital gains, reward the usurer,
and look for new plunder—leaving a mill town devastated,
workers idle on streetcorners, broken equipment, no cash
for repair or replacement, no inventory or credit.
Then vote for the candidate who abolishes foodstamps.

I embrace the creation, not for what it signifies,
but for volume and texture thrusting up
from the touched places. I marry the creation that stays
in place to be worked at, day after day.
The sparrow lights on my fire escape once and once only;—
there is only the one self; my day is to carve it
That my mother disintegrated while I watched her
flies past my window once; that I burned white houses
in middle life flies past my barred window once.
To know how the sparrow flies turns hours to marble.

After the Constitutional Convention in Philadelphia
the delegates started for home on horseback and in carriages,
for the former colonies of Massachusetts and Virginia,
for York State. They visited with friends telling stories.
They traveled all day; at nightfall they rested in taverns.
The moon waxed and waned; days grew long and shortened again;
it snowed; spring melted snow revealing gray grass.
Some sold horses to board steamboats working the rivers,
then disembarked for trains that shook out sparks
setting fire to grassy plain, sheepbarn, and farmhouse.

Some delegates hitched rides chatting with teamsters;
some flew standby and wandered stoned in O'Hare
or borrowed from King Alexander's National Bank: None
returned to plantation, farm, or townhouse.
They wandered weary until they encountered each other
again, converging on Hollywood Boulevard bordered with bars
in their absurd clothing like movie extras, Federalist
and Republican descending the cloverleaf together
to engage another Convention at the Hollywood–La Brea Motel—
wearing their nametags, befuddled, unable to argue.

There are ways to get by. When we bought this grownover
orchard from Bone's widow, we burnt birch the first winter
and worked odd jobs part-time: sugaring, logging, substitute
teaching, schoolbus driving. The first summer we culled
old trees past saving (next winter we kept ourselves warm
in the scent of applewood); others we trimmed and topdressed.
Next spring we set out three hundred semidwarves
in the old hayfield that sloped north by the disused
railroad under the pasture turned into woodlot: McIntosh
mostly, New Hampshire's goodness, October's fiery compacted

appleflesh; Cortland, Empire, Strawberry, Astrakhan,
Baldwin, Spy . . . We order our days by the paradisal
routine of apples: from winter of pies and cider
through spring's trim and exaltation of blossom,
through summer's attention and repair: then picking
with neighbors, selling at roadside, packing for market . . .
We age among apples—in dread of icestorm, wet snow
in May, drought, August wind forcing early drops; wary
of bark-eating deer, of bears that break branches climbing.
From the first orchard to the last is one day and forever.

Smoke rises all day from two chimneys above us.
You stand by the stove looking south, through bare branches
of McIntosh, Spy, and Baldwin. You add oak logs
to the fire you built at six in the castiron stove.
At the opposite end of the same house, under another chimney,
I look toward the pond that flattens to the west
under the low sun of a January afternoon, from a notebook
busy with bushels and yields. All day in our opposite
rooms we carry wood to stoves, we pace up and down, we plan,
we set figures on paper—to converge at day's end

for kisses, bread, and talk; then we read in silence,
sitting in opposite chairs; then we turn drowsy.
Dreaming of tomorrow only, we sleep in the painted bed
while the night's frail twisting of woodsmoke assembles
overhead from the two chimneys, to mingle and disperse
as our cells will disperse and mingle when they lapse
into graveyard dirt. Meantime the day is double
in the work, love, and solitude of eyes
that gaze not at each other but at a third thing:
a child, a ciderpress, a book—work's paradise.

From north pole and south we approach each other;
Atlantic encounters Pacific, up meets down:
Where extremes meet we make our equator:—your body
with narrow waist and carved shoulders, hips
comely, breasts outswooping; my body intent,
concentrated, and single. We enter this planisphere
without strangeness, betrayal, or risk; our bodies
after bright tumult float in shadow and repose
of watery sleep, skin's fury settling apart
and pole withdrawing to pole: A bed is the world.

Or: Buy fifty acres of pasture from the widower:
Survey, cut a road, subdivide; bulldoze the unpainted
barn, selling eighteenth-century beams with bark
still on them; bulldoze foundation granite that oxen sledded;
bulldoze stone walls set with lost skill; bulldoze the Cape
the widower lived in; bulldoze his father's seven-apple tree.
Drag the trailer from the scraggly orchard to the dump:
Let the poor move into the spareroom of their town
cousins; pave garden and cornfield; build weekend houses
for skiers and swimmers; build Slope 'n' Shore; name the new

road Blueberry Muffin Lane; build Hideaway Homes
for executives retired from pricefixing for General Electric
and migrated north out of Greenwich to play bridge
with neighbors migrated north out of Darien. Build huge
centrally heated Colonial ranches—brick, stone, and wood
confounded together—on pasture slopes that were white
with clover, to block public view of Blue Mountain.
Invest in the firm foreclosing Kansas that exchanges
topsoil for soybeans. Vote for a developer as United States
senator. Vote for statutes that outlaw visible poverty.

I crashed like my daredevil pilots; it was what
I wanted. For two years I moved among institutions,
admitted because of barbiturates (I took pills
to keep from dreaming), alcohol, and depression.
Electroshock blanked me out. If I worked my hands shook;
when I carved, my chisel slipped making errors:—
I contrived art out of errors. For five years I talked
with a white-haired woman three times a week.
Once toward the end I complained: "Is it possible, ever,
to be single-minded?" I spoke in discouragement, glimpsing

the erratum slip on my psyche: "For love read hate
throughout; for hate read love." White eyebrows wavered:
"In this life?" But later she added: "One day
you will love someone." I wept the whole hour with relief
and without confidence. If singleness is impossible, how
do we discover its idea that mocks us? Our longing
for being, beyond doubt and skepticism, assembles itself
from moments when the farmer scything alfalfa fills
with happiness as the underground cave fills with water;
or when we lose self in the hourless hour of love.

The one day clarifies and stays only when days depart:
"The days you work," said O'Keeffe, "are the best days."
Whole mornings disappeared through my hand into elmwood
before me. I did what I wanted: As my hand
strengthened I lost day after day that did not return
doubled and burnt in drug-time's cindery lapse.
No longer did I rage at my young father dying
in the wrecked car. I slept all night without murder:
I talked with my friend; with my children I visited
the zoo on Wednesday; teasing I cooked them dinner.

When I was forty I married again. I kept him twelve years
until the occlusion snapped him off like a light. Now when
I am discontent, when the beekeeper's shadow approaches
up the desolate block, I number his disappearance
among the griefs and cinders where it belongs;
but neither the howl of loss nor ecstatic adventure remains
largest in store: My grainshed keeps the single
repeated green-valley day, repose of imaginable summer,
long hours not hours at all, vacant of number:
Like great Holsteins we chewed the voluptuous grass.

From burnt houses and blacked shrubs, green rises
like bread. Because the Revolution failed; because men
and women are corrupt and equal; because we eat topsoil
and Massachusetts smokes Virginia's tobacco; because
dancers twist in Alexandrine and millennial light
and lemons grow smaller in the groves; because the old
house burnt, because I burnt it, we carry green inside
from the hill: Potted plants on shelves braced
at every window or hanging in rope fingers take sunlight:
We drowse on a green bed in the valley of the third thing.

Here, among the thirty thousand days of a long life,
a single day stands still: The sun shines, it is raining;
we sleep, we make love, we plant a tree, we walk up and down
eating lunch: The day waits at the center when I reached out
to touch the face in the mirror, and never
touched glass, touched neither cheekbone nor eyelid,
touched galaxies instead and the void they hung on.
The one day extended from that moment, unrolling
continuous as the broad moon on water, or as motions of rain
that journey a million times through air to water.

The one day speaks of July afternoons, of February
when snow builds shingle in spruce, when the high sugarmaple
regards the abandoned barn tilted inward, moving
in storm like Pilgrims crossing the Atlantic under sail.
Nebuchadnezzar and the grocer fish with the same pole;
Nebuchadnezzar listens to his chief of staff complaining;
the grocer's son has broken his arm in Texas.
Leave behind appointments listed on the printout!
Leave behind manila envelopes! Leave dark suits behind,
boarding passes, and soufflés at the chancellor's house!

The great rock at the side of the road reminds us.
Long ago we slipped, rodents among ferns like redwoods;
elongating our claws we climbed the baobab;
for millennia we hung by one hand eating with the other
until we dropped to hide in lengthening grass;
by the waterhole we walked upright sniffing for cats;
we chased elephants into the bog with our brothers;
for ten thousand years we scudded beneath bushes: I leaned
from ladder into tree; you watered the Burgundy Lily.
When we die it is the cell's death in a hair-end.

I walk around a corner in the strange town and arrive
at the first street of my childhood—the house of half-blue,
half-yellow, the black Pierce-Arrow beside it. The tomcat
plays with his mother, sucking and teasing; he cuffs
his mother's jaw. The tomcat limps home in the bloody
morning, ear torn. The tomcat sleeps all day
in a portion of sun, fur tatty over old scars, pulls
himself to the saucer of milk, and snores going back
to sleep, knowing himself the same. The kitten leaps
in the air, her paws spread like a squirrel's.

The one day stands unmoving in sun and shadow:
like the tuft of grass left behind in the pasture
when the Holstein heard the farmer call her for milking
and remembered fresh millet; like Tunisian aqueducts
and butcherblock counters; like Blackwater Pond
with its dirt road; like the committee's styrofoam cup
that lives so briefly to contain coffee and its whitener
for ten minutes between the cellophaned stack
and the trash compactor; like the granite boulder
that the glacier deposited by the orchard's creek.

We return to inhabit this old house over Bone's orchard
that we will abandon in death only, our bodies slow
to assemble each morning as we gaze north at our trees.
We congregate, we grow to diminish again, we drowse.
I remember the dead fox warm on the barn floor,
inexplicably dead, and how my grandmother tenderly
lifted the body on her pitchfork, strands of hay
under the delicate corpse of the young red fox,
to the burying place by the willow at the garden's edge
where we left the barncat's kittens killed in the road.

Now the lost friend or the repudiated self
sinks into wood of the table, throat heaving with veins,
hands trembling to hold the beer for waking up with,
tumbler of whiskey to steady his hands until lunch.
He is fat now, transparent hanging flesh, and he sighs
for lost love and betrayed day:—for what he wanted.
Or he walks the criminal's yard in the penitentiary
at Clinton, cursing and mumbling, seeing no one,
tracks on his arm scrabbled over—that one shaking there,
gray-faced, who once was eager in pursuit of honor:

He walks delicately, impeccably, trembling in outrage,
among criminals in New York, like a sick fox
seeking the hay floor. When my sister drowns
my lungs fill also: We are one cell perpetually
dying and being born, led by a single day that presides
over our passage through the thirty thousand days
from highchair past work and love to suffering death.
We plant; we store the seedcorn. Our sons and daughters
topdress old trees. Two chimneys require:
Work, love, build a house, and die. But build a house.

When I was ninety I spent my days beside the window,
looking at birds from my wheelchair; sometimes I sketched.
To go to the White House for the President's Medal
I needed help, and the Secret Service was helpful.
I omitted my diuretic that morning; that day I fasted.
A limousine took me to the air base where I was hoisted
into Air Force One for the brief flight to Andrews.
I remember little of the day, although with old friends
gathered for the ceremony I chatted about the past.
I felt no pain except when I stood for the medal.

This morning we watch tall poppies light up
in a field of grass. At the town dump, one styrofoam cup
endures eight hundred years. Under the barn,
fat and ancient grandfather spider sleeps
among old spoked wheels: Our breathing shakes his web:
It is always this time; the time that we live by
is this time. Together we walk in the high orchard
at noon; it is cool, although the sun poises upon us.
Among old trees the creek breathes slowly,
bordered by fern. The toad at our feet holds still.

7  The Height and House of Desire

Tubes

1

"Up, down, good, bad," said
the man with the tubes
up his nose, "there's lots
of variety ...
However, notions
of balance between
extremes of fortune
are *stupid*—or at
best unobservant."
He watched as the nurse
fed pellets into
the green nozzle that
stuck from his side. "Mm,"
said the man. "Good. Yum.
(Next time more basil ...)
When a long-desired
baby is born, what
joy! More happiness
than we find in sex,
more than we take in
success, revenge, or
wealth. But should the same
infant die, would you
measure the horror
on the same rule? Grief
weighs down the seesaw;
joy cannot budge it."

2
"When I was nineteen,
I told a thirty-
year-old man what a
fool I had been when
I was seventeen.
'We were always,' he
said glancing down, 'a
fool two years ago.'"

3
The man with the tubes
up his nostrils spoke
carefully: "I don't
regret what I did,
but that I claimed I
did the opposite.
If I was faithless
or treacherous and
cowardly, I had
my reasons—but I
regret that I called
myself loyal, brave,
and honorable."

4
"Of all illusions,"
said the man with the
tubes up his nostrils,
IVs, catheter,
and feeding nozzle,
"the silliest one
was hardest to lose.
For years I supposed
that after climbing
exhaustedly up

with pitons and ropes,
I would arrive at
last on the plateau
of walking-level-
forever-among-
moss-with-red-blossoms.
But of course, of course:
A continual
climbing is the one
form of arrival
we ever come to—
unless we suppose
that the wished-for height
and house of desire
is tubes up the nose."

MOON CLOCK

Like an oarless boat through midnight's watery
ghosthouse, through lumens and shallows
of shadow, under smoky light that the full moon
reflects from snowfields to ceilings, I drift
on January's tide from room to room, pausing
by the wooden clock with its pendulum that keeps
the beat like a heart certainly beating, to wait
for the pause allowing passage
to repose's shore—where all waves halt
upreared and stony as the moon's Mycenaean lions.

CAROL

The warmth of cows
    That chewed on hay
And cherubim

Protected Him
    As small He lay.

Chickens and sheep
    Knew He was there
Because all night
A holy light
    Suffused the air.

Darkness was long
    And the sun brief
When the Child arose
A man of sorrows
    And friend to grief.

PERSISTENCE OF 1937

After fifty years Amelia Earhart's Lockheed fretted with rust
still circles over the Pacific. From her skull's scrimshaw
she peers downward, looking for a lane through permanent
    weather
while a sixty-year-old man carves her story onto whalebone,
slowly incising the fifth-grader who paces from kitchen
through livingroom to parlor back to kitchen, eating unbuttered
slices of Wonder Bread, listening to the Philco for bulletins
from the Navy: *After fifty years her Lockheed still circles.*

SIX NAPS IN ONE DAY

1

In the nap there are numerous doors, boudoirs, a talking hall
of sisters who gesture underwater, and bricked-up memoirs
with closets inside. There are bikes and desks in the nap,

2

corridors of glory, water, and pots of ivy hooked to ceiling
or ocean floor. Apes play with papers on the busy desk
I swim up to, through laborious sleep water. Rex the butcher

3

wears a straw hat sleeping on sawdust. When the extinguished
U-boat, flapping bat wings, settles under millennial silt,
whose eyes gleam through the periscope? They are Regina's.

4

Two squadrons of black biplanes dogfight over the trenches
of nineteen seventeen, death's-heads graven on engine cowlings,
helmeted pilots' faces turned into skulls, and their bones

5

as shadowy blue as underwater feet in the shoestore x-ray.
The gibbon's cry hobbles on the wooded shore, like the cry
of this bed. He walks by the ocean's tide a thousand years

6

in his gown of claws and hair, a deposed king searching
for sleep's bosom and the tall queen of dunes: Regina
skulks hiding in salt grass—while the halt gibbon howls.

THE COFFEE CUP

The newspaper, the coffee cup, the dog's
    impatience for his morning walk:
These fibers braid the ordinary mystery.
    After the marriage of lovers
the children came, and the schoolbus
    that stopped to pick up the children,

and the expected death of the retired
    mailman Anthony "Cat" Middleton
who drove the schoolbus for a whole
    schoolyear, a persistence enduring
forever in the soul of Marilyn,
    who was six years old that year.

We dug a hole for him. When his widow
    Florence sold the Cape and moved to town
to live near her daughter, the Mayflower
    van was substantial and unearthly.
Neither lymphoma nor a brown-and-white
    cardigan twenty years old

made an exception, not elbows nor
    Chevrolets nor hills cutting blue
shapes on blue sky, not Maple Street
    nor Main, not a pink-striped canopy
on an ice cream store, not grass.
    It was ordinary that on the day

of Cat's funeral the schoolbus arrived
    driven by a woman called Mrs. Ek,
freckled and thin, wearing a white
    bandana and overalls, with one
eye blue and the other gray. Everything
    is strange; nothing is strange.

This Poem

1

This poem is why
I lie down at night
to sleep; it is why

I defecate, read,
and eat sandwiches;
it is why I get
up in the morning;
it is why I breathe.

2
You think (and I know
because you told me)
that poems exist
to *say* things, as you
telephone and I
write letters—as if
this poem practiced
communication.

3
One time this poem
compared itself to
new machinery,
and another time
to a Holstein's cud.
Eight times five times eight
counts three hundred and
twenty syllables.

4
When you require it,
this poem consoles—
the way a mountain
comforts by staying
as it was despite
earthquakes, presidents,
divorces, and frosts.
Granite continues.

5

This poem informs
the hurt ear wary
of noises, and sings
to the weeping eye.
When the agony
abates itself, one
may appreciate
arbitrary art.

6

This poem is here.
Could it be someplace
else? Every question
is the wrong question.
The only answer
saunters down the page
in its broken lines
strutting and primping.

7

It styles itself not
for the small mirror
of its own regard—
nor even for yours:
to fix appearance;
to model numbers;
to name charity
"the greatest of these."

8

All night this poem
knocks at the closed door
of sleep: "Let me in."
Suppose all poems

contain this poem,
dreaming one knowledge
shaped by the measure
of the body's word.

Praise for Death

1

Let us praise death that turns pink cheeks to ashes,
that reduces father from son and daughter, that sets tears
in the tall widow's eye. Let us praise death that gathers
us loose-limbed and weeping by the grave's edge in the flat
yard near the sea that continues. Let us praise death

2

that fastens my body to yours and renders skin
against skin sometimes intolerably sweet, as October
sweetens the flesh of a McIntosh apple. Let us praise
death that prints snapshots, fixing an afternoon forty
years ago on a sandy lane. While we stand holding

3

each other, let us praise death as a dog praises
its master, bowing, paying obeisance, rolling over;
let us praise death as a spaniel praises a pitbull.
What remained of her at the end, compared to my friend
eight months before, was the orange peel to the orange:

4

as if the shard of fruit—once pungent and moist, now smeared
with coffeegrounds—pulsed, opened an eye, and screamed
without stopping. As we enter the passage of agony,
imagining darkness prepared underground, we recollect
Jesus who drank from the cup: "Why have you forsaken me?"

5

Praising death we sing parts with Between-the-Rivers,
with the King of Uruk, dole's aboriginal singer.
The Victorian with his imperial figleaf praises death
like the Inca, or like the first emperor of Qin
who models a deathless army in terra cotta. Let us

6

praise rictus and the involuntary release of excrement
as the *poilu* does, and Attila, and the Vestal Virgin.
We remember the terrified face behind the plexiglass mask
as Hadrian remembers Antinous. Are you rich, young,
lucky, and handsome? Are you old and unknown?

7

Are you Mesopotamian, suburbanite, Cossack, Parisian?
We praise death so much, we endow our children with it.
At seventy-eight, Henry Adams spent the summer of 1916
discussing with Brooks "the total failure of the universe,
most especially *our* country." From London he heard

8

that Harry James was dead, who "belonged to my wife's set,"
he wrote Elizabeth Cameron, "and you know how I cling
to my wife's set." Thirty years before, he discovered Clover,
still warm, her lips damp with potassium cyanide.
"All day today," he wrote, "I have been living in the '70s."

9

By the river abandoned factories tilt like gravestones.
Mills collapse behind broken windows over soil broken
to build them, where millhands wore their lives out
standing in fractured noisy stench among endless belts
and hoses steaming waste to the fish-killing river.

10

Commerce dies; and commerce raises itself elsewhere.
If we read the Boston *Globe* on a Monday, we find fixed
to the business section the part-index: *Deaths, Comics.*
The old father's dignity, as he daily and hourly rehearses
the lines of his pain, stiffens him into a tableau vivant.

11

All day he studies the script of no-desire, scrupulous
never to want what he cannot have. He controls speech,
he controls desire, and a young man's intense blue eyes
look from his face as he asks his grandniece to purchase,
at the medical supply store, rubber pants and disposable pads.

12

Let us praise death that raises itself to such power
that nothing but death exists: not breakfast nor the Long
Island Expressway, not cigarettes nor beaches at Maui,
not the Tigers nor sunrise except under the aspect
of death. Let us praise death that recedes: One day

13

we realize, an hour after waking, that for a whole hour
we have forgotten the dead, so recently gone underground,
whom we swore we would mourn from the moment we opened
our eyes. All night in sleep I watch as the sinewy, angry
body careers and hurtles in harmless air, hovering

14

like a hang glider over the western slope of Kearsarge,
fired from the Porsche that explodes, rips open, settles,
and burns while the body still twists in the air, arms
akimbo, Exxon cap departing frail skull, ponytail out
straight, until it ends against granite. Let us praise

15

death that bursts skull, lungs, spleen, liver, and heart.
Let us praise death for the piano player who quit high school
in 1921 and played *le jazz hot* through France and Italy;
who recorded with *Lud Gluskin et son Jazz* four hundred
sides of a barrelhouse left hand; who jammed with Bix

16

at Walled Lake in 1930; who tinkled foxtrots for Goldkette
and Weems, suitcase depression nights of Wilkes-Barre
and Akron; who settled down to play clubs, give lessons,
run the musician's Local, and when he died left
a thousand books behind, with the markers still in them.

17

Let us praise the death of dirt. The builder tells us
that the most effective way to preserve topsoil
is to pave it over. Petersen's farm in Hamden raised
corn, beans, and tomatoes for sale at New Haven's markets.
For a hundred years they ripened in Adams Avenue's

18

countryside among the slow cattle of dairy farms.
Now slopes extrude hairy antennae; earth conceals itself
under parking lots and the slimy, collapsing sheds
of STOP & SHOP, BROOKS, BOB'S, CALDOR, and CRAZY EDDIE.
The empire rots turning brown. Junkyards of commerce

19

slide into tar over dirt impervious to erosion, sun, wind,
and the breaking tips of green-leafed, infrangible corn.
Beside his right eye and low on his neck shiny patches of skin
blaze the removed cancer. The fifty-year-old poet and I
drink seltzer together in the Grasshopper Tavern; he rants

20

like Thersites denouncing his Greeks. Probably it won't
kill him, but toadstool up each year: *"I want"*—he looks
longingly; desire remakes his face—*"I want so much to die."*
Let us never forget to praise the death of a red tomcat.
Downstairs her nieces gather weeping among soft chairs

21

while neighbors bring casseroles and silence;
in the bedroom the widower opens the closet door
where her dresses hang, and finds one hanger swaying.
At Blackwater Farm beside Route 4 the vale bellies
wide from the river, four hundred acres of black dirt

22

over glacial sand, where Jack and his uncles spread
a century of cow manure. They milked their cattle
morning and night, feeling them grain, silage, and hay
while the renewable sisters drank at the river's edge,
chewed cuds, bore yearly calves, bounded and mooed

23

to praise each other's calving, and produced a frothing
blue-white Atlantic of Holstein milk. Yesterday the roads
went in, great yellow earthmachines dozing through loam
to sand, as Jack's boy Richard raises fifty Colonial Capes
with two-car garages and driveways, RIVERVIEW MEADOW FARMS

24

over smothered alluvial soil. "Death tends to occur,"
as the Professor actually said, "at the end of life."
When I heard that his daughter coming home from her job
found Clarence cold in his bed, I remembered the veiny
cheeks and laconic stories: For one moment I mourned him.

25
Then I felt my lungs inflate themselves deeply, painfully:
I imagined my own body beneath the disordered quilt.
For the first time in a year I felt myself collapse
under the desire to smoke. Like you, I want to die:
We praise death when we smoke, and when we stop smoking.

26
After the farmer fired him, the drunk farmhand returned
at nightfall and beat him to death with a tire iron
while his wife and six-year-old son stood watching.
As his father's body flopped in the wet sand, as blood
coiled out of ears, the boy—who had observed

27
hens without heads, stuck pigs, and a paralyzed mule
twitching in a stall—cried, "Die! Please die. Please."
Let us praise St. Nihil's Church of the Suburban Consensus;
at St. Nihil's we keep the coffin closed for the funeral;
when we take Communion at St. Nihil's, the Euphemism melts

28
in our mouths: *pass, pass away, sleep, decease, expire.*
Quickly by shocking fire that blackens and vanishes,
turning insides out, or slowly by fires of rust and rot,
the old houses die, the barns and outbuildings die.
Let us praise death that removes nails carpenters hammered

29
during the battle of Shiloh; that solves the beam-shape
an adze gave an oak tree; that collapses finally
the settler's roof into his root cellar, where timber sawn
two centuries ago rots among weeds and saplings. Let us
praise death for the house erected by skill and oxen.

30

Let us praise death in old age. Wagging our tails,
bowing, whimpering, let us praise sudden crib-death
and death in battle: Dressed in blue the rifleman charges
the granite wall. Let us praise airplane crashes.
We buried thirty-year-old Stephen the photographer

31

in Michigan's November rain. His bony widow Sarah, pale
in her loose black dress, leaned forward impulsively
as the coffin, suspended from a yellow crane, swayed
over the hole. When she touched the shiny damp maple
of the box, it swung slightly away from her

32

as it continued downward. Stephen's mother Joan
knelt first to scrape wet dirt onto the coffin lid;
then his father Peter lifted handfuls and let them drop,
then his sister Sarah, then his widow Sarah. Under
scraggly graveyard trees, five young gravediggers stood

33

smoking together, men tattooed and unshaven, wearing
baseball caps, shifting from foot to foot, saying
nothing, trying never to watch in Michigan's November rain.
"Bitterly, bitterly I weep for my blood-brother Enkidu.
Should I *praise* master death that commanded my friend?

34

"I wander hunting in the forest weeping salt tears;
in my anger I slaughter the deer. Bitterly I cry:
'Nowhere can I lay my head down to rest or to sleep!
Despair sucks my liver out! Desolation eats bitter meat
from my thigh! What happened to my brother will happen to me.'

35
"I stood by his body eight days. I implored him to throw
death over, to rise and pull his gold breastplate on.
On the ninth day worms crawled from the skin of his neck.
Now, therefore, I climb to the sun's garden, to Utnapishtim
who alone of all men after the flood lives without dying."

SPEECHES

1
Two old men
meet at the lunch
    counter

of Blackwater Bill's
after the first
    hard

frost: "And how
did your garden
    fare?"

2
"Sherm never
was afraid
    of work."

3
Chester Ludlow
told me stories
    about my

two great-grand-
fathers Chester
    remembered,

about frogging
one hundred
   bullfrogs,

about his old
steam-tractor
   Greta

that blew up
on the Fourth
   of July—

and when I stood
to go, Chester
   asked, "You

going to write
this down
   in a book?"

"May be." "Told
you a lot
   of lies."

   4
"It's down to
the store up by
   Wilmot way."

   5
If you asked,
"Does it look
   like rain?"

during the year's
worst downpour,
   Kate said,

"Maybe, I guess,
perhaps, I
   suppose so . . ."

     6
At Wilmot
town meeting,
   Bob the town

moderator asked,
"All those in
   favor of

buying Henry
his new front-
   loader?"

     7
Wes said, "Saw
a piece about you
   in the paper."

I told him,
"Oh, I turn up
   everyplace."

"Yup," said
Wes. "Just like
   horseshit."

8
Lila dialed
Bertha to tell
   her go

look out her
parlor window
   east:

"It's as pretty
as a picture
   postcard."

9
"Fellow lost
his bobhouse,
   works

down to Henry's,
's he the Budd
   boy's wife

ran off with
the bread driver
   hates beaver?"

"Blows up dams with
TNT? No, that's
   not him."

10
At Blackwater
Bill's, Jenny
   yells to Claude

in the kitchen, "Hey,
Froggie, nuke us
   some beans."

The Night of the Day

Cool October, Monday night. I waited for kickoff
at nine o'clock as the long day declined
when I turned older than my dark-haired father
ever got to be. I leaned back sleepy in my chair
as the Dallas Cowboys kicker approached the tee
and was startled to hear a pickup in the drive.
At the door I found Larry Lamorte, agitated
and pointing backward down dark Route 4.
"Dawn!" he shouted. "Dawn! There's something
in the road! Heifers! Bulls!"
                    Looking past him
into the moonless night, I saw bulky forms
that moved heavily on blacktop, as incongruous
as battleships on Eagle Pond. Larry's old Datsun
shuddered as he apologized, "Sorry not to help.
I promised Earlene I'd watch that show about apes."
   I stared through the dark at the creatures:
heifers? Bulls were unlikely. Through the dark
I watched their ruminant motion, black on black,
and thought: If a late-night Plymouth hurried
over the hill at sixty-five, somebody could die.
Inside I woke Jane to telephone Peg Smith,
our constable who usually rounded up black Labs,
not Holsteins, and to wake our neighbors
downstreet. After I walked back out, approaching
cow shapes that hovered over macadam, I heard
Dave Perkins's door slam and watched father and son
walk toward me, black moving against blackness,

and heard David hallo through the silence,
"Whose heifers do they be?"
                        When David and I
were boys—and I visited for the summer, up
from Connecticut—all the old Route 4 farmers
kept a few cattle, raised one or two heifers,
and sitting on stools alongside runty Holsteins
squeezed out two cans of bluish milk a day;
the milk truck stopped at dawn. In return
for the old men's haying, milking morning and night,
hauling ice from the pond for summer's milk,
and raising field corn, H. P. Hood & Co.
mailed them a monthly check, sometimes as much
as twenty dollars. The summer I was thirteen,
my grandfather and I spent an August day chasing
two wild heifers that escaped from a pasture,
but tonight's skinny creatures were tame. Whose
could they be? Nobody raised cattle nowadays
in this valley of old pastures becoming woodlots
(houselots sometimes, and sometimes video
outlets) with only a few fields flat enough
for a tractor to work in; now, to break even,
you needed to milk fifty registered pedigreed
Holsteins—and borrow from Fleet to buy
a milking machine, a stainless-steel cooling tank,
a Macintosh computer, and a frontloader
to spread manure on three hundred hayable acres—
and still you worked sixteen hours;
or you labored all week at the mill to support
your addiction to Holsteins.
                        David and Paul and I
cowboyed the seven heifers from Route 4
to the field beside our barn where their ancestors
had chomped for a hundred years. Whose could
they be? I called my cousin Sherman Buzzle

—selectman, deer hunter, carpenter, pig raiser;
who knew every voter in Wilmot by name—
and woke him where he lived two miles away
in a white Cape with many sheds that our common
great-grandfather built, and asked him
if anybody nearby still kept a herd of cattle.
Sherman was curious. Right after I hung up
(Jane bundled herself into three sweaters
and came outside to help), Sherm's 4 x 4 GMC
maneuvered into the driveway, and he swaggered
to join us—forty years old, hitching green
workpants under his belly, burly or maybe fat
but strong—and peered through darkness
at loose heifers munching asters by the barn.
    Then Peg Smith's new Ford braked at the margin
of the road with her flashers flashing,
and she heaved uphill to join us. Just behind,
her deputy Ned Buttrey parked his Plymouth van,
sparking another cadence, and approached
grinning with one tooth. Ned looked back
at Route 4's shoulder blinking on-and-off,
said, "Looks like quite some party," and laughed,
joining our circle.
                    We gossiped together,
mostly ignoring the heifers that mostly
ignored us back as they moseyed to browse.
Now I saw the cattle clearly enough: young,
not yet bulked-out, bony, old-style Holsteins.
Somebody driving down Route 4 saw car lights
pulsing; he braked, backed up, parked, turned
his flashers on, and joined us. Now we were eight,
but David said goodnight; he needed to load
his truck at five; and Paul went to high school,
David reminded us, who had left school at fourteen.
The quiet father and son walked home together.

I noticed how, not thinking of anybody watching,
they were holding hands.
                              Sherman listed neighbors
who kept cows: Bill Marcik across the pond,
who raised sheep for the wool that his wife Sally
spun and wove, kept a few decorator Holsteins;
but *seven* heifers? We agreed it couldn't be Bill.
Jane mentioned Willy DeLord; when she said his name,
everyone laughed. Sherman spoke common knowledge:
"Willy likes to fence the front of his pasture.
He never gets around to fence the back."
But Willy's disheveled hill farm straggled
on Ragged Mountain five miles north, too far
for Willy's heifers to wander. Peg had a thought:
"Maybe perhaps Ed Ek keeps cows?" Knowingly
Sherman nodded. "Penelope," he said. "But Penny
died on Ed last year November. Old age."
Ned remarked that Sherm remembered names of cows
even though they never voted, "or hardly ever."
We laughed and stomped our feet. The stranger
said maybe these cows were wild, like the bears
that came back to our woods after a hundred years.
I told him I liked the notion of feral cows
returning to this New Hampshire valley
of disappearances.
                              Then I went back inside
to telephone Bill Marcik, just to *do* something,
and Bill answered, "Well, let me see.
Mother and daughter were there at eight o'clock.
Want me go see? I'll take a look." I told him no;
I doubted even *his* two cattle could multiply
into seven so fast. "Do you have an idea
whose they might be?"
                              "Try Willy," Bill said.
Walking back, I heard the sound of stories

in a laugh that rose abruptly from the circle,
from pale faces over sweaters and down jackets
beside the barn—a laugh that ended a story
with gaiety's flare, like a wooden match striking
gold inside a stove. I said, "They're not Bill's.
Bill said try Willy." Nobody had an idea;
nobody fretted. Somebody started to tell the one
about the bull butting the vet that brought syringes.

    Well, *I* fretted: "What do I *do* with them?"
Sherm offered: "Feed them poems. They tell
you've got extra. They tell you keep old bales
of poems stacked in the hayloft."

                              We kept a roof
over our tie-up, but no cows stirred under shingle
since my grandfather's heart gave out
thirty years ago. Did I want to wear overalls?
For a moment I milked the cattle of daydream
morning and night; but no: I knew how I wanted
to spend my day. I farmed in the summers of boyhood
and that was enough of farming.

                              But whose heifers
were they? I jogged inside to ring up
Willy DeLord, asleep five miles away or not.
When I told him who I was, and said I was sorry
to wake him, and mentioned the heifers,
Willy's doleful voice ascended to interrupt me:
"Ohhh, *darn.* Ohhh, *darn.* I'll be down—*darn!*
darn!—as soon as I find my pants."

                              With Willy
on his way, Jane and I alone could have kept
the heifers in place, but nobody wanted
this impromptu party to end; we felt giddy,
the way children do when something extraordinary
keeps them up past bedtime and rules are broken,
all rules are broken, as they are in Paradise.

Sherm told about plowing one February morning
at three o'clock as a snowstorm finished:
"I was scraping Jones's driveway up near Willy's
and saw the electric light in Willy's tie-up."
He found Willy sound asleep, snoring, his head
rising and falling on a Holstein's ribcage.
I remembered my grandfather's tales of Pete Butts,
the Willy DeLord of another day. Peter Butts
planted corn in August and stacked hay in his barn
mixed with snow: Pete's hay turned black, rotting
in his rotting loft, and he died in the poorhouse.
   Peg Smith was telling how Willy's father
was a martinet of whitewashed tie-ups
and exact routines—while Willie can't sell his milk
because his barn would never pass inspection.
Sherm told how he and his brother Grant
took three days to muck out decades of cowshit,
black straw, and spiderwebs from Willy's tie-up
after H. P. Hood & Co. mailed its ultimatum.
"It took Willy one week to make it dirty as ever.
So Willy can't pay town taxes, July and December"
—he farms to feed his family: growing a garden,
churning butter the way his grandmother did,
feeding milk to pigs in order to smoke bacon,
slaughtering Holsteins to grind for hamburger—
"and every year in the fall, for taxes" (Sherman
said it aloud), "Willy sells another piece
of his daddy's farm."
                         No one spoke. Changing
the subject without changing it, Ned Buttrey
remembered how Peter Butts never cut stovewood
one winter, "so instead Pete burned old bed frames
that he hauled down from the attic, busted
rocking chairs, spinning wheels, picture frames,
and wooden chests that saved dead people's

frocks and union suits." He burned broken tables
enough to stock ten antique shops, or enough
to buy himself an oil furnace, but Pete
never thought of attic things as ANTIQUES FOR SALE.
He used up useless stuff, and the green captain's
chair his great-granddaddy dozed in burned hot,
real hot, in the rusted Glenwood kitchen range.
The last thing he burned that year—Peggy tells us;
all of us know these stories—was his outhouse.
Pete pulled it down with the nineteen twenty-four
John Deere Model D that he used for a tractor,
and sawed it up for the stove, ending
with the five-holed ancient plank, "which didn't
smell too good when it burned, is what
they say."
        Each of us waited to add a story,
this storytelling night—it was so dark
we never saw each other's faces except
when Sherman lit a Camel; we knew each face
by its voice's shape—but before we told another,
Willy DeLord's enormous rusting Buick
sang on its dying bearings into the driveway.
(Sherm took time to mention, dropping his voice,
that Willy never changed his motor oil.
"You know that row of wrecks behind his barn . . .")
Then Willy bounced from his car, grinning, cringing
with apology, and groaning, "Gol darn it to heck!"
Victoria drove the car. Stepping out,
she followed Willy a pace behind, smiling faintly
to let you know it was Willy's predicament,
not hers. (*Willy* was hers.) "Sorry we took so long,"
she said. "We couldn't find Willy's pants."
In Victoria's headlights we watched Willy, garlanded
with rope, creep up on his loitering creatures.
He wore pinstriped gabardine trousers, muddy black

wingtip shoes, brown suspenders that rounded up
over his belly, and a Sears workshirt with many darns.
Our circle tightened to watch him as he roped
his cattle one by one, tying quick knots
around each black-and-white neck, his bulky body
agile and quick, until he hitched his heifers
together and straightened up—smiling, puffing,
and proud.

        By now it was midnight, three hours
after kickoff: no more traffic, which was good
because Willy had to drive his cattle now
five miles home, tapping their sluggard backs
with a birch sapling. Would Willy repair
his fence tonight? No, no. Maybe tomorrow
his seven heifers would graze Route 4 again.
He waved goodbye, driving his cattle, as Victoria
rolled the Buick three miles an hour behind him,
headlights on bright to forewarn an oncoming car.
Now Peggy, Ned, Sherm, and the stranger made goodbyes
and headed to their machines; one by one, starters
whirred, engines caught, headlights lit, flashers
stopped flashing, and cars U-turned to vanish.
Jane went inside, to bed and electric blanket.
Silence and darkness returned, blessed dark silence,
interrupted again by Larry Lamorte's rusty Datsun
crushing the driveway's gravel. "Dawn! Dawn! Dawn!
Who belonged to them bulls?"

        Then I had the night
to myself. No moon, no stars, no trucks, no heifers,
no friends, no stories, and no sound: Only dark fields
and darker road, black on black, and I was alive, older
than my dark-haired father ever got to be, sleepy,
not wanting to sleep, happy, startled by happiness.

Another Elegy

In Memory of William Trout

> "O God!" thoughte I, "that madest kynde,
> Shal I noon other weyes dye?
> Wher Joves woll me stellefye,
> Or what thing may this sygnifye? . . ."
>
> —Geoffrey Chaucer, *Hous of Fame*

> The task and potential greatness of mortals reside
> in their ability to produce things which are at home in
> everlastingness.
>
> —Hannah Arendt, *The Human Condition*

> Both one and many; in the brown baked features
> The eyes of a familiar compound ghost . . .
>
> —T. S. Eliot, "Little Gidding"

It rained all night on the remaining elms. April soaked
through night loam into sleep. This morning, rain delays
above drenched earth. Whitethroated sparrows shake
wet from their feathers, singing in the oak, while fog
snags like lambswool on Kearsarge. The Blackwater River
runs high. The blacksnake budges in his hole, resurrecting
from winter's coma.
                    Now green will start from stubble
and horned pout fatten. By the pond, pussywillows
will labor awake to trudge from darkness and cold
through April's creaking gate.
                    Bill Trout remains
fixed in a long box where we left him, a dozen years ago.

❧

July, nineteen sixty: Three friends with their families
visited Bill at his Maine cabin secluded among scrub pines—
setting up tents, joking, frying pickerel in cool dusk.

Only Bill was divorced, drinking all night, living alone
on his shabby acre. Drunk the whole week, he recited
Milton's syllables of lament, interrupting our argument,
told Nazarene parables, and wept for his friends
and their children. While the rest of us dove from a dock
or played badminton with our wives, Bill paced
muttering, smoking his Lucky Strikes. Later the rest
divorced and paced.
                        We fished the river for horned pout,
Bill standing with a joint by the dam, watching the warm
water thick with fish, black bodies packed, flapping
and contending to breathe. Dropping hooks without bait,
we pulled up the horny, loricate fish, then flipped them
on grass to shrivel as we watched and joked, old
friends together. Continually sloshed, Bill proclaimed
that life was shit, death was shit—even *shit* was *shit*.

        ∽

Idaho made him, Pocatello of hobos and freightyards—
clangor of iron, fetor of coalsmoke. With his brothers
he listened for the Mountain Bluebird as he dropped worms
into the Snake River, harvesting catfish for a Saturday
supper in the nineteen thirties.
                        Two Sisters of the Sacred Heart
cosseted him when he strayed from the boys' flock
to scan the unchanging dactyls of Ovid. Landowska set out
the Goldberg Variations on a hand-wound Victrola.

When he was fifteen he stayed home from fishing to number
feet that promenaded to a Union Pacific tune, A B A B
pentameters. At the university his teacher the disappointed

novelist nodded his head—in admiration, envy, and pity—
while Bill sat late at a yellow dormitory desk, daydreaming
that his poems lifted through night sky to become stars
fixed in heaven, as Keats's poems rose from Hampstead
lanes and talks with Hunt and Haydon.

                                       When he considered
the cloth, Bill saw himself martyred. The ambition
of priest and poet!—innocent, and brainless as a shark.

    ∽

Sculptors make models for touch; singers raise voices
to the possible voice; basketball players improvise
humors of levitation. They jump, carve, and sing in plain
air as we do dreaming.

                                 Because emblems of every calling
measure its aspiration, the basketball player shoots
three hundred freethrows before breakfast; the mezzo
exists in service to the sound she makes, without eating
or loving except for song, selfish and selfless together;
the novice imagines herself healing a dozen Calcuttas
as Mother Teresa smiles from a gold cloud, and violates
holiness by her daydream of holiness.

                                      Bill Trout
woke up, the best mornings of his life—without debilities
of hangover, without pills or panic—to practice joy
at four o'clock dawn: to test words, to break them down
and build again, patient to construct immovable objects
of art by the pains of intelligent attention—remaining
alert or awake to nightmare.

                                 But the maker of bronzes
dies decapitated in the carwreck; the whitefaced mime
dozes tied to the wheelchair; the saint babbles and drools;
carcinoma refines chemist, farmer, wino, professor, poet,
imbecile, and banker into a passion of three nerves
and a feeding tube.

                                 At the Bayside Hospice Bill's body

heaved as it worked for air; IVs dripped; bloody phlegm
boiled from the hole punched like a grommet in his throat.

∞

Another fisherman writes me: "A man's death is his own;
you take Bill's death away, for public tears." I remember
Bill depressed, drinking double Manhattans straight up,
taunting himself: "Compassion's flack! Elmer Gantry
of Guggenheim grief!" In Coleridge's *Notebooks*,
he underlined: "Poetry—excites us to artificial feelings—
callous to real ones."
                          Commonly Bill recited, from John 14,
"I go to make a place," then shrugged and sang the Wobbly
hymn, "You'll get pie in the sky by and by—when you die."
After reciting Thomas Hardy, he went on to mimic Oliver.

Two years after the Maine summer, he worked for SNCC
in Alabama, in a cadre of Christians and Jews, beaten bloody
and jailed, declaiming Amos as gospel of anger and love.

Angry he married again; loving he wrote "Selma with Hellfire."

A decade after, as we sat late in a bare Port Townsend room,
bossily I reminded him to eat the wax-paper'd hamburger
cooling by his ashtray. Bill delivered a line, in his voice
as lush as an old Shakespearean's: "Ohhhh . . . to think
of the mornings I've waked with a cold cheeseburger beside me!"
He walked into water and out again; he woke in the drunktank
heaving; he trembled after electroshock; he made the poems.

∞

If ambition is innocent, nevertheless it impairs those
it possesses, not to mention their irretrievable children.
In the interstices of alcohol and woe, Bill vibrated
awake to a room that surged, shook, and altered shape.
He secreted vowel-honey in images dangling from prepositions;

he praised survival.

     When he finished his sojourn
at McLean, where Very and Lowell had paced before him;
when Margaret left him, removing their daughter, and Bill
declared bankruptcy; when he was unable for five years
to take Communion—he drank two Guggenheims and snorted
an NEA. He quoted Amos: ". . . as if a man fled from a lion
and a bear met him."

     From his house in Oakland, USIS
flew him to Prague, then home to detox. Once I visited him
just back from drying out, shuffling from chair to table
like a ninety-year-old, shaking as he tried to light
his Lucky, barely able to speak.

     Then in middle age
he fell in love again. He listened again to Chaucer
and recited Spenser's refrain as he stood by the Thames,
holding his Hindu love by the hand; or walking arm in arm
by a lake where Wordsworth walked;

     or, happy in Delhi,
reading the Gita, he breathed each morning India's fetid
exhausted air, filling his notebook in warm dawn
as parrots flashed and his throat opened with gold
vowels, line after beautiful line, all the last summer.

  ∽

The week before he died he handed me a clutch of poems.
Speechless, syllables occluded in his throat, he raised
a yellow pad and wrote, "That's it." Eyes protruded
from bone sockets; neck cords strained; trunk heaved
as he looked for his love who gazed out the window
of the room, bare except for a crucifix, downward to the bay
and the brown edges of March.

     After he died Reba gave me
his Modern Library Dickinson, in which editors corrected
the poet's lines. I imagine Bill in Eugene, penciling,

neat in the margin, restorations of Amherst.
                                        Each year
his death grows older. Outside this house, past Kearsarge
changing from pink and lavender through blue and white
to green, public language ridicules "eager pursuit of honor."

Do I tell lies? ". . . in middle age he fell in love . . ."
Did he never again tremble from chair to table? At night
Bill delivered his imagination and study to *Laverne*
and Shirley, laughing when a laughtrack bullied him
to laugh—while Reba groaned an incredulous Bengali groan—
in order not to drink.
                        Yet again he walked in a blue
robe in detox, love's anguish and anger walking beside him.

              ∽

It is twelve Aprils since we buried him. Now dissertation-
salt preserves *The Collected Poems of William Trout*
like Lenin. Here is another elegy in the tradition
of mourning and envy, love and self-love—as another morning
delivers rain on the fishbone leaves of the rotted year.
Again I measure the poems Bill Trout left on the shore
of his scattery life: quatrains that scrubbed Pocatello
clean, numbers of nightmare and magic, late songs in love
with Reba and vowels—his lifelines that hooked and landed
himself and his own for his book.
                                But if a new fixed star
resurrects Bill's words who labored and excelled, not even
Chaucer's or Ovid's accomplishment—"Joves woll me stellyfye"—
will revise electrodes, jail, and death at fifty.
Bill Trout is incorrigible, like the recidivist blacksnake,
sparrow, and high water that turn and return in April's
versions—cycles of the same, fish making fish—
                                        "unless,"
Bill dying, shriveled and absolved, wrote on a yellow
pad, "Jesus who walked from the tomb has made us a place."

8 Baseball

The First Inning

1. I would like to explain baseball to
Kurt Schwitters, Merz-poet and artist,
whose work was clothing, office, bedroom,
and carapace, who glued together
assemblages of ordinary
things—cigarette wrappers, bus tickets,
ads—first to make collage, and then to
inhabit. I would like to linger
with Schwitters in the Fenway bleachers,

2. explaining baseball. But, as poets
tell us, the man is dead, and I—call
me K.C.—lack his German, much less
death's German. Well, there are nine players
on a baseball team, so to speak, and
there are nine innings, with trivial
exceptions like extra-inning games
and games shortened by rain or darkness,
by riot, hurricane, earthquake, or

3. the Second Law of Thermodynam-
ics. Rilke feared the death of the sun;
then we exploded the sun. The Merz-
collagist expired in England, of
emphysema originally
contracted during poverty and
inflation, when he smoked the deutschemark.
Rilke died of leukemia, his
blood clarified to spiritual

4. water. When Jennifer walks down the
driveway, absently posting letters
in the mailbox or strolling across
the road to water the chickens, I
lean after her narrow waist—the swell
undulant above it, below it
the smooth slender outcurving outswoop—
the way July's daylily buds tip
south from Ragged's green hill, following

5. the risen sun, and swell to erupt
orange. Tonight, after baseball, she
looks Chinese, skin under her eyes puffed
from her morning tears. As she totters,
she touches bookcase and tabletop
with the tips of dubious fingers.
Depression is the blood's own journey,
by its own map. There is only one
thing to do; happily we do it.

6. From home plate to the pitcher's rubber,
as the actress said to the bishop,
takes sixty feet and six inches. Of
course you will recognize Being: It
looks just like Nothingness except that
it wears a striped Thai-silk four-in-hand.
As the poet says, "Words cannot tell,
cannot express . . . Words falter . . . Words are
inadequate to describe . . ." Poets

7. woo the unspeakable to their desks,
listening to radio baseball.
Meantime the cells or constituent
molecules go on sunning themselves
in the pure daylight of unconscious
punning and dancing, now slowing down,

now jetting Cambridge blue electrons—
the enterprise of ongoingness.
This condition resembles baseball

8. in its laboratory method
or purity, physics of nine times
nine times nine times nine. We hanged three deer
behind the new 7-Eleven
beside lions Flaubert crucified.
I am not interested in words
without sentences, or sentences
without meaning. Every meaningless
sentence says the same thing. Igitur,

9. they pave the green mountain for progress
while they grow hairy vert chemicals
into grass cement for the diamond
and Newfound Lake newly obscured by
sawtooth-shingled condominia
at x thousand thousand dollars each
to prohibit view of the wind's lake.
Kurt, when the pitcher makes a false start,
the runners move up: It is a balk.

The Second Inning

1. When I wake each morning, each morning
points itself like a dog at the fowl
of baseball. My father who adored
the game died on the year's shortest day,
on December the twenty-second
at six-twenty P.M., long after
sundown. When we buried him, Christmas
Eve, the day was already longer.
His hands were long and always busy:

2. like dachshunds, like the wooden carvings
in old churches, like bowls of cashew
nuts. Although Cincinnati's ballpark
is symmetrical and horrific,
its execution of the German-
American wurst is exceeded
only by Milwaukee's. When I first
wrote about rising and pointing, I
arrived instead at the bird of work.

3. Baseball is not my work. It is my
walk in the park, my pint of bitter,
my Agatha Christie or Zane Grey—
release of the baby animal's
energy into the jungle gym
of a frivolous concentration.
Also I dictate letters between
pitches—as I observe the Red Sox
or whatever game's on satellite.

4. Who can say what his or her work is?
I write out these tentative verses
—K.C. at the Desk, Mudville at bat,
last of the ninth—working in the dark
morning while a cat climbs on my lap
nibbling at pen and paper. For sure,
my pleasure is a habitual
recreational tapping at blocks
of the language, absentmindedly,

5. even when "there is no language there"
(Jenny says)—frustration frustrated
by counting on fingers of almost
two hands. Don't forget, Kurt: Use two hands
when you catch the ball, and don't ignore

the starved cat. In the multiplying
gossip of cells, catch the Sprechstimme
of the spheres. A baseball is a sphere,
or near enough. The pitiful quarks

6. turn charming: meiosis, mitosis,
off and on. It was light and motion
before Moses was, before you are,
and I am. Entropy contracts cold;
density implodes: Let there be light
and chattering membranes of discourse.
Rain for seven innings at Fenway
Park, mist and drizzle, drizzle and mist
on umbrellas in front-row boxes:

7. Most of us withdrew to remote seats
under cover while the straight youthful
men of the outfield splashed through puddles,
mudsliding for fly balls. After six
innings and an hour's wait, the umpires
called the game off, tied one to one. We
struggled wetly out to Kenmore Square
after a game without issue. Young
ballplayers partied and slept, to rise

8. tomorrow for a doubleheader
starting at five-thirty. All night long,
asleep, I practiced how to focus
my eyes to catch the light rain falling
slant against green grass and uniformed
boys: rain like time in dowels of light.
K.C.'s omnium-gatherum (in
New English we call it "town dump") weds
the East Side to Langton Street. I dreamed

9. of old Ezra Pound after meeting
Olga Rudge at Orono, Maine. A
peregrine falcon flew in and out
of my dream. Just twenty-five years back,
I interviewed Pound as he entered
the house of silence. But the dream bird?
The next day I understood: I felt
troubled about another old man:
Henry Moore wheelchaired at Perry Green.

The Third Inning

1. Alexander, first over the wall,
collapsed battered by stones. Instantly
the Macedonian companions
gathered their shields over his body
and these athletes of honor and brawn
withstood repeated iron assault—
to defend, to survive, to triumph.
When the king's wound healed, he divided
the known world among his companions.

2. At the center of a baseball, Kurt,
is ten pounds of cat intestine, packed
into a tiny marble-sized sphere.
While I write "Baseball," Prudence the cat
rubs at my ankles to inform me
that nothing whatever bothers her.
Jennifer and I make love at night;
afterward, happiness continues,
as if the radio, turned on low

3. at three A.M., told about baseball
all night long in Japanese or Spanish,
with crowd noises the same as Fenway.

The next morning, as Jenny pauses
by the kitchen sink and looks idly
out the window, I gaze at her ass;
then she squeezes an orange: Its bright
gelatinous membranes rupture to
fill her blue cup with sunny ichor.

4. The ship made twenty-five knots into
a fifty-knot wind over hot gulf
water. I climbed to the topmost deck,
tilting my weight into the hot wind,
poising my heavy body into
the wind's weight, pulling myself along
rails with both hands to push against wind
that scudded black clouds into blackness
with the moon down and few stars showing.

5. Wind flattened my beard and my nostrils.
Wind gathered my shout and shuffled it.
It is ecstasy beyond pleasure
to watch Jennifer squeeze orange juice.
All night the kitten walked back and forth
on top of us, biting and poking.
Meantime the old cat hissed and added
new disloyalties to her lifelist,
as when the Dodgers left Ebbets Field.

6. So the new dog's pet is the kitten.
All day she hurls herself at his huge
muzzle, bigger than she is, her mouth
wide open and her claws stretched. He snaps
without biting, love bites; she pauses
in her fury to lick his jaws clean.
Then she hides—to leap from her secret
branch onto the great boa of his
wagging magnificent golden tail.

7. All winter aged ballplayers try
rehearsing their young manhood, running
and throwing in Florida's sunshine;
they remain old. In my sixtieth
year I wake fretting over some new
failure. Meeting an old friend's new wife,
I panicked and was rude. Or I ache
mildly, feeling some careless anger
with my son I cannot push away.

8. The bodies of major league baseball
players are young. We age past the field
so quickly; we diminish, watching
over decades, observing the young
as they dodder. The old cat hisses
at the kitten and pokes the new dog;
her life is ruined and she declines
bitterly toward death. At night she purrs
briefly, lying restored on our bed.

9. The leg is the dancer and the mouth
the sculptor. The tongue models vowels
or chisels consonants. Pause, pitch, pace,
length, and volume patine a surface
of shapes that the mouth closes over.
Behind our listening lips, working
the throat's silent machine, one muscle
shuts on/off/on/off: the motionless
leg of the word that leaps in the world.

THE FOURTH INNING

1. As the moment's vowel rolls itself
out, mind entertains intelligence
for body's sake. Word-skin and muscle-

shape dance to the corporal music
of sententia or anecdote.
Syntax is sinew. In the aroused
mouth, sweet juices accumulate verbs,
adjectives, and nouns lolling in luxe,
calme, et volupté like Miami.

2. In nineteen seventy-three, Dock said
that pitcher and poet were up to
the same tricks. "All I'm trying to do,"
he said, "is fool 'em." When you expect
robinsegg blue, I suppose, you get
rubberized cement instead. Always
remember, Kurt, that Sandy Koufax
spoke of pitching baseball as "the art
of intimidation." To instill

3. fear, what do poets do? Robert Frost
said that the thing was to *score*, to *win*,
and his ambitious or murderous
eyes frightened anyone who took them
in. Sixty, he played vicious softball.
The pitcher stares at the catcher's mitt
and appears, Kurt, to glare once in the
batter's direction. The batter's eyes
concentrate on body, arm, and ball.

4. John Tudor was annoyed by the press
after his second World Series win
in nineteen eighty-five. For Tudor,
success's discomfort reversed it.
Heraclitus affirmed reversals
and the truest poem exposes
itself in a fury of self-love
and flagellation. In the last game
John Tudor's team never got it up.

5. If the destination is always
a lie, because (1) we cannot stop,
(2) there is no *there* there, and (3) there
is no (3), is the journey also
mendacious? Doubtless, conceptual
propositions make no never-mind
and K.C.'s traveling metaphor
dies the usual death. Let us go
back to gazing at Jennifer's shorts.

6. This poem is necessarily
dedicated to Gerald Burns, the
commissioner of "Baseball." Former
dispensations necessitated
sequences of eighty sonnets, then
one further. When Lefty Gomez died,
Bill Dickey remembered a story:
Gomez shook off his signs as Jimmie
Foxx stood at the plate; at the mound, Bill

7. asked what his pitcher *wanted.* "Nothing,"
said Gomez. "I thought he might get tired
of waiting and go away." Walking
on the island of Inishbofin,
eight miles into the Atlantic off
Galway, we strangers met an old blind
woman in black who, just to be safe,
scratched a cross in the dirt path with her
blackthorn stick. That day on the island

8. there was a rumor that a boatload
of tourists from Spain would drop anchor
in the bay. Annie Morin fixed us
with blank eyes and asked: "Be ye the Moors?"
When Wade Boggs took BP he heard them
chanting "Margo," and as he finished

showering and climbed onto the team
bus, a small boy yelled "Margo" at the
window. With a single-edge razor,

9. a Gem, I sliced the printed sheets of
balsa; I glued; I stretched lavender
tissue paper over frail wing-ribs;
I sanded propellers. But the glued
ribs and struts sprung and the paper tore.
My planes like my baseballs never flew—
or my best fastball *flew* over the
backstop; I struck out; I dropped the ball:
Airplanes crashed on my feckless sandlot.

THE FIFTH INNING

1. Kurt, last night Dwight Evans put it all
together, the way you made collage,
with an exemplary catch followed
by an assist at first base, a hit
in the seventh inning for the tie,
and another in the last of the
ninth to pull it out at Fenway Park
and win the game. The madness method
of "Baseball" gathers bits and pieces

2. of ordinary things—like bleacher
ticket stubs, used Astroturf, Fenway
Frank wrappers, yearbooks, and memory—
to paste them onto the bonkers grid
of the page. I stood at the workbench
after school and all day on weekends
—and I stand there still, in the gloomy
cellar on Ardmore Street, cutting and
gluing, my tongue protruding from my

3. lips, and nothing flies. When my daughter—
bored at thirteen by the grown-up talk
at the fancy picnic outside the
theater in Stratford, Ontario—
remarked frequently on the paddle-
boats skimming the lake ("Oh, look!" "That looks
like fun!" "I wonder where they start from."),
I understood: I said, "Let's go find
the dock or whatever and rent one."

4. Her face livened up, but she was smart:
As we walked toward the pier together,
she asked: "Are you certain you want to
do this, or are you doing it just
to be mean?" In nineteen thirty-eight,
the hurricane lifted Aunt Clara's
cottage at Silver Sands and carried
it twenty yards to deposit it
in a salt meadow; the tidal wave

5. overwhelmed the Thimble Island where
Uncle Arthur lived. When rain started
in the second inning at Fenway
Park, it drizzled on umbrellas raised
in boxes by the field. Most of us
climbed to remote seats back under the
overhang to watch the (I wrote this
before, back in the second inning)
puddles pocked by raindrops. In the lights

6. we made out straight up-and-down falling
pencil lines of rain that the pitchers
squinted through to see the catchers' signs;
batters peered to watch how the ball spun.
After six innings it rained harder

and the umpire suspended play—game
tied three to three—then called it an hour
later. We struggled wetly out from
a game without issue. The young men

7. partied and slept, to make tomorrow's
doubleheader at five. All night I
slept and woke practicing—obsessive
even in sleep, just as I bully
notes into lines—how the slow rain fell
like time measured in vertical light.
When I was a child, Connecticut
of the thirties and forties, we drove
to Ebbets Field or the Polo Grounds,

8. a couple of hours down the newly
constructed or incomplete parkways
to Brooklyn especially, dense with
its tiny park and passionate crowd.
After Billy Herman brilliantly
stopped a ground ball and flipped to Pee Wee
for the force, I turned immediate
attention to a vendor and my
father thought I missed the lucky play.

9. While that was happening, Kurt, I guess
you left Germany for Norway. Good.
As I thought about Curt (sic) Davis,
you were building a Merz-apartment.
I watched the first game of the nineteen
forty-one World Series in the Bronx,
when Joe Gordon took Curt Davis deep
and we lost three to two, unable
to rally back. Then the long drive home.

1. Sometime, Kurt, you ought to come along
to Danbury Elementary
School when I umpire a softball game.
I call balls and strikes, safe and out, foul
and fair. When I blow a call, I make
it up on the next one. Once when I
intoned "Strike one!" a small batter said,
"Hey, that's your 'Casey at the Bat' voice,
Mr. Hall." (I dislike it, having

2. a poetry voice—but I have one.)
Danbury goes through the sixth grade, and
the best game of the year is the last,
when the sixth grade plays the P.T.O.
reinforced by teachers. Serious
athleticism and revenge combine
to dissipate in the ethical
disorder of prejudiced calls by
an undisinterested umpire.

3. Before we left Spring Glen Grammar School
for high school, the eighth grade played hardball.
I tried out for catcher, knowing that,
aside from a good first-string player,
nobody wanted to wear the mask.
They cut me anyway, and I slunk
off to my familiar province of
tears, failure, and humiliation
where I lived until Harvard College.

4. Sometimes I take naps as shallow as
puddles on cracked sidewalks in Spring Glen
after a summer shower when sun
will lift the dampness soon and restore

dryness to white cement. And sometimes
I nap the rare nap as profound as
the Pacific Ocean, where fathoms
of fault steam from a crack in the deep
floor: Napoleon! Napoleon!

5. After fifty years of images
and symbols (watch out, kids; here comes a
symbol), it is difficult to keep
oneself head-bent-down to the language
only, as if language were a grid
for athletes, Kurt, as in parts of speech.
If a coincidence of noises
suggests the possibility of
interjecting a French emperor

6. onto a suburb confounded with
an ocean composed of shifting plates
and geological moral terms
multiplied by alliteration,
what have we gained except, perhaps, the
grid's distracted polymorphous joy
in evasion? I insinuate
notions despite my resolution,
of many years, to remain aloof

7. from disputes over the usefulness
of this method of generation
or that. I know from experience
that the matter of least import is
what you *think* you are doing. Still, I
exercise control by not making
public, by crossing out, perhaps to
some degree by concealing myself—
but mostly by keeping my silence.

8. Thus K.C. becomes Napoleon,
Nap Lajoie's first name. In the Book of
Dead Cats, dishes of Nine Lives Super
Supper petrify. A permanent
odor of tomcat establishes
ownership in the next world of twelve
volumes of the *OED*, snapshots
breathe three times a year, and the armchair's
clawmarks reify practices of

9. rodent control listed in the Book
of Dead Mice. Soft columns of tanned skin
descend from her pink shorts this morning:
Jennifer's. I stare happily at
linen that covers her slender hips,
at her thighs and knees. What good fortune
to touch Jennifer's limbs—delicate,
supple, smooth, and skinny as a deer's—
that twist with a grown woman's passion.

THE SEVENTH INNING

1. Baseball, I warrant, is not the whole
occupation of the aging boy.
Far from it: There are cats and roses;
there is her water body. She fills
the skin of her legs up, like water;
under her blouse, water assembles,
swelling lukewarm; her mouth is water,
her cheekbones cool water; water flows
in her rapid hair. I drink water

2. from her body as she walks past me
to open a screen door, as she bends
to weed among herbs, or as she lies

beside me at five in the morning
in submarine light. Curt Davis threw
a submarine ball, terrifying
to right-handed batters. Another
pleasure, thoroughly underrated,
is micturition, which is even

3. commoner than baseball. It begins
by announcing itself more slowly
and less urgently than sexual
desire, but (confusingly) in the
identical place. Ignorant men
therefore on occasion confuse beer-
drinking with love; but I have discussed
adultery elsewhere. We allow
this sweet release to commence itself,

4. addressing a urinal perhaps,
perhaps poised over a white toilet
with feet spread wide and head tilted back:
oh, what delicious permission! what
luxury of letting go! what luxe
yellow curve of mildest ecstasy!
Granted we may not compare it to
poignant and crimson bliss, it is as
voluptuous as rain all night long

5. after baseball in August's parch. The
jade plant's trunk, as thick as a man's wrist,
urges upward thrusting from packed dirt,
with Chinese vigor spreading limbs out
that bear heavy leaves—palpable, dark,
juicy, green, profound: They suck, the way
bleacher fans claim inhabitants of
box seats do. The Fourth of July we
exhaust stars from sparklers in the late

6. twilight. We swoop ovals of white-gold
flame, making quick signatures against
an imploding dark. The five-year-old
girl kisses the young dog goodbye and
chases the quick erratic kitten.
When she returns in a few years as
a tall shy girl, she will come back to
a dignified spreading cat and a
dog ash-gray on the muzzle. Sparklers

7. expel quickly this night of farewell:
If they didn't burn out, they wouldn't
be beautiful. Kurt, may I hazard
an opinion on expansion? Last
winter meetings, the major leagues (al-
ready meager in ability,
scanty in starting pitchers) voted
to add two teams. Therefore minor league
players will advance all too quickly,

8. with boys in the bigs who wouldn't have
made double-A forty years ago.
Directors of player personnel
will search like poets scrambling in old
notebooks for unused leftover lines,
but when was the last time anyone
cut back when he or she could expand?
Kurt, I get the notion that you were
another who never discarded

9. *anything*, a keeper from way back.
You smoked cigarettes, in inflation-
times rolled from chopped-up banknotes, billions
inhaled and exhaled as cancerous
smoke. When commerce woke, Merz was awake.
If you smoked a cigar, the cigar

band discovered itself glued into
collage. Ongoing life became the
material of Kurtschwittersball.

THE EIGHTH INNING

1. Kurt, terror is merely the thesis:
Ten years later the guerrilla chief
swears himself in as President for
Life, appointing Commando Plastique
his Minister for Health and Welfare.
Meanwhile former Emperor Pluto
wags his tail at the Zurich Hilton,
attended by his secretary,
Miss Universe-*und*-Swiss-Bankaccount.

2. However, Kurt, we must inform you
with regret (you will not be surprised)
that the Committee of Reconcil-
iation finds itself unable
to attend the ceremonies, nor
will it observe the Riviera
reunion of the secret police:
The peacemakers have been moldering
in their mass grave for a decade. I

3. cherish the photograph on my wall,
Kurt, where you embrace Bambino Babe
Ruth (Tokyo, nineteen twenty-eight).
Photography's dolor is common:
We are forever older than our
photographs. Even a Polaroid—
by the time the fish of the image
has swum to the surface and settled
into its fins and fortunes for all

4. eternity—measures another
sixty seconds fading toward the grave.
Baseball, like sexual intercourse
and art, stops short, for a moment, the
indecent continuous motion
of time forward, implying our death
and imminent decomposition.
Did you ever marry the bottle?
I married Scotch when I was forty.

5. For two years we kept house together.
She constructed pale renewable
joy when twilight was summer; she was
impassive, agreeable, faithful,
forgiving; she was church and castle,
princess and dragon, Eden and Elm
Street, hell and heaven poured together.
If it were not God's will, the baseball
would disintegrate when the pitcher

6. touched it. Grace before dinner implores
food to remain among visible
things: Only His will sustains peapods.
Flying over China we saw base-
ball diamonds in the sun. Guangzhou and
Shenyang, the smallest of our cities,
each kept four million people. We pale
anomalous tall phantoms with big
noses walked at night in the glow from

7. small shops among the polloi that roiled
multitudinousness everywhere.
In Chengdu at night the scroll sellers
played flashlights over their wares—bamboo,
dragons, snapdragons—that hung from ropes
strung between poplars. In the full moon

the fox walks on snow, black prints of fox;
but the chicken's head has migrated
to the pigsty already. Oink. Oink.

8. Baseball in the winter is our dream's
retrospective summer, and even
(D. V.) the summer of prospect, game
perfectly mental that we control
by the addition of our wishful
selves throwing, catching, hitting, running
bases, staring with the same eyes back
and forth as pitcher and as batter.
No game plays its theater so nightly:

9. It never rains on this Wrigley Field;
in this Tiger Stadium it is
always Ebbets Field, the Polo Grounds,
Forbes Field, Griffith Stadium, Braves Field,
and Comiskey Park. Whatever's green,
it's not grass; those aren't hot dogs either;
but when we depart the old within-
Fenway of January and snow,
we find ticket stubs in our wallets.

THE NINTH INNING

1. My dog and I drive five miles every
morning to get the newspaper. How
else do I find out when the Sox trade
Smoky Joe Wood for Elizabeth Bishop?
He needs persistent demonstration
of love and approval. He cocks his
head, making earnest pathetic sounds.
Although I praise his nobility
of soul, he is inconsolable

2. when I lift my hand from his ear to
shift. Even so, after the reading
the stranger nods, simpers, and offers
to share his poems with me. Dean Gratt
confided, at the annual Death
and Retirement Gala: "Professor
McCormick has not changed: A Volvo
is just a Subaru with tenure."
Catchers grow old catching, which is strange

3. because they squat so much. "The barn is
burning, O, the barn is burning on
the hill; the cattle low and blunder
in their stalls; the horses scream and hurl
their burning manes." Jennifer remains
melancholic. Do you start to feel,
Kurt, as if you're getting it? I mean
baseball, as in the generations
of old players hanging on, the young

4. coming up from triple-A the first
of September, sitting on the bench
or pinch-running, ready for winter's
snow-plowing and cement-mixing, while
older fellows work out in their gyms
or cellars, like George "Shotgun" Shuba,
who swung a bat against a tethered
ball one thousand times a day, line drives
underneath his suburban ranchhouse.

5. By twenty twenty-eight, when K.C.
turned one hundred, eighty-three percent
of American undergraduates
majored in creative writing, more
folks had MFAs than VCRs,

and poetry had passed acrylic
in the GNP. The NEA
offered fellowships for destroying
manuscript and agreeing "*never*

6. to publish anything jagged on
the right side of the page, or *ever*
described as 'prose poems.'" Guerrillas
armed with WordPerfect holed in abstract
redoubts. Chief of Staff Vendler mustered
security forces, a k a
death squads, and issued cheerful reports
nightly on lyric television.
Hideous shepherds sing to their flocks

7. under howling houses of the dog.
At the Temple Medical Center
in New Haven I wait. My mother
at eighty-six goes through the upper
and lower GI again. My mind
jangles, thinking of my sick son in
New York and his sick one-year-old girl.
This afternoon, if the x-rays go
all right, I drive back to New Hampshire.

8. In New Hampshire, late August, the leaves
turn slowly, like someone working to
order—protesting, outraged—and fall
as they must do. The pond water stays
warm but the campers have departed.
By the railroad goldenrod stiffens;
asters begin a late pennant drive
in front of the barn; pink hollyhocks
wilt and sag like teams out of the race.

9. No Red Sox tonight, but on Friday
a doubleheader with the Detroit
Tigers, my terrible old team, worse
than the Red Sox who beat the Yankees
last night while my mother and I watched
—the way we listened, fifty years back—
spritely ghosts playing in heavy snow
on VHS 30 from Hartford,
and the pitcher stared at the batter.

9 ∤ The Museum of Clear Ideas

OR SAY:
HORSECOLLAR'S ODES

For the poet is light, winged, and holy. There is no invention in him until he has been inspired, out of his senses, and has no mind.

—Socrates to Ion

Poets refuse to *utilize* language. Since the quest for truth takes place in and by language, it is useless to imagine that poets look for truth.

—Jean-Paul Sartre, *What Is Literature?*

One morning W.B. came back from the post office. "I don't understand," he cried. "It's closed! No one is there!"
   "But Mr. Yeats," I replied, "It is Christmas Day."

—Dorothea von Kreicke, *The Swan's Wife*

I am quite deaf now. Such a comfort.

—Evelyn Waugh to Nancy Mitford

DECIUS — WHOSE GUILEFUL

Decius—whose guileful agency sustains
and decimates me—I know that some people
require fame as athletes; still others demand
election to office or every gadget
for sale on 42nd Street; Tanaquil
enjoys dozing in the British Museum
and its pub; she prefers them to Disney World,
while her Chair, who won an all-expenses-paid
weekend in Rome, Italy, would have favored
Las Vegas. Marvin enjoys drinking himself
quadriplegic, Joan backpacks through Toledo,
Kim helicopters into Iranian
deserts, and Flaccus shoots tame wild antelope
in a hired game preserve. As Horsecollar nods,
"It takes all kinds," Madonna continues to
writhe in public, doing what she wants; Max finds
fire hydrants to piss against; Senator Hell
displays risky photographs in a cloakroom;
and Fidelia lowers her artificial
eyelashes in the direction of Tu Fu,
who sits cross-legged in his hut, composing,
oblivious that he is starving. Glaucus
urges American men to go bowling
together—to discover Mister Zero
of the bowling alley. Arbogast daydreams,
Camilla tends peonies ten hours a day,
and Julia with net and binoculars

treks through jungles and over Himalayas,
adding to her collection of deities.
I know that some people exist to look thin,
others stare at television sets all day
until they die, and others expend their lives
to redeem the dying. As for Horsecollar,
Decius, he'll take this desk, this blank paper,
this Bic, and the fragile possibility
that, with your support, the Muse may favor him.

WE'VE COME TO EXPECT

We've come to expect earthquakes, fires, hurricanes,
and tidal waves from our whitecoated brothers
whose laboratories shed radiation
        on land and landscape,

disabling cities. Foresighted citizens
outfit granite arks in Idaho's brown hills,
stocked against flood, famine, pestilence, war, and
        hunger of neighbors,

with bulgur, freeze-dried Stroganoff, and Uzis.
Let's remember: Our great-grandfathers holed up
in mountains with pistols and pemmican, their
        manhood sufficient,

should they avoid peritonitis and gan-
grene, to perform the mechanic alchemy
which liquefied landscape, dirt to nuggets, and
        sluiced a state golden.

Let's remember not only the local wars
over claims but a late conflict of siblings

in aristocracy and the stock market,
      sharing destruction.

Or recollect the brothers who stayed back east
laboring in the shoe factory, or their
bosses who summered hunting in Scotland and
      reside forever

in the Protestant Cemetery at Rome
among cats, the pyramid of Cestius,
and Keats's grave. What use are those forefathers
      to our condition?

We want comfort: Shall we consult Jefferson?
Alas, he's busy conducting a call-in
show for Republican-Democrats. Franklin?
      He is occupied

obliterating SIN from Webster's project.
If we approach doddering George Washington,
he only smiles at us in his foolishness.
      Shall we call upon

Abraham Lincoln for succor? No: The Great
Emancipator succumbs to Grant's whiskey.
As we approach the present, passing double
      Roosevelts, we do

not help ourselves—not with old Eisenhower
cursing at caddies; not with Nixon cursing.
But if we return past Jonathan Edwards,
      past Cotton Mather,

to the Israelites of the *Mayflower*—
who make covenant with Jehovah's promised

wilderness and the manna of Indian
       corn, who stay secure

in Adam's fall and the broken promises
of the remnant—we discover ancestors
appropriate to our lapsarian state:
       Their rage sustains us.

Let Engine Cowling

Let engine cowling rivets
       adhere. Let hydraulic systems operate
flaps without interruption
       and electric signals work as expected.

O 747
       that carries Glaucus across the Atlantic
and slants down over the brief
       Mediterranean to the Grecian shore,

keep him safe. Not long ago
       flying required noticeable bravery
as a bold Frenchman, not to
       say Dayton, Ohio's bicycle-making

brothers, ascended on frail
       boxes into an alien windstream, never
questioning propriety
       but taking air on challenge as their domain.

When their eyes teared with the wind,
       did they fear wind? Although they climbed the breezes
of our own century, they
       seem ancient as Leonardo or Fulton.

They were gallant without guilt
        as they rose up, and expected to return—
after ingenuity
        and courage sustained them their moment's release

from the ponderable weight
        of gravity—to accept the gratitude
of their descendants. But they
        prepared us Dresden's fire and Nagasaki's.

Are we grateful for the death
        that drops on us from flying mental engines
the Renaissance invented
        with enlightened conceit? If we beg pardon,

as we dig holes for ourselves,
        all right; but if we ascend, separated
from grief's ground without terror
        or foreboding, we add complacency to

wickedness, idiocy,
        and engineering. Fear death. Anxiety
mothers and fathers souls
        giddy with vacuum—otherwise orphaned.

WINTER'S ASPERITY MOLLIFIES

Winter's asperity mollifies under the assault of April.
        Now the trout fisherman flexes stiff waders;
now cattle and sheep clamber out of barns that kept them warm all winter;
        now the countryman no longer seeks comfort

by sleeping on his Glenwood, for ice has departed the coldest field.
        Under the new moon animal bodies play,

cavorting on tender grasses that the breezes caress and embrace.
  Each morning we gaze at daffodils, closing

our eyes in languor. Soon we will inspire the July garden's densest
  effluence and shuffle to drowse in maple
shade and the shade of birches, convening where soft mosses are
  to build with our bodies temples for Venus

as summer suggests: We sigh, we are easy—because we understand
  that we must squeeze every moment: The truest
aphrodisiac is our certain knowledge that we will die: We sweat,
  we pant, we drop our pants whenever we touch

the subject of dying—because dead people rarely appear content;
  because they want energy; because they lack
desire for each other's bodies. In response to death's deplorable
  likelihood, we bed each other down in spring.

∾

Or say: In spring (and for that matter in summer, fall,
and winter) each of us dreadfully desires to die.
However, our conventions consider this longing morbid
and in the worst possible taste: Therefore we dress up
in costumes of lust to distract ourselves; we pound
and jab ourselves into each other—we flail, we froth,
our cup runneth over—in order to provoke blood chemistry
that, for the moment, relaxes our lust for oblivion
by substituting oblivion. As Horsecollar says, adopting
the style of his alternative Citizen Zero, "Love
and death, love and death: How do you tell them apart?"

Who's This Fellow

Who's this fellow wearing the aftershave lotion
with the slim figure embracing you, Fidelia,
      in the rose garden beside
         the artificial hill?

I suppose that he's nameless and legion, for whom
you loosen your golden abundant sensuous
      hair. For the rest of his life
         he'll weep over this hour,

whimper himself green deploring inconstancy,
make hack metaphors that associate fickle
      seas with storms and dread shipwrecks—
         this same amorous boy

who sighs with pleasure now, credulous of yellow
tresses, loyalty, and unfading loveliness—
      ignoring the Oedipal
         weather of history.

Ridiculous that he suffers this ecstasy
over you! Horsecollar knows, who points a moral
      of shipwreck and survival
         as he drips saltwater.

I'm Not Up to It

I'm not up to it. Oh, it would require Dante
to tell your story, even Gore Vidal himself
to describe, Professor, the filth and corruption
      of your critical maneuvers!

Others drain swamps, you swamp the drains. In Manhattan,
you leave muddy crocodiles asleep where Elm Street
used to cross Maple; your depraved taste and judgment
   effect this metamorphosis.

Commissioner, how can I sing adequately
of the gross self-seeking that beats to enable
your cardiovascular system? How can I
   —pastoral, gentle, good-natured—

recount the conflicts of interest and favor-
trading that distinguish your abuses of power,
O Eulogist of Whatever Crawls on Twelve Legs?
   My petty Muse lacks energy

to reveal feculent praises supplied as blurbs
to be bartered for Guggenheims and Pulitzers.
The major industry of the Scilly Islands
   is doing each other's laundry.

∾

Or say: Ancient Maître Zero, toothless
and seamed as corduroy, sipping brandy
on Montparnasse, answers Horsecollar's
question for the *Paris Review*—"What keeps
you alive?"—with one word, and a sneer
as venerable as Tutankhamen's: "Revenge!"

LET MANY BAD POETS

Let many bad poets praise the Grand Canyon, the Panama
   Canal, the Statue of Liberty, Mount
Hood, the Napa Valley with its products of fermentation,
   Sicily, Connecticut, and themselves.

Some of us spend our whole lives praising Danbury, New Hampshire,
　　　　or Mount Fuji: Praising our places, we
praise ourselves while pretending to look outward. We build Tu Fu's
　　　　Chengdu cottage as a shrine for ourselves

in every *Poetry*, by printing reflections, in free verse
　　　　without noticeable attention to
line breaks, on snapshots of the poetic mother and father,
　　　　in their weird clothes, on vacation, before

the poet was born: How poignant it is, how remarkable
　　　　that one's parents were older than oneself!
Then they died. Oh. Because I have nothing to say, and nothing
　　　　deeply pitiable to whine over,

I program my poem-processor for irony, malice,
　　　　envy, loathing, and the decent pleasure
of breaking anyone's Mont Blanc who disturbs my solitude.
　　　　While others probe an already sore place

with the pickaxes of guilty ululation, I relax
　　　　with a good book on the soul's wooden porch,
or, as they advised Amos some ages ago, I eat bread
　　　　and prophesy. It happens I predict

myself, praising my villa as Horace did, praising Ragged,
　　　　Camilla, Eagle Pond, and Max the dog.
I prophesy the country I invent by shutting the door;
　　　　I praise citizenship in the nation

of myself. You too can withdraw into a granite valley
　　　　defended by the troops of history,
learning, sexual luxury, diligence, and narcissism.
　　　　Just remember: Never knock on this door.

In the Name Of

In the name of Madonna,
    Tanaquil, why do you find it necessary to ruin
Marvin for love? Now he loathes
    the streets of his city who used to delight in running them;

Marvin goes bowling no more;
    no longer does Marvin drag-race his Buick on the back roads;
no longer does Marvin slurp
    sweet wine while playing jokers wild with pals from the
        department.

This was the manly Marvin
    renowned for drinking a case of Hamm's while going four for fou
or making strikes with one hand
    while spilling a Seven-and-7 from the hairy other.

Now he lies low, Tanaquil,
    concealing secondary sexual characteristics
that were famous. His mother
    dressed Achilles as a girl, to keep him from dying at Troy.

Mount Kearsarge Shines

Mount Kearsarge shines with ice; from hemlock branches
snow slides onto snow; no stream, creek, or river
        budges but remains still. Tonight
            we carry armloads of logs

from woodshed to Glenwood and build up the fire
that keeps the coldest night outside our windows.
        Sit by the woodstove, Camilla,
            while I bring glasses of white,

and we'll talk, passing the time, about weather
without pretending that we can alter it:
                      Storms stop when they stop, no sooner,
                                leaving the birches glossy

with ice and bent glittering to rimy ground.
We'll avoid the programmed weatherman grinning
                from the box, cheerful with tempest,
                        and take the day as it comes,

one day at a time, the way everyone says.
These hours are the best because we hold them close
            in our uxorious nation.
                       Soon we'll walk—when days turn fair

and frost stays off—over old roads, listening
for peepers as spring comes on, never to miss
                the day's offering of pleasure
                        for the government of two.

CAMILLA, NEVER ASK

Camilla, never ask when it will happen, for we'll never know
how it comes or when. Leave divination to Julia, our friend
who orders predestination from catalogues of remaindered
theologies. Let us determine to take what comes, hot or cold,
whether we stay alive into old age or drop dead next Tuesday,
which is doubtless as good a day as any. Tonight let us fill
our wineglasses without fretting about the future, which only
sours the Beaujolais. Forget tomorrow's blueberries; eat today's.

The times are propitious for fake religions.
Today let's decide which priest, beauty, athlete,
moviestar, or Jungian to celebrate
      by electing him

God. Hype springs eternal in the human breast.
Let's diversify spiritual options,
play New Age rock, and improvise jargon with
      Julia, founder

of the God-of-the-Month Club, who keeps busy
shamaning around in her medicine man
costume, afterward to go Sufi dancing
      with Jerry Falwell

outside the Zen temple just dedicated
to Kali, Martin Luther, and Orphée, who
plays for the waltzing of Mithra, Hercules,
      and Joseph Campbell

wearing his benign suit. Our bewitching friend
mumbles and invokes, imploring the oak trees
to accept worship—or should we say workshop?
      It's literary.

Polytheism pays tribute to singleness
by proclaiming Zeus CEO. Julia
has always found him authoritarian;
      if Julia feels

humble toward one god, she makes up another,
as her suburban divine rotten boroughs
grant Julia an Olympic parliament's
      perpetual rule.

Now with her biorhythm calculator,
organic vitamins, ouija board, yoga
exercises, mesmerism, Iroquois shells,
      Obeah routines,

Zen meditation, Tantric sexgames, Shirley
MacLaine, phrenology, Fletcherizing, I
Ching, and crucifix, she's in total control.
      Unless she isn't.

Gibbon published the first volumes of *Decline*
in 1776. When he praised
the Antonine who, although quite sensible,
      believed that planets

controlled destinies, he assured Jefferson
that until recently quite a few *almost*
intelligent folk believed such idiot
      junk. What sign are we,

Julia? Whatever superstitious trek
you follow today, you'll find a new Tibet
by nightfall tomorrow. Have you learned to mold
      Aztec sugarskulls?

The Apostate rises from his magician's
cave, cobwebbed and fusty, hearing your summons:
to expunge the light of the centuries' wit,
      to bring in his train

a hobgoblin horde of devils and monsters
carrying bronze tridents, disreputable
strongmen, giants, gargoyles, licentious shepherds,
      nymphs, dragons, satyrs,

saints with fake wounds, messengers—the revenant
discredited minor athletes of magic
and bêtise, rabble of nothing, who proclaim:
     "Let there be darkness."

                     ∾

Or say: The much-esteemed Gibbon and his Virginian
colleagues by cheerful error calculated
that civilization motored a tidy upward turnpike
to culminate in the city of Guess Who's worldly
intelligence. But from A.D. 300, for a millennium,
every daughter knew less than her mother, every
son less than his father. Now, as we dispute
over the exact moment when we engaged this autobahn
downward again—hurtling in a tinny Volkswagen fueled
by idleness, greed, and superstition—our great-
grandfathers (the ones who could read and write)
drape themselves white to hear our diminished
chicken-cackle language in the parliament of fools.

DRUSILLA INFORMS

Drusilla informs young Libo
       about her former lover's gross pectorals
and biceps. Does she want the man
       to expire of a terminal jealousy?

He shakes, his vision blurs, his skin
       whitens and turns cold; a repulsive teardrop,
unbidden and deplorable,
       slips down his cheek in evident dishonor.

Will this acknowledgment serve? When
       she adds that her thighs were bruised and blue, heaving

under her temporary hunk,
        and that his teeth marked her neck, need her Libo

roll on his back wagging his tail?
        "Please extend your constancy backward," he begs,
"removing this fellow's swart grunts
        who brutalized the body of your young skin.

"Retrospective fidelity,"
        he declares, "will obliterate earlier
error. O Drusilla, let us
        unscrew the past." "Where is my suitcase?" she says.

SHIP OF STATE, HIGHTIDE

Ship of state, hightide rising
carries you off again, far
        from land. When you packed
            black traffic

to Virginia's shore, whole
cloth expanded under blue
        heaven. New England's
            enlightened

gentry constituted you
of stout pine and steam-bent oak
        for the seasonal
            hurricane

but not to withstand the rage
that your cargo turns on you
        as you divagate
            uncaptained

on the greedy fitful winds
of your final century.
        I beg you to sink
            abruptly.

                  ∾

Or say: We catch sight of you through the rain
and wind, Yankee clipper, as the tide's
defeat carries you off your mooring and out
to sea—from the Museum of Clear Ideas
into twenty-foot waves of Atlantic rubbish.
You're unfit for traffic, *Philosophe,* which is all
you were fitted out for. Where the wind leans,
your rational rudder takes you—the wind
is your helmsman—and neither intelligence nor will
takes passage with you, who were constructed for
eternity and Philadelphia by the reasonable will.

WHEN THE YOUNG HUSBAND

When the young husband picked up his friend's pretty wife
in the taxi one block from her townhouse for their
first lunch together, in a hotel dining room
            with a room key in his pocket,

midtown traffic gridlocked and was abruptly still.
For one moment before klaxons started honking,
a prophetic voice spoke in his mind's ear despite
            his pulse's erotic thudding:

"The misery you undertake this afternoon
will accompany you to the ends of your lives.
She knew what she did when she agreed to this lunch,
            although she will not admit it;

and you've constructed your playlet a thousand times:
cocktails, an omelet, wine; the revelation
of a room key; the elevator rising as
                    the penis elevates; the skin

flushed, the door fumbled at, the handbag dropped; the first
kiss with open mouths, nakedness, swoon, thrust-and-catch;
endorphins followed by endearments; a brief nap;
                    another fit; restoration

of clothes, arrangements for another encounter,
the taxi back, and the furtive kiss of goodbye.
Then, by turn: tears, treachery, anger, betrayal;
                    marriages and houses destroyed;

small children abandoned and inconsolable,
their foursquare estates disestablished forever;
the unreadable advocates; the wretchedness
                    of passion outworn; anguished nights

sleepless in a bare room; whiskey, meth, cocaine; new
love, essayed in loneliness with miserable
strangers, that comforts nothing but skin; hours with sons
                    and daughters studious always

to maintain distrust; the daily desire to die
and the daily agony of the requirement
to survive, until only the quarrel endures."
                    Prophecy stopped; traffic started.

                              ∽

Or say: Why this whining? You liked
your nooky well enough, back when
you had your teeth. Agreed, you
enjoyed the performance of rage

and disloyalty as much as orgasm;
still, you cherished the first time
a new one reached behind her back
to unfasten her bra, or slipped her
pants down hooking thumbs over black
silk. You devoted the greatest part
of the intelligence and energy of your
middle years to security measures:
maildrops, codes, and safehouses.
Do you croon guilt's anthem now
—after twenty years of diligence
and a gold watch—because your bald
agent retires from the company?

Old Woman Whom I

Old woman whom I remember beautiful
and young, I who am still older recollect
        words that shame me: Sink my abusive
           words under the Pacific Ocean.

Nothing is so ruinous as revenge's
rage—not whiskey, not the imagination,
        not love of country. In rage's house
           nothing rules but rage, and the waters

cannot drown it nor the winds blow it away
nor the fires burn it down. In our human minds
        ferocities gather and enlarge
           that we attempt to call inhuman:

The starved lion's hungry fury as he tears
the antelope resides in us: These rages
        destroyed Socrates and Stalingrad
           together, Masada and Emma

Bovary and Troy. Lion men burn houses
with their bushes and gardens until cities
        become cinder heaps that stink of meat.
            When I was forty animals walked

inside me. I was their cage, and when the gate
swung open I swung it. My lions loosened
        blood in the suburbs. I wrote those words
            to tear you with the five claws of rage.

It was love that grew eyeteeth, not for love bites;
it was love that made war. What other destroys
        so thoroughly as love does? Revenge
            and destruction are love's two faces.

When the Fine Days

When the fine days migrate east from Ohio,
climbing Vermont's greenest mountains and fording
        the Connecticut at White River
            Junction; when our meadows take relief

from inversions and July's lamentable
heat, you and I hike in fortuitous air
        up-mountain on logging roads—our dog
            Max leading us, bouncing, looking back

with mild impatience, making sure we follow—
and kneel taking joy of tiny red blossoms
        in moss. Here are no snakes to beware;
            here the shy black bear conceals himself;

here the glory of creation loosens our
spirits into appropriate surrender.

Looking down past a clearing, we fill
            with the fullness of the valley's throat,

where the slow cattle grind the abundant grass
and their laboring stomachs turn green to white;
            where the fat sheep graze without budging,
                    like soft white boulders. Now Max settles

alert, his nostrils twitching to read calm air.
Let us descend, Camilla, to the long white
            house that holds love and work together,
                    and play familiar music on each

other's skin. Today we won't worry about
weather, depression, or war; about bad luck
            for our labors; about heart attacks
                    or metastasis to the liver.

When I Was Young

When I was young and sexual
            I looked forward to a cool Olympian age
for release from my obsessions.
            Ho, ho, ho. At sixty the body's one desire

sustains my pulse, not to mention
            my groin, as much as it ever did, if not quite
so often. When I gaze at your
            bottom as you bend gardening, or at your breasts,

or at your face with its helmet
            of sensuous hair, or at your eyes proposing
the text of our next encounter,
            my attention departs from history, baseball,

food, poetry, and deathless fame.
　　　　Let us pull back the blanket, slide off our bluejeans,
assume familiar positions,
　　　　　　and celebrate lust in Mortality Mansions.

FLACCUS, DRIVE UP

Flaccus, drive up from Providence to see us.
I'll buy some bargain Scotch at a New Hampshire
liquor store and we'll celebrate your new book
　　　　　　and that good review

in the *New York Times*, which you'll complain about
—I don't see how—while you denounce your old friends
for their usual treacheries; but after
　　　　　　two hours of kvetching

you'll quiet down; you'll begin to laugh. I know
you can do better for Scotch in Rhode Island,
but no one there puts up with your complaining.
　　　　　　We miss you. Come soon.

LET US MEDITATE THE VIRTUE

Let us meditate the virtue of slogans.
Let us declare onomastic solutions
to difficulties largely unnameable,
　　　　　　and by the mottoes

of euphemism contract verbal righteousness.
Let's indite bulletins to tell everyone
the Jargon of Things, to name Lifestyles, to learn
　　　　　　the Tongue of High Coy:

Do you desire to purchase a beverage?
We thank you for not smoking. Have a nice day.
May we share these suggestions with you? Let us
       praise exaltation,

never calling a route salesman a milkman,
nor an officer of the law a cop, nor
a senior citizen old, nor a starving
       freezing bagwoman

poor. When we can't alter ills that upset us,
we will change their names to prevent compassion
from disturbing our ungulate composure:
       words to deny worlds.

Vocabulary voids original sin;
cavalry of the lie reaches Calvary
just in time—to bugle Christ down from the cross.
       But: no nails, no Christ.

WE EXPLORE GRIEF'S

We explore grief's borders, boundaries of mourning
and lamentation, wild cries and unending tears,
when the unexpected and unacceptable
       death happens. Henry King, teach us

to grieve with gratitude, who mourned for your young wife
in a Christian elegy. It is our habit
to continue by daydream to contradict death,
       so that continually we

imagine our friend smiling to hear our stories
or taking pleasure in some piece of good fortune

until her death leaps out of the corner again
to jeer at us: *No, no, you don't!*

The whole village weeps. Where shall we take our pleasures
for validation? Houses and farms and hamlets
mourn her absence, and no one more than Camilla,
who studied, watching her, the craft

of growing old with dignity and amusement.
Still we dream to whisper: "The coast is clear. Please come
out! This underground business has lasted too long:
Relent. Relent. Relent. Relent."

I SUPPOSE YOU'VE NOTICED

I suppose you've noticed, Fidelia, that drunks
rarely bang on your door anymore. You sleep
straight through, no longer aroused every few hours
by an amorous

clamor. Your telephone no longer jangles
at three A.M., breathes in your ear, and hangs up.
No more does your latest victim, or maybe
the victim before

last, wake you by asserting that you're heartless
for sleeping while he dies, much worse by sleeping
with someone else. If it was unfair that your
lovers tormented

you for your beauty, cheer up: Worse suffering
derives from age's ruin. It's not your fault
that your skin puckers, sags, and gathers, but now
men turn away when

you expect homage. When you lust—lust never
relents—your wet fury finds no complaisant
organ. You whine; you drink vodka; and your old
        lovers groan: revenged.

Sabina—Who Explored

Sabina—who explored internal continents for decades
        of poetry, bourbon, and night—molders
in a patch of Oregon far from her Vermont. For thirty
        years she made poems out of her troubles

and places—out of Middlebury, West Los Angeles, and
        Happy Valley—poems that stay alive
years after her early death. But Sabina was born to die
        like her poetic mothers and fathers,

like the sisters and brothers of our more ordinary lives
        and would-be making. Even the great ones?
Maybe great ones especially die. We the still surviving
        belittle ourselves at the funerals

of genius that offered us pause. We understand that we will
        also die, but claim, or wish to believe,
that women and men who appear to stop time by their products
        never depart entirely from being.

Nonetheless, Sabina disintegrates in her bare graveyard—
        as much as airline pilots whose planes crash,
or sailors who drown, or the greater number of us who stop
        breathing and turn blue in attended beds.

                    ∾

Or say: Good master Horsecollar
At Dartmouth-Hitchcock and in terror

Removed a carcinoma, D.V.
    Timor mortis conturbat me.

Sabina died ten years ago.
Flaccus endures, Death's sworn foe,
As Marvin burns melanoma away.
    Timor mortis conturbat me.

Kim died of the cure. My old teacher
Inhaled a carton of throat cancer
And each generation learns to die.
    Timor mortis conturbat me.

Frank was the first: He was run over;
Glaucus leapt underearth for cover.
Great ruth it were that it should be.
    Timor mortis conturbat me.

Go Write a Poem

"Go write a poem about it." Dutiful
Horsecollar, hastening to obey, invokes
the male Muse and tutelar of Parnassus:
        "Peter Mark Roget,

"breathe in for this inarticulate maker
of the temporary verb; supply language
as he makes up strophes fit to be counted
        Parnassian song.

"Figure him help from Brooklyn, from Cumberland
Street's wiry spinster if not the yawpmaster;
not the campy ocean but a syllabic
        exactitude, O

"numerical testudo of Athena!"
By administration of your amplitude,
Horsecollar counts on his eleven fingers
              beautiful numbers.

Nunc Est Bibendum

Nunc est bibendum. To condescend the phrase
into the preferred demotic—Latin that
          plain folks talk, picking up Anglish from
                    the cowboy and High Dutch from the sergeant—

we may translate the suggestion, "Let's get burnt,"
or choose the style of C. E. Bennett (Cornell
          University, nineteen fourteen):
                    "Now is the time to drain the flowing bowl."

However you say it, let us grab this hour
to float glorious magenta peonies
          in blue bowls on festival tables
                    as we gather to cherish victory.

Until this afternoon, it seemed unlucky
to break out the cider we pressed last autumn.
          We feared that Senator Hell might win,
                    wagging his sullied tail to celebrate

fund-raising, bigotry, merde, contempt for art,
and detestation of the First Amendment.
          Fundamental J. Virtue, D.D.,
                    joined forces with Representative Roar

and tobacco's senator to assemble
checks and attention by denouncing poets,

homosexuals, painters, Marxists,
    thieves, violinists, and people like that

except for Andrew Wyeth. They lost the vote
and their boats burn in the harbor. Let us drink
    to the survival of liberty—
        but remain vigilant: The enemy

always survives, for Egyptian solutions
don't wash in Washington. Senator Hell knows
    no humiliation in defeat:
        He sniffs, looking for something to roll in.

I, Too, Dislike

I, too, dislike it—the mannerism of plain,
natural, or idiomatic language
McPoets go in for. Horsecollar prefers
    chatting in Latin,

"Iowa delenda est," par exemple.
Squish the demotic underfoot, Arbogast.
When you take up syntax and semicolons,
    then show me your stuff.

             ∾

Or say: Rain on the weatherman who announces that
"we may experience shower activity" while others
claim that "it looks like rain" and Horsecollar
grumbles about "pluviosity." Now Libo disappears
from the pages of his existence, as void as Sabina
or Tu Fu who composes and decomposes together
with Camilla, Glaucus, atque Fidelia of syllabic
prurient fantasy. Horsecollar occupies his mornings

with a chisel, concentrating his stylus on language,
cutting square letters into stone, to avoid thinking
about aging, death, sexual loss, the countryside's
vanishing, replacement of affection by greed,
Mister Zero's prophylactic smirking dog-cynicism,
betrayals of love, and disappearance of the good
mothers and sisters, brothers and fathers, into dirt.

10 *Extra Innings*

The Tenth Inning

1. My friend David tells me that Jasper Johns
never takes his advice, so when David
suggests "Extra Innings," K.C. picks up
a bat. Last April the Boston Red Sox
beat Toronto opening day, then lost
three straight. At least, Kurt, the season started,
and even losing three out of four is
preferable to off-season—as life
despite its generic unpleasantness
appears under almost all conditions

2. more attractive than its alternative.
Batter up. We know what wins in the end,
in "Extra Innings." Therefore, many folks
settle for conditions of middleness,
lukewarm descending as far as lukecold,
pitch neither high nor low, volume neither
loud nor soft. Without a life, who fears death?
Even the season is out of season
unless we relish baseball, daydreaming
a game each night; then the morning paper.

3. After the bald surgeon making his rounds
removed the bandage from Jennifer's neck,
he pressed tiny bandaids over drainholes
side by side like snakefang punctures. As we
drove home we sat together in silence,

touching each other lightly, as if touch
were safety. Our ecstatic young dog leapt
to see her home—and pawed her incision
open. All night I reached in the darkness
to feel her familiar body again

4. and at dawn brought coffee to her bedside
as ever. All morning we sought comfort
in the blessedness of the resumed hour,
in the dear repetition of daily
gestures and tasks. We breathed calmly again
until like a sudden front from the north
we remembered the word cancer. That night,
while baseball lingered on the set, my mind
reran the last days, as a crow returns
to the perfume of putrescent carcass:

5. The drive to the hospital, admissions,
gown, bed, and a quick night's arduous sleep.
At six-thirty the following morning
I walked by her gurney to the metal
swoon of the elevator, then returned
to this house to wait for the surgeon's call.
In dread of consciousness I dozed beside
the telephone; I dreamt of a garden
where tomatoes sagged erupting black juice,
where squash lapsed softly drooling corrupt lymph

6. and seed, where Kentucky Wonders curled up,
cankered, and dropped from the derelict vine.
When the phone rang with the surgeon's message,
I would not have anyone else tell her:
I drove to the hospital to tell her
that the growth in her neck was malignant—
and that pathology's slow slides required
six days to deliver a prognosis

on the likelihood of metastasis
or probability of recurrence.

7. The entire history of human thought,
Western and Eastern, remembers and codes
our efforts to declare the real unreal.
Kurt, I almost forgot about baseball:
How would the Red Sox fare with the Yankees?
In my contracted heart Jennifer died
a thousand times. As I watched her alive,
I held her dying. Again and again,
I looked covertly at the small bandage
over the smooth skin I kissed so often

8. while we made love and I nuzzled her neck—
the skin swollen, with its row of stitches
like a zipper—and I trembled, dreading
that a black cell divided and split there.
In self-pity I watched the widower
weep by her grave: lamenting, lamented.
Sometimes a manager in a tight game
brings in a new relief pitcher for each
batter, two or three in a row—left, right,
left; meanwhile the other team's manager

9. answers with his pinch hitters—right, left, right—
after each pitcher faces one batter
until somebody runs out of bodies
on the bench or arms in the bullpen. Kurt,
do you know what a bench is? a bullpen?
Pathology telephoned its words: "a
muco-epidermoid carcinoma,
the size of a grape, intermediate
in virulence, encapsulated in
the membrane of the salivary gland"—

10. with no likelihood of metastasis
and little for recurrence. Next morning,
we woke alert in the pink-and-green dawn,
aware of joy at waking for the first
morning in weeks, in blissful consciousness
cherishing the settlement of the day:
Routine was paradise—walking the dog,
newspaper, coffee, love, rye toast, work, grape
juice, the Yankees beaten three straight, Cleveland
coming to town for four, a big series.

The Eleventh Inning

1. In nineteen ninety, Kurt, I picked the Red Sox
for fourth and they won the East. (But let's forget
the Oakland playoffs.) In nineteen ninety-one,
when I daydreamed before opening day that
the Red Sox took the World Series, we started
by losing four out of five. Baseball—the Sport
of Hope and Resignation: "Wait till next year."
"Next year we'll be dead, thanks; let's win it this year."
K.C. has been posthumous for twenty years
like everybody else in the universe.
The first time I died I was forty, whining

2. commonplace miseries of whiskey and love
as the Tigers kept winning; in a blurry
fury of bourbon I cheered Denny McLain
and Mickey Stanley on. Two innings ago,
at the end of the ninth, I drove my mother
for the upper GI. We dreaded cancer;
but I felt fatigued all day, taking six naps,
and it was I who constructed a quiet
carcinoma at the top of my colon.

The posthumous recognize each other at
store or postoffice: *that* one, with the pale shroud

3. wound invisibly around her body, who
exudes an aroma of continual
termination in a sickroom of terror
and gratitude. We nod at each other; we
acknowledge pain, baseball, lethargy, and cracks
in the bedroom ceiling. Do you remember
the Poverty Year of eighteen sixteen? Crops
froze twelve months out of twelve; we hungered all year
whether the Red Sox provisioned our daydreams
or froze them black. Now in the mild risen sun
we take deliberate pleasure breathing air;

4. every hour of our lives we inhale deeply
to reassure ourselves that lungs still expand
and contract. In the day we smell horsemanure
or lilac, we feel sun or hail equally,
with indifferent skin so long as synapses
fire. If a worm nibbles at the underside
of tissue, never mind: It is zero to
zero, the eleventh inning of a blue
April day. The posthumous never complain.
Kurt, I begin to understand what matters
in this daily game. Listen: Baseball is types

5. of continuousness, simultaneous
hours not consecutive ones, independent
temporalities that gather ongoing
moments into a perpetual present
that invalidates the inexorable
business of clocks. (Copy, *Sports Illustrated.*)
Five hundred years before Jesus and Caesar,
Xenophanes of Colophon recounted

what strangers said to each other, "fit topics
for conversation among men reclining
at the wineshop after a meal." The doctor

6. with thick glasses and cheerful manner mumbled,
"Fine, all clear," during the colonoscopy—
then quieted. Withdrawing his instrument,
solemn, he spoke with a summoned dignity,
looking in my eyes: "You have colon cancer,"
September 18, 1989, and
we contracted a surgeon and a schedule.
I still hear his clear inadmissible voice.
Over the season, games are quotidian
from the morning paper through extra innings
from the West Coast—fading with the pale grasses

7. of October, returning with the yellow-
green of April—measuring a timelessness
day by day and as dayless as paradise,
lacking the hour: "Before Adam was I am."
Lung cancer killed my father at fifty-two.
"A stranger asks: 'What is your family name?
How old were you when the Persians invaded?'"
Six months later, Kurt, we sat at the bedside
of Jack Jensen as he lay dying, mid-March,
while spring training thawed under Florida sun
and snow darkened by New London Hospital.

8. As his breaths grew quicker, abrupt and panicked
even in sleep, he woke smiling to offer
assurance, showing affection by smiling
because he could no longer speak. As I held
his cold hand, I felt my own hand turning cold.
My pulse slowed and energy flowed from my hand
into his hand, under blue skin to his heart;

my breath turned shallow and my dying body,
in pain of cold and good estate, drained itself
into his body. Frightened, watching my grave
open and suggest that I might enter it,

9. as if an owed death assumed me to itself,
I withdrew my hand. I warmed my aching hand
in my other hand still warm, and paced outside
his room on squares of the hospital hallway
while my friend in his pale skin snored into death.
We lay on the same bed, but I stepped away
from Jack in my fear. I prayed for forgiveness,
and next morning ate peanut butter again
for breakfast, read the *Globe,* and wrote at my desk.
When wrinkled flesh warmed itself again, I made
love with Jennifer in her grieving body.

10. In the apothegm of Baltimore Earl Weaver,
"This ain't football; we play this game every day."
Each day twenty-five men, older and younger,
throw, hit, catch, run, circle the bases; they take
BP, run wind-sprints, do infield, play pepper,
sign autographs, and chatter with young women
who lean over the dugout. Then they are old,
although they believed it would never happen:
They sell used cars, real estate, and insurance;
they pray, they eat peanut butter, they weep tears;
they practice love, sleep, work, cancer, and baseball.

11. When you drove me back home from the hospital,
you had strung tiny lights over the painted
Victorian bed. I slept. For the Series,
we moved a recliner in front of the box.
Over the weeks as I grew stronger, as pain
diminished, brother dread kept vigil by me.

But slowly the day returned; my skin returned
to rub against your skin and we touched again
in the complacency of the ecstatic
day's routine, inhabiting this clapboard,
quotidian, rare, sensible paradise.

The Twelfth Inning

1. Before lights, Kurt, baseball games were sometimes delayed
on account of darkness. Usually, as I
remember, they were continued and concluded
before another game began. On occasion,
now, games are suspended because of a curfew.
Really, who can finish a series like this one?
Therefore I declare that this Merzball game will stop
after twelve innings of play—although, as Nolan
Ryan puts it, pitching for Advil, "Ah could *pitch*
another *nine innings.*" In nineteen fifty-five,
the Dodgers beat the Yankees in the World Series
for the first time, as Johnny Podres won three games.

2. I watched with my father on a seven-inch screen,
borrowed from a neighbor's attic, in the guest room
where he coughed toward his death on a hospital bed.
He was happy—we were happy—minutes on end,
despite the losses of voice, eyesight, and hearing.
Winning distracted us; we looked for distraction.
Kurt, did you ever observe Dr. Naismith's game?
Basketball is the performance of miracles—
levitation, luck, opposites turning into
each other, primary-process as sports event—
while baseball remains the alternative to days:
twilight on the porch, lemonade, and sleepiness.

3. Dock Ellis performed pointguard for his high school team
but pitched for a profession. He threw a no-no
for Pittsburgh against San Diego—on acid,
having forgotten that he was supposed to pitch
until almost too late. Years later Gene Clines told
the story of Dock's change-up that a prospect swung
through so humiliatingly he was finished—
sent back to triple-A, never heard from again.
In-your-face is more common in basketball, where
wonders and stunts are ordinary, good-natured,
and devastating. When we fake this way, fake that,
break past the body leaping midair to block us,

4. and lay it up behind his back, we are deathless.
Among enormous bodies, alert eyes, and hands
that flap like manta rays, dandy delicate guards
are minnows outwitting whales, or sons their fathers,
and basketball is Austrian psychodrama—
expressionist in its distortion of physics,
grand-operatic in its bipolarity—
while baseball is De Stijl: orderly, obsessive,
the meeting ground of arithmetic and beauty
or the daily grid of manic pastoral song.
In September the Red Sox have an outside chance
if Toronto keeps on clutching, if the Tigers

5. lose games they ought to lose. Today as the leaves fall
red and amber, our town's yellow schoolbus returns
up the gravel road in a mild September rain
for the waiting child who wears her yellow slicker
and carries last year's beat-up Big Bird lunchbox, first
day of school. Chill nights at Fenway bring April back
with annual ironies of remembered dreams
and retrospective foresight—as gardens go down
behind the house, under the hill. Here Jennifer

last spring raised a wild dazzlement of daffodils,
and under the high sun of July prodigious
peonies of privacy, whiter than winter;

6. where buttercups flourished by a stony wellhead,
now dry stalks wither. Hurricane Bob shut Fenway
two days in a row, pity, with Cleveland in town.
On Jennifer's neck it is impossible to
detect the scars of her cancer: virgin again.
K.C. monitors a possible recurrence
by checking the level of his blood's CEA
each quarter, raising anxiety to lose it
for three months more of Jennifer's shorts, poetry,
and baseball. My father is thirty-five years dead,
buried on Christmas Eve. For twenty years his death
provoked the choices of my life. I use mornings

7. to work in, and afternoons for reading and love,
and do desultory chores nights during baseball—
paying bills, dictating letters. When the Red Sox
play on the West Coast, K.C. takes an evening nap,
eight-thirty to ten-thirty, then watches the game
until one A.M. Five drugs together control
Jennifer's depression: She can't sleep or hold still
or watch baseball but her mood is enterprising;
joyously she writes poems that render despair
and gardens until dark encloses the garden.
She weeps to recall Jack, who turned into ashes,
remembered by a granite bench with flowering shrubs.

8. It is the season for blackberries that prosper
at roadside in thorny tangles and in the trench
of the abandoned railroad. Mrs. Roberts walks
from early spring to late fall by the asphalt's edge,
toting a Shaker basket for wild strawberries
and volunteer asparagus, for dandelion

greens in spring, for blackberries from August into
hard frost. David inquires: What does K.C. stand for
(besides the vainglorious Irishman Casey
mocked by the millowner's Harvardman son and heir)?
Prizes for best answers: Kurt Carcinoma? Kid
Chumpleheart? Kitsch Champion? Kitchen Cat? Kup Cake?

9. Steve Blass was a control pitcher one year, the next
season—after his friend Roberto Clemente's
plane crashed in a winter sea—couldn't throw a strike.
John Singer Sargent defined a portrait as "that
form of painting in which there is always 'something
a little *wrong* about the mouth.'" When I was young,
I covered my mouth when I felt a difficult
subject approach—or when I lied; with age I stopped
lying. Kurt, while you built your Merz-house, the Dodgers
played the game of baseball with Red Barber's guidance,
who still talks baseball for NPR on Fridays
from Tallahassee. His voice was soft and nervous,

10. his affection luminous. Baseball is better
than model airplanes, and poems are better still—
preferable to conceited demonstrations
that poems cannot exist and authors are dead.
Blass lost his control because he was terrified
of hitting batters—after his friend's plane went down.
He said he felt like Secretariat: All that
money and he couldn't get it up. Next year Blass
sold class rings to Connecticut high school seniors.
The farmhouse where we live straggles back to Ragged
Mountain from an ox path that became the Grafton
Turnpike in 1803, later Route 4. The Cape,

11. in its almost two hundred years of adjustment
and generation, wandered from yellow to red
to white and green on the same squared-off oaken sills.

Our unpainted barn remains upright. Beside it
my grandfather and I threw baseballs back and forth
in nineteen forty-two while firebombs descended
on England, Spitfires shot down Messerschmitts, and Kurt
coughed beginning slow death. In September maples
turn yellow and red against the black-brown rusty
barnboards; now Jennifer's sunflowers feed the autumn
chickadees, nuthatches, and slate-colored juncos;
soon grosbeaks with yellow chests will peck at the seeds.

12. In September the Red Sox lose games in the ninth.
The season ends. Even if you win the Series,
the season ends, O, and games dwindle to Florida's
Instructional League where outfielders without wheels
learn to be catchers. From Florida north will truck
oranges that Jennifer squeezes in the cold
light of a low sun. I wear my yellow sweater;
we eat scrambled eggs from blue and white dishes; her
hair's kerchief is yellow. We gather yellow days
inning by inning with care to appear careless,
thinking again how Carlton Fisk ended Game Six
in the twelfth inning with a poke over the wall.

The Thirteenth Inning

1. John Singer Sargent's *The Daughters of Edward D. Boit*
renders three reticent sisters and a silk infant
whose mother escapes citation. We study its fierce,
darkling, upright, mysterious, slick, Victorian
sexuality. I called Jane "Camilla" when I
was Horace Horsecollar, and "Jennifer" while K.C.
explained baseball to Kurt Schwitters, deceased and German,
who cared nothing for baseball or my voice nattering.
As we drive home to New Hampshire, leaving the daughters

in the permanent museum, the game starts again
that ceased in the twelfth inning, although the multitude
has dispersed and Fenway Park is empty and silent.
In darkness and silence the game continues itself.

2. When the moon rises, light standards cast eldritch shadows
on players who cast no shadows, and we observe four
transparent pitchers superimposed on each other,
from ghostly Babe Ruth past Cy Young and Smoky Joe Wood
to Parson Ted Lewis. "A thousand years a city,
a thousand years a desert," as the Hindus put it,
who recede distantly enough in antiquity
to say such things. Aphorisms, epigrams, apothegms,
and proverbs: "It is better to bend a strawberry."
In the Protestant Cemetery at Rome, near Keats,
Shelley, cats, and the pyramid of Cestius, we
find a stone marker for "Ned" Boit, father of daughters
and painter of eternal Rome. The thirteenth inning

3. elapses as I do play-by-play for Kurt, while we
wander in dark Fenway among boxes and bleachers,
reviewing baseball's enterprise of ongoingness,
which is the name of everything assembled together.
Sometimes on Sunday afternoons my father and I
drove half an hour to watch the West Haven Sailors play
baseball for a crowd innocent of television—
sometimes as Class D minors, sometimes as semipro.
Once they advertised in the *New Haven Register*
that Ralph Branca's *brother* would pitch. All losses are one:
In the Gra-Y camp I wept for loneliness; now I
dread death. At Rome, William Wetmore Story lies under
his own carved marble near Constance Fenimore Woolson.

4. She leapt from a balcony in Venice; Henry James
buried his friend whose suicide roared like a lion

in Lamb House: *too late, too late, too late.* As I entered
the hospital to lose the right lobe of my liver,
a fourth granddaughter was born. I thought of Boit's daughters
as Abigail followed on Emily, Allison,
and Arianna. Two weeks after I returned home,
the lesion excised, Peter Hall was born in Boston—
large, male, and redheaded like his sister Emily
and his cousin Allison, as if the beautiful
daughters of Edward D. Boit, lurking in such shadow,
were completed by a fifth and masculine presence,
foregrounded, laughing, wearing a joyous milk mustache.

5. What may I pray for grandchildren? That the sun never
set and they never suffer? Like euphoria but
more frequent and more ineluctable, suffering
is universal and incomparable. May they
survive to cherish and make their children's children laugh,
telling them stories: When their great-grandfather Dean Smith
pulled a chain through the lumberyard and somebody asked,
"Why's Dean pulling that chain?" the boss answered, "You ever
see anybody *push* one?" Dr. Sutton performed
resection. Morphine in ICU, five minutes sleep
alternating with five minutes writhing, tubes twisted
like spider legs. I remembered my friend William Trout
and Reba, who crawled into his deathbed carefully

6. to administer her warm body. For "writhing" read
"writing" throughout, as Hanuman and Ganesh appeared
bringing floral pots and intravenous nirvana.
When I woke in ICU—Abigail six days old—
I thrashed among seven tubes and hoses. Unable
to speak for respiring, I punched buttons to raise up
the Red Sox playing the Orioles. Who won that game?
In the cemetery at Rome, avenues of damp
and ivied marble clutter with cats and eminent

Protestant dead. Last year at the White House I observed
Ted Williams and Joe DiMaggio, both tall and gray,
leaning in the doorway and smiling while the awkward
president alluded to seasons fifty years past.

7. "Live Free or Die." Because Queen Elizabeth the First
was shortsighted and old, courtiers could paint her cheeks
green and compliment her on a healthy complexion.
Hospitals are benign engines of paranoia:
Suffering is the privacy that accompanies
us on our cold excursion; even if it becomes
public, we examine its degree in solitude.
As I recover, spring exaggerates its vigor
and turns to baseball. Does it weary of annual
return? When Charlie Whittemore asked my grandfather,
during an August drought, if he reckoned it might rain,
Wesley Wells looked south over the blue mountain and paused
to consider the matter: "It always *has*," he said.

8. The Spring Glen Barbershop is vacant, clean, and empty,
not even a TO LET placard leaning in the blear
plate-glass window, but the blue-red-white pole still spirals,
days and nights. Go turn the fucking thing off; go summon
Salvatore the barber back, swiveling from Sally's
—nobody knows where the switch is—oily grave of hair.

೦౪

It starts raining and the umpires call time. We enter a rain delay.

In Madras, the drive to the airport should have taken half an hour;
because of the monsoon it took an hour and a quarter. Jennifer and
I were nauseated. With the windows closed, the taxi was hot; with the
windows open, the air entering the taxi carried six-sided chunks of ex-
haust.

When Carlton Fisk catches, he is master at annoying hitters, interrupting their concentration. Fisk has been called the Human Rain Delay.

The baby sitting in front is Julia Overing Boit, who became a painter like her father; she was born in Soisy, France, 15 November 1877, and survived in Newport, Rhode Island, as late as 1969. Jane Hubbard Boit hovers above her baby sister; she was born in 1870 and died in Connecticut in 1955. Leaning against the great Chinese urn is Florence, the eldest; born in Newport in 1868, she died in Paris in 1919. On the left of the painting is Mary Louisa Boit, born 5 June 1874 in Paris and dead in Newport in 1945. None of them married.

Outside Bombay, a man sits on the sidewalk at noon with a hand-operated sewing machine making shirts. Another man pounds tin making pots and pans. A cow walks between tailor and tinker, nosing at thread but not eating. Where a baker discards a blackened edge of bread, the cow pauses to chew. Turning full circle, we see three other cows, a camel, five dogs, a pig, an elephant hauling a shrub, twelve hens, and a bullock.

During a rain delay on television we return to the studio and run highlights of the nineteen seventy-five World Series. Carlton Fisk, twenty-seven years old, hits a pitch into the screen again, ending the game in the twelfth inning. But this time something goes wrong in the mechanics of electronic reproduction: The game continues into the thirteenth inning—in total darkness, the players transparent, dead, and multiple, the audience also . . .

At the Agra railroad station, a teenage boy, bent into a semicircle, walks on all fours like an ambulatory arch, clip-clops attached to his hands. A little girl with a cute marketable smile looks up with her palm outstretched; glancing down to look away, I see that the feet of this four-year-old are as large as a basketball player's.

During a rain delay on radio, the announcers improvise their own
game; no one has any idea what really happens. The game is collage,
Kurt: smells of Calcutta pasted next to shreds of a liver biopsy, Ted Wil-
liams wriggling in two dimensions on a nineteen forty-one baseball
card thumbtacked with a swatch of red hair swept from Salvatore's
floor, catpiss from the Protestant Cemetery, Ganesh pitching with six
baseballs at once, Mary Louisa Boit in pigment, and Bill Trout drunk as
dirt in the empty bleachers as the rain stops.

∽

Edward D. Boit's four pretty daughters, who are buried
not in Rome but in Connecticut, Paris, and Rhode
Island, gave this painting to the Boston Museum
thirty-seven years after Sargent painted it. Why
did none of them marry? They were representative
rich Americans who lived in Italy and France
for a hundred years while Henry James wrote about them.

9. When Reba came to his bed at the Bayside Hospice,
Bill clasped her hands and stared steadily into her eyes,
his jaw grinding sideways as if it would dislocate;
he gazed memorizing her face for recitation
in the imminent grave. "How many lines was Reba?"
Kurt, for a moment let us sit behind the dugout.
Don't look, but I think that's Carl Yastrzemski coming up.
It's hard to tell, because he's as flimsy as we are.
In nineteen forty-eight, lunching in Eliot House,
I noticed two students waving their arms as they marched
the dining room's length, displaying oblongs of cardboard
they offered for sale. No one paid attention but me:
Thus I attended the Cleveland-Boston playoff, which

10. we lost when Boudreau hit two home runs. Kurt died that
        year,
and like Eliot House he didn't give a goddamn.

It was a bright September afternoon, cool and clear
at woeful Fenway Park; I lamented more deeply
for the lost Dodgers of Brooklyn than for Boston's team.
Last night I went to bed early, Red Sox on the coast,
and nightmared chemotherapy all night. Dread of death
consumes later life, when eros is unavailing.
On an August weekday late in the nineteen forties
my middle-aged father drove my grandfather and me
from New Hampshire to Boston and Fenway Park, so that
Wesley Wells could watch Ted Williams address a baseball.
In eighteen ninety-eight he took the morning train south

11. to see the Boston Nationals; Parson Ted Lewis
pitched and won. Haying, he told me stories of that game
fifty years on. In nineteen ninety-two I enter
the infusion room—where I observe the long circle
of cots and couches like sofas set for Roman feasts
with vomitoria supplied at every bedside
for bald skeletons with flesh hanging slack from their bones,
for fetal half-moons rigid in this twisted district.
Leukovorin drips into my wrist-back for two hours.
Before the registered nurse administers eighteen
cc's of 5FU into the coiled transparent
IV tubing, I take my antinausea pill.
In the infusion room, caritas tempers anguish.

12. At my mother's house on Ardmore Street I take four naps
a day as we set her up again, at eighty-nine,
returning from another journey when she turned blue
while paramedics siren'd her to Yale—New Haven.
Jennifer freezes soup, rubs me down daily, and sees
a man at the corner of her eye who vanishes.
She recognizes the face of my father, who died
thirty-seven years ago in this airless guest room
where we sleep for a week. She says: "He looks after you."

Does he look *for* me? Today I am a dozen years
older than my father ever became. I recall
nineteen fifty-five when the Dodgers beat the Yankees
four out of seven, and my namesake died on this bed.

13. Kurt, the players of the thirteenth inning have vanished
into white dawn. I dread that it's time to stop talking
and leave Fenway, you for your grave in England, and I
to Jennifer's passionate weeping that comforts me
in my grief at leaving her. I long to stay alive
for her careful hands, for poems, for four granddaughters
and one grandson. I know: John Singer Sargent is dead,
and Boit's daughters, and Mrs. Fiske Warren, whom I met
as an old lady with a jeweled velvet choker
while Warren Spahn pitched for the Boston Braves, whose portrait
as a beautiful middle-aged woman Sargent made.
Breathing I glue together these anthems and cutouts
of the thirteenth inning although the game is over.

14. But not the poem. The thirteenth inning goes to fourteen
stanzas. In Pondicherry's Good Guest House the Mother's face
looked down from every wall. Stepping out into Lansdowne Street,
Kurt and I meet a visitor from another poem,
Horace Horsecollar, avid to join this last enterprise,
who metamorphoses into his muttering alter
ego, Manager Zero the cynic philosopher,
who barks as the traffic of daylight visits Kenmore Square:
"Everyone dies. Blubbering never deterred a last breath
from blurring its elegy on a redundant mirror.
The narcissist believes that his death is the only death,
and remorseless self-pity makes music of self-regard.
There is something a little wrong about the sitter's mouth.
You roll like a dog in the rotted carcass of your death."

11 The Old Life

Spring Glen Grammar School

Sitting in the back seat
of a nineteen thirty-five Packard
            with running boards, I held
my great-uncle Luther's blotchy hand.
            He was nine for Appomattox
and remembered the soldier
            boys coming home from the war.
When I pressed the skin of his hand
            between thumb and forefinger,
the flesh turned white as Wonder Bread.
            It remained indented
for a few seconds and then rose up,
            turning pink, flush to the surface
of his veined hairless mottled
            hand. Then I pressed it again.
Luther would stay old forever.
            I would remain six, just
beginning first grade, learning to read.

            For weeks we learned
the alphabet—practicing it, reciting
            in unison singsong,
printing letters in block capitals
            on paper with wide blue
lines, responding out loud to flash cards.
            Then she said: "Tomorrow
you'll learn to read."
                              Miss Stephanie Ford

               wrote on the blackboard
in large square letters: T H A T. "That,"
            she said, gesticulating
with her wooden pointer, "is 'that.'"

               Each year began
in September with a new room and a new
               teacher: I started with
Stephanie Ford, then Miss Flint, Miss Gold,
               Miss Sudel whom I loved,
Miss Stroker, Miss Fehm, Miss Pikosky . . .
               I was announcer
at assemblies. I was elected class
               president not because
I was popular but because I
               was polite to grown-ups, spoke
distinctly, held my hands straight down
               at my sides, and kept
my shirt tucked in: I was presidential.

               Eight years in this
rectangular brick of the nineteen thirties:
               If I survive to be eighty,
this box will contain the tithe
               of a long life.
In the glass case, terra is miniature:
               tiny snails and mosses,
wooden houses with sidewalks, small trees,
               and Spring Glen Grammar School.
See, pupils gather around a boy
               in black knickers
who shoots an agate, kneeling in the circle.

THE HARD MAN

My father wept easily,
laughed loudly when his friends teased him,
        and blustered like a basso—
but *his* father was "a hard man."
        H.F. was strict, handsome,
silent, and severe. When his stallion
        Skylark ran away
with my young uncle and threw him, H.F.
        galloped to a stop
beside his son's body, bellowing, "Are
        you trying to kill
the horse?" I remember the time we called
        on H.F. after church
to find him sitting upright, staring
        straight ahead without
expression, as my uncle cut his boot
        away with the carving
knife that sliced white and dark at Christmas;
        I remember the leather
curling like a black rose petal.
        That morning Skylark
slipped on clear ice that H.F. neglected
        to notice, and the horse,
falling, rolled on his leg. Jagged pink
        bone was sticking out
through H.F.'s paper-white leg skin as he
        sat stiff, resolute,
without complaint or excuse for error.

VENETIAN NIGHTS

There were joys, even
in Connecticut; there were miracles
in the suburbs. Snow
still lay in patches on Ardmore's north side
when the mailman brought
the catalogue—with pages as flimsy
as a comic book's,
four colors printed askew—from the Bliss
Fireworks Company
of East Valparaiso, Indiana.
I became scholar
of smudged images: SPECIAL MAJESTIC
VENETIAN NIGHTS
and GOLDEN ETERNAL SHOWERS OF ECSTASY.
I put checks by Roman candles
and skyrockets that dropped lead
soldiers under tissue
parachutes.
My father printed out
the form in his neat letters.
When the box came I unpacked it
and lined up pinwheels and bombs,
sorting the fountains and green fire.
On the Fourth we drove
to a county where fireworks were legal
and parking on a dirt
road after dark flared our paradise
of fire.
The next day
I began right away to plan ahead
for next year, foreseeing
fireworks always with my young father,
slender rockets unpacking

their quick shoots of burning petals,
      green gold, as we two
became one person, ecstatic and joint,
      blossoming together
into smoke that enlarged and expired.

BLUE

      In Spring Glen, nineteen
forty-one was melancholy. Were all
      these years so sad?
My father hated his job at the Dairy,
      working for his father,
and came home weeping. When my mother
      recovered from an operation,
she took to bed again
      with a "nervous stomach."
That Christmas we experimented:
      Our window candles had blue bulbs;
the lights on the tree burned blue.
      We sat in the dark house,
blue in its hollow darkened by shrubs
      and trees, in the blue
darkness of the den, blue gazing at blue.

MY AUNT LIZ

      My aunt the English teacher,
who wrote verses for Hallmark cards
      and looked like my mother
only younger and plumper, took me
      walking in the woods
when I was five. She stirred me with stories

about a one-eyed
giant outwitted by a clever Greek
sailor; about a wooden
puppet whose nose elongated
when he told a lie.
Aunt Liz was pretty, generous, moody,
and fierce in affections
and desires. I cherished her. When I
was eleven or twelve,
one summer when she was without love
and lonely in her thirties,
she visited the farm. She took
to crawling into
my bed for a cuddle as I woke up
until one morning,
as she squeezed herself against me, Liz flushed
and leapt from bed, saying
I was grown up now; she was sorry.

SCREENPLAY

When I was twelve I bused
alone from Hamden to New Haven
to go to the movies,
to worship at the Church of Corpses:
The Wolf Man in brute
carnations, *Frankenstein, Dracula, Bride
of Frankenstein*. The boy
next door's name was Billy Harris, three
years older; he said, "If you like
that sort of stuff, you should read
Edgar Allan Poe."
With this advice my life began. I tried
writing poems and stories

imitating Poe. Because I
        constructed myself,
I consulted Hervey Allen's thousand-
        page biography
Israfel, which made much of young Edgar
        reading Keats and Shelley
at fourteen. I saved my allowance
        to buy, for a dollar
twenty-five, the Modern Library
        Keats and Shelley, and read it
straight through, resolute—and two years
        smarter than Poe—to script
the home movie of the chosen life.

THE PROFESSION

        As a Boy Scout
I never owned a uniform. At fourteen
        I went to Scout meetings
as a way to get out of the house.
        Talking one night
with David Johnstone—uniformed, ironic,
        sophisticated, First Class,
sixteen—we proved ourselves members
        of the Teenage Ambition
Club, in whom "the desire to be
        extraordinary,"
as the Autocrat of the Breakfast
        Table put it, "is
commonplace." I bragged that in my high school
        study hall that morning
I had written a poem. Dave's eyes
        quickened with passion.
"Do you write *poems?*" he said. "Yes," I said.

"Do you?" Pulling
himself up, he uttered a noble sentence
that dictated the rest
of my life: "It is my profession."

On the *Advocate*
in nineteen forty-eight, we argued all
night about whether
a poem was decent enough to print.
John Ashbery sat
in a chair, shelling pistachio nuts;
Robert E. Bly wore a three-
piece suit and a striped tie; Kenneth
Koch was ever sarcastic.
Once as we pasted an issue
together we discovered
a blank page and teased Ashbery
to give us a new poem.
John disappeared to Dunster House.
When he dawdled back
with his lines about fortunate Alphonse,
we admired it
and pasted it up. Later he admitted
that he had gone back
to his room and improvised the poem
on his Olivetti.
When I told him the story forty
years later, John laughed.
"Yes," he said, sighing. "I took longer then."

THE GIRLFRIEND

When I came home for Christmas
halfway through college, my girlfriend
        from Simmons wrote me
a note: She'd had her period. Of course
        my mother read the letter,
and my father with a broad smile
        —anxious, loving, terrified—
suggested we have a talk. "One
        thing," he said to begin with.
"You mustn't go back to Boston
        for the New Year's party."
It was A Turning Point in our lives.
        I knew it; he knew it.
Our hearts thudded; tears cornered our eyes.
        I Dug In My Heels;
he Lost His Composure—telling me that
        "if you go to the party,
you will be kicking your mother's
        body." They drove me to Boston
—reproach by kindness—and next
        morning at breakfast,
after two hours' sleep, I was filial
        and affectionate, tired,
happy, smelling love on my fingers.

THE GIANT BROOM

My last spring at college
I bought a beat-up wire recorder
        and with my friends
invented a radio quiz program called
        The Giant Broom.

Each contestant told a lachrymose story.
　　　　Murmuring his sympathy,
the MC would explain the rules:
　　　　"If you answer
the question correctly, you get a million
　　　　dollars tax-free; but if
you fail, the Giant Broom will sweep you
　　　　into our Incinerator
where you will burn to death for
　　　　the entertainment
of our studio audience." The questions:
　　　　"Who is Sylvia?" "How
can we know the dancer from the dance?"
　　　　"Oh, I'm *so* sorry ..."
As the Broom swished, we recorded screams of
　　　　terror and agony,
as well as applause from spectators.
　　　　We played the game
all night, in the weeks before graduation,
　　　　waiting for honors,
graduate school, partnership in Morgan
　　　　Stanley, or
possibly a police action in Korea.

MR. ELIOT

　　　　Mr. Eliot at sixty-
three—Nobel Laureate and Czar—
　　　　kindly suggested
that I drop by his office at Faber's
　　　　in London on my way
to Oxford. In dazed preparation,
　　　　I daydreamed agendas
for our conversation. At his desk,

the old poet spoke
quietly of "the poetic drama,"
and "our literary
generations," as if I had one.
After an hour, he scraped
his chair back. I leapt up, and he leaned
in the doorway
to improvise a parting word. "Let me see,"
he said. "Forty years
ago I went from Harvard to Oxford,
now you from Harvard
to Oxford. What advice may I give you?"
He paused the precise
comedian's millisecond as I
reflected on the moment,
and then with his exact lilting
English melody inquired:
"Have you any long underwear?"

LE JAZZ

In the nineteen forties
I wore my Blue Notes down to scratches
and visited the Savoy
Saturday nights to hear Wild Bill,
Vic Dickenson, Teddy Bunn,
Pops Foster, and Big Sid. The spring
of nineteen fifty-two,
in Paris, I hoarded black-market
francs to hire a table
at Vieux Columbier for *le jazz
hot de* Sidney Bechet.
Afternoons, I sauntered past Hôtel
Montana on Rue Saint-Benoît

where the man from New Orleans
    tilted back on a wooden
chair by the door. When I tried out
    "Good afternoon," he agreed.
In the dark nightclub he played "Dear
    Old Southland"
and "Summertime" on clarinet and soprano
    sax. One Pernod warmed
beside me as I heard Sidney Bechet
    announce in his Cajun
French, *"Et maintenant,* 'Muscat Ramble.'"

JUST MARRIED

    It was the year when
everybody got married. I was there
    with my tall beautiful
bride when Tom McElroy went berserk.
    When he reached
the getaway car after the silk reception,
    Tom found his ushers
gathered to decorate the Cadillac
    the usual way—with *Just*
Married, pie plates, ribbons, and straw.
    He was furious. He rushed
forward to kick Geoff, who padlocked
    tire chains to an axle,
then swung at me, who sprayed silver paint.
    When we all understood
that Tom was drunk or crazy—drunk *and*
    crazy—we stepped back.
He sped off toward the airport, *Just Married,*
    Maggie relentlessly
and appropriately blubbering
    beside him as he

grumbled in a continuous outrage
      while they started their
decade's trip toward the usual divorce.

DREAD

      My mother said, "Of course,
it may be nothing, but your father
      has a spot on his lung."
That was all that was said: My father
      at fifty-one could never
speak of dreadful things without tears.
      When I started home,
I kissed his cheek, which was not our habit.
      In a letter, my mother
asked me not to kiss him again
      because it made him sad.
In two weeks, the exploratory
      revealed an inoperable
lesion.
      The doctors never
      told him; he never asked,
but read *The Home Medical Guidebook.*
      Seven months later,
just after his fifty-second birthday
      —his eyesight going,
his voice reduced to a whisper, three days
      before he died—he said,
"If anything should happen to me . . ."

THE FRAGMENTS

      After dinner at Crispi's
we drove around Rome. "There's the *scene—*

307

of the *crime,*" he said
as we passed a building, in the accent
        or melody that sounded
like W. C. Fields. "Where you broadcast
        the talks?" "Where I *gave* 'em—
the *scripts.*" When he couldn't remember
        the way to Hadrian's
tomb, he sank back in diffident woe.
                But when, with his yellow
Confucian scarf slung on his shoulders,
        he bought gelati
and we strolled a piazza together,
        old Ezra Pound cocked
his lionish head like a gallantman
        captain of mercenaries
hired by a Sforza.
                Answering
        my knock the first day
I arrived from Thaxted, he addressed me
        in small bursts like sporadic
gunfire: "Mr. Hall—you have *come*
        —all the *way*—from *England*—
and you *find* me—nothing but *fragments.*"

FAME

        When I interviewed Henry
Moore's old friends for a *New Yorker*
        profile, Edward
Bantam invited me to dine at his house.
        I brought whiskey. The old
man remembered forty years back, young
        art-student roommates
arrived from Yorkshire to London, sculptor

308

and portrait painter:
Edward Bantam's portrait of Moore's mother
        hung in the dining room
at Henry Moore's house.
                        But Ned Bantam
        at forty converted
to surrealism. I looked; I looked
        away. He told
anecdotes of friendship in bohemia
        as we drank Glenfiddich
until his head fell forward, he wept,
        and complained that Henry
remembered nothing of the old times,
        but had to send me,
a stranger, to ask him about the years
        friends worked side by side
for fame that would divide them forever.

FORTY YEARS

        Forty years ago this
spring Robin and I made the journey
        from Oxford to Charterhouse
on a bright day, changing trains twice,
        talking continually
as we strolled the paradisal
        sward of his school
among daffodils in an English April.
        Last October I saw him
at the London Clinic: confused,
        skeletal, panicked,
and confident of recovery. In
        November Monica
scattered his ashes from a dinghy

into the Channel.
That day in nineteen fifty-two we rode
                back to the college
in a van of House cricketers who stopped
                for pints of bitter
at every pub. Robin and I were tired,
                but talked as men in their
twenties talk about what they will do,
                friends now and always,
or until we died, if that could happen.

What Counts

                Moore was sixty when I
met him. Before tea—when he had worked
                eight hours on maquettes,
waxes, an eight-foot reclining figure
                in elmwood, and a
monumental two-part shaped like the skull
                of an elephant—we played
Ping-Pong. He was quick, resourceful,
                wiry, competitive,
thirty years older, and I beat him.
                When I smashed the ball
to his backhand, before he could swing his
                paddle to meet it,
he swatted the ball back over the net
                with his naked left hand.
"That counts," he said quickly, "doesn't it?"

                He liked to repeat
advice that Rodin gave to young sculptors:
                "If you're working
on a maquette, and it doesn't go right, don't

keep picking at the clay,
making little changes here and there.
Drop it on the floor.
See what it looks like then." And he liked it
that Rodin remembered
tips from the craftsman who counseled him
when they labored
together in an artisan's shop. "Rodin,"
said Adolph Constant
to the apprentice, "your leaves are too flat.
Make some with edges pointing
straight up at you. Never think of
a surface except
as the extremity of a volume."

MOON SHOT

With a drink in my hand
and my mouth turned down, I sat with Min
and Bill looking
at the television picture in July
of nineteen sixty-nine
as my life emptied like a bottle
on its side, glug glug
glug. In two months I would turn forty-one:
Hopeless, divorced,
abandoned, without love or my children, I
understood that my losses
were my own contrivance. I sat
drinking gin while snowy
Neil Armstrong fixed his indefinite
heavy enormous boots
to a ladder's rungs and wobbled down
toward the moon's scattered

rubble and boring surface. Who cared? If
      he spoke from a sound-
stage in Arizona, who the fuck cared?

7 ½

      If I press Play instead
of Record, and howl that the machine
      has busted, or if I plug
the two ends of one extension
      cord triumphantly
together, or if I discard the fresh
      milk and drink the sour
without noticing there is a difference,
      I am addressed with
affection as Old Seven and a Half.
      Jane and Philippa
recall the time a university
      telephoned for
my hat size; I didn't have an idea.
      The helpful caller
suggested, "Maybe seven and a half?"
      I was overheard to ask,
"Would that be the circumference?"

ELBOWS

      I walked from the yard
into the kitchen of my mother's house
      on a hot morning, hearing
footsteps approach from the sunporch
      through the parlor
in a familiar cadence. When the person

entered the kitchen,
it was someone who looked like me, just like
        me. I gazed into this face
that stared back, puzzled or annoyed,
        me but not me: I who was
thinking, or who write these lines now,
        lived inside a body
that felt its feet touch linoleum,
        that heard its own heart
beating in panic, not the other's heart.
        When we stepped closer,
we held each other fast by the elbows.

THE WEDDING COUPLE

        Fifteen years ago his heart
infarcted and he stopped smoking.
        At eighty he trembled
like a birch but remained vigorous
        and acute.
                When they married
fifty years ago, I was twelve.
        I observed the white lace
veil, the mumbling preacher, and the flowers
        of parlor silence
and ordinary absurdity; but
        I thought I stood outside
the parlor.
        For two years she dwindled
        by small strokes
into a mannequin—speechless almost, almost
        unmoving, eyes open
and blinking, fitful in perception—
        but a mannequin that suffered

shame when it stained the bedsheet.
Slowly, shaking with purpose,
he carried her to the bathroom,
undressed and washed her,
dressed her in clean clothes, and carried her back
to CNN and bed. "All
you need is love," sang John and Paul:
He touched her shoulder; her eyes
caressed him like a bride's bold eyes.

Rain

Curled on the sofa
in the fetal position, Jane wept day
and night, night and day.
I could not touch her; I could do nothing.
Melancholia fell
like the rain over Ireland for weeks
without end.
I never
belittled her sorrows or joshed at
her dreads and miseries.
How admirable I found myself.

Beans and Franks

When Newberry's closed
in Franklin, New Hampshire—homely lime front
on Main Street, among the closed
storefronts of this mill town depressed
since nineteen twenty-nine;
with its lunch counter for beans and franks
and coleslaw; with its

bins of peanuts, counters of acrylic,
        hair nets, underwear, workshirts,
marbled notebooks, Bic pens, plastic
        toys, and cheap sneakers;
where Marjorie worked ten years at the iron
        cash register, Alcibide
Monbouquet pushed a broom at night.
        and Mr. Smith managed—
we learned that a man from Beverly
        Hills owned it, who never saw
the streets of Franklin, New Hampshire,
        and drew with a well-groomed hand
a line through "Franklin, New Hampshire."

REVISIONS

        I woke to a bluish
mounded softness where the Honda was.
        I broomed off the windshield
and drove to the Kearsarge Mini-Mart
        before Amy opened
to yank my *Globe* out of the bundle.
        Back, I set a cup
of coffee beside Jane, still half-asleep,
        murmuring stuporous
thanks in the aquamarine morning.
        Then I sat in my blue chair
with blueberry bagels and strong
        black coffee reading news,
the obits, the comics, and the sports.
        Carrying my cup
twenty feet, I sat myself at the desk
        for this day's engagement
with the revisions of a whole life.

315

ROUTINE

In the bliss of routine
—coffee, love, pond afternoons, poems—
we feel we will live
forever, until we know we feel it.

12 *ALL*

HER LONG ILLNESS

Daybreak until nightfall,
he sat by his wife at the hospital
     while chemotherapy dripped
through the catheter into her heart.
     He drank coffee and read
the *Globe*. He paced; he worked
     on poems; he rubbed her back
and read aloud. Overcome with dread,
     they wept and affirmed
their love for each other, witlessly,
     over and over again.
When it snowed one morning Jane gazed
     at the darkness blurred
with flakes. They pushed the IV pump
     which she called Igor
slowly past the nurses' pods, as far
     as the outside door
so that she could smell the snowy air.

                    ∾

Home a week. He looked
back in the calendar. February
     was slashed kitty-corner
with Jane's shaky large block capitals
     staggering eight letters
out: L E U K E M I A

                    ∾

"This morning Gussie
woke me up. I let him out, fed Ada,
      took Gus back in again,
and fed him. Then I went to the bathroom
      to pee, and saw myself
in the mirror. I had forgotten
      the bald woman with
leukemia who stared back at me."

                    ∾

This time they put Jane
in the East Wing—no room in the Bubble—
      but he kept forgetting.
One afternoon, absent-mindedly
      approaching Pod 4.'s glassed-in
comfort and safety, he saw someone
      hurl through the heavy door
howling, erupting tears, staggering,
      followed by a nurse
who touched her and led her away.
      When he returned to Jane,
he did not tell her what he had seen.
      Later an orderly told them
there was a bed for her in the Bubble.

                    ∾

Alone together a moment
on the twenty-second anniversary
      of their wedding,
he clasped her as she stood
      at the sink, pressing
into her backside, rubbing his cheek
      against the stubble
of her skull. He gave her a ring
      of pink tourmaline
with nine small diamonds around it.

She put it on her finger
and immediately named it Please Don't Die.
    They kissed and Jane
whispered, "Timor mortis conturbat me."

                    ∾

    When they courted, Jane's hair
was short and straight, easy to care for.
    Later she grew it long,
below her shoulders, and wrote poems
        from the cave behind it.
In New Hampshire, as she grew older,
    her hair flourished—thick,
curled, sensuous, massed with its white
        streak around her exaggerated
features. He slipped through its waterfall
        to the mossy darkness
behind its flowing. When she was forty
    she came into her beauty
as into a fortune—eyes, cheekbones, nose,
        and thickwater hair.
                        Today,
she looked at her bald head and at
        her face swollen
with prednisone: "I am Telly Savalas."

                    ∾

    When he roiled in Recovery
after the surgeon cut out half his liver
        two years earlier,
Jane pushed the morphine bolus.
    She brought him home,
a breathing sarcophagus, then rubbed his body
        back to life with her hands.
Now, rocking on the bed in their horror,
        they wept and held on

against the proliferation of her blasts,
    murmuring together
of what adhered them. This ardent
    merging recollected
old passionate connections at two
    in the afternoon:
brief, breathless, ecstatic, then calm.

          ∾

    He hovered beside Jane's bed,
solicitous: "What can I *do?*"
    It must have been unbearable
while she suffered her private hurts
    to see his worried face
looming above her, always anxious to *do*
    something when there was
exactly nothing to do. Inside him,
    some four-year-old
understood that if he was good—thoughtful,
    considerate, beyond
reproach, *perfect*—she would not leave him.

          ∾

    Why were they not
contented, four months ago, because
    Jane did not have
leukemia? A year hence, would he question
    why he was not contented
now? Therefore he was contented.

          ∾

    They flew all day across
the country to the hospital for hard cases.
    The night before Jane
entered isolation in Seattle for chemo,
    TBI, and a stranger's

bone marrow—for life or death—they slept
       together, as they understood,
maybe for the last time. His body
       curved into Jane's,
his knees tucked to the backs of her knees;
       he pressed her warm soft thighs,
back, waist, and rump, making the spoons,
       and the spoons clattered
with a sound like the end man's bones.

              ∾

       As they killed her bone
marrow again, she lay on a gurney
       alone in a leaden
room between machines that resembled
       pot-bellied stoves
which spewed out Total Body Irradiation
       for eleven half-hour
sessions measured over four days.
       It was as if she capped
the Chernobyl pile with her body.

              ∾

       The courier brought
bone marrow in an insulated bottle
       from the donor, a nameless
thirty-nine-year-old female who
       sent along words
"To the Recipient." Jane's
       "For the Donor" flew back
somewhere, where a stranger lay flat
       with an anesthetic
hangover and pelvic bones that ached—
       and with disinterested
love, which is the greatest of these.

Jane lay silent on her back
as pink liquid leached through a tube
        from a six-inch-square
plastic envelope. It was Day Zero.

                    ∾

By Day Eleven, mucositis
from the burn of Total Body Irradiation
        frayed her mouth apart
cell by cell, peeling her lips and tongue.

To enter her antibiotic
cube, it took him fifteen minutes
        to suit up, wearing a wide
paper hat, yellow mask, long white
        booties like a Dallas
Cowgirl, blue paper surgical gown,
        and sterile latex gloves.
Jane said he looked like a huge condom.

                    ∾

He woke at five, brewed
coffee, swallowed pills, injected insulin,
        shaved, ate breakfast, packed
the tote with Jane's sweats he washed
        at night, filled the thermos,
and left the apartment on Spring Street
        to walk a block and a half
to the hospital's bone marrow floor.
        Waiting for the light
to cross the avenue, briefly he imagined
        throwing himself in front
of that bus. He knew he wouldn't.

                    ∾

Discharged at last,
she returned to sleep with him again
        in the flat jerry-built
for bald tenants and their caregivers.
        He counted out meds
and programmed pumps to deliver
        hydration, TPN,
and ganciclovir. He needed to learn
        from Maggie Fisher the nurse
how to assemble the tubing, to insert
        narrow ends into
wide ones. "From long experience," Maggie
        told him, "I have learned
to distinguish 'male' from 'female.'"

                    ∽

        As Dr. McDonald plunged
the tube down her throat, her body thrashed
        on the table. When she
struggled to rise, the doctor's voice cajoled,
        "Jane, Jane," until
blood-oxygen numbers dropped toward zero
        and her face went blue.
The young nurse slipped oxygen into Jane's
        nostrils and punched
a square button. Eight doctors burst
        into the room, someone
pounded Jane's chest, Dr. McDonald
        gave orders like
a submarine captain among depth charges,
        the nurse fixed
a nebulizer over Jane's mouth and nose—
        and she breathed.
                    Meanwhile,
understanding that his wife might be dying

before his eyes, he stood still,
careful to keep out of everyone's way.

∽

At four every afternoon
Jane started to fret or panic.
On a Monday he lay
on the sofa with mild vertigo,
but Jane was sure
it was a heart attack or embolism,
no matter what he said.
Paramedics from an ambulance took
his EKG for Jane's sake.
A day later, Jane couldn't stand or walk.
Back in the hospital
she believed that she had never been sick
and would be discovered,
that Blue Cross and the hospital would sue
and take away their house.
It did not matter what he told her,
but Haldol and Klonopin
mattered. For two hours she dozed; when
she woke, she no longer
insisted, "I am a wicked person."

∽

A volunteer drove them
to baggage, wheelchair, and USAir
frequent traveler
first-class seats. In Pittsburgh a cart
delivered them to the gate
for Manchester, New Hampshire, where
the children held up posters
and placards that their children had crayoned.
They waved and leapt
as Jane walked without help down the ramp

to the wheelchair,
to the heated car, to the hour's ride home.

∾

At home each day budged
forward—more calories (Ensure Plus,
        cream cheese and jelly,
macaroni and cheese), more exercise
        (two hundred yards'
joyous walking with Gus), and, tentatively,
        the first phrases
dictated toward what might be a poem.

∾

They hired a movie each
afternoon—Jane could read a short story
        for half an hour—and at bedtime
he helped her take off her sweatpants
        and pull on the blue-striped
flannel nightgown Caroline gave her.
        It was reasonable
to expect that in ten or twelve months
        she would be herself.
She would dress and eat her breakfast.
        She would drive her Saab
to shop for groceries.
                        He felt shame
        to understand he would miss
the months of sickness and taking care.

∾

"It was reasonable
to expect." So he wrote. The next day,
        in a consultation room,
Jane's hematologist Letha Mills sat down,
        stiff, her assistant
standing with her back to the door.

"I have terrible news,"
Letha told them. "The leukemia is back.
    There's nothing to do."
The four of them wept. He asked how long,
    why did it happen now?
Jane asked only: "Can I die at home?"

∾

Home that afternoon,
they threw her medicines into the trash.
    Jane vomited. He wailed
while she remained dry-eyed—silent,
    trying to let go. At night
he picked up the telephone to make
    calls that brought
a child or a friend into the horror.

∾

The next morning,
they worked choosing among her poems
    for *Otherwise*, picked
hymns for her funeral, and supplied each
    other words as they wrote
and revised her obituary. The day after,
    with more work to do
on her book, he saw how weak she felt,
    and said maybe not now; tomorrow?
Jane shook her head: "Now," she said.
    "We have to finish it now."
Later, as she slid exhausted into sleep,
    she said, "Wasn't that fun?
To work together? Wasn't that fun?"

∾

He asked her, "What clothes
should we dress you in, when we bury you?"

"I hadn't thought," she said.
"I wondered about the white salwar
        kameez," he said—
her favorite Indian silk they bought
        in Pondicherry a year
and a half before, which she wore for best
        or prettiest afterward.
She smiled. "Yes. Excellent," she said.
        He didn't tell her
that a year earlier, dreaming awake,
        he had seen her
in the coffin in her white salwar kameez.

                        ∾

        Still, he couldn't stop
planning. That night he broke out with,
        "When Gus dies I'll
have him cremated and scatter his ashes
        on your grave!" She laughed
and her big eyes quickened and she nodded:
        "It will be good
for the daffodils." She lay pallid back
        on the flowered pillow:
"Perkins, how do you *think* of these things?"

                        ∾

        They talked about their
adventures—driving through England
        when they first married,
and excursions to China and India.
        Also they remembered
ordinary days—pond summers, working
        on poems together,
walking the dog, reading Chekhov
        aloud. When he praised
thousands of afternoon assignations

that carried them into
bliss and repose on this painted bed,
          Jane burst into tears
and cried, "No more fucking. No more fucking!"

∽

          Incontinent three nights
before she died, Jane needed lifting
          onto the commode.
He wiped her and helped her back into bed.
          At five he fed the dog
and returned to find her across the room,
          sitting in a straight chair.
When she couldn't stand, how could she walk?
          He feared she would fall
and called for an ambulance to the hospital,
          but when he told Jane,
her mouth twisted down and tears started.
          "Do we have to?" He canceled.
Jane said, "Perkins, be with me when I die."

∽

          "Dying is simple," she said.
"What's worst is . . . *the separation.*"
          When she no longer spoke,
they lay alone together, touching,
          and she fixed on him
her beautiful enormous round brown eyes,
          shining, unblinking,
and passionate with love and dread.

∽

          Leaving his place beside her,
where her eyes stared, he told her,
          "I'll put these letters
in the box." She had not spoken

for three hours, and now Jane said
her last words: "O.K."
                    At eight that night,
    her eyes open as they stayed
until she died, brain-stem breathing
        started, he bent to kiss
her pale cool lips again, and felt them
        one last time gather
and purse and peck to kiss him back.

            ∾

    In the last hours, she kept
her forearms raised with pale fingers clenched
        at cheek level, like
the goddess figurine over the bathroom sink.
        Sometimes her right fist flicked
or spasmed toward her face. For twelve hours
        until she died, he kept
scratching Jane Kenyon's big bony nose.
        A sharp, almost sweet
smell began to rise from her open mouth.
        He watched her chest go still.
With his thumb he closed her round brown eyes.

BARBER

    Jane's brush cut looked
    like a Marine recruit's
    as she sat skinny
    and pale at the table,
    interrupting our chore
    to vomit in a china bowl.
    We picked through jumbles
    of medical supplies,
    filling two garbage bags

with leukemia's detritus.
When I lifted up leftover
disinfectant or Duoderm,
she shook her head
no, and I tossed it away,
as I did with the Ziploc
of her massy hair,
cut off the year before
when it started to shed.
The young barber trembled.

THE PORCELAIN COUPLE

When Jane felt well enough for me to leave her
a whole day, I drove south by the river
to empty my mother's house in Connecticut.
I hurried from room to room, cellar to attic,
looking into a crammed storeroom, then turning
to discover a chest with five full drawers.
I labeled for shipping sofas and chairs,
bedroom sets, and tables; I wrapped figurines
and fancy teacups in paper, preserving
things she had cherished—and in late years dreaded
might go for a nickel at a sale on the lawn.
Everywhere I saw shelves and tabletops
covered with glass animals and music boxes.
In closets, decades of finery hung in dead air.
I swept ashtrays and blouses into plastic sacks,
and the green-gold dress she wore to Bermuda.
At the last moment I discovered and saved
a cut-glass tumbler, stained red at the top,
Lucy 1905 scripted on the stain. In the garage
I piled bags for the dump, then drove four hours
north with my hands tight on the steering wheel,
drank a beer looking through the day's mail,

and pitched into bed with Jane who slept fitfully.
When I woke, I rose as if from a drunken sleep
after looting a city and burning its temples.
All day, while I ate lunch or counted out pills,
I noticed the objects of our twenty years:
a blue vase, a candelabrum Jane carried on her lap
from the Baja, and the small porcelain box
from France I found under the tree one Christmas
where a couple in relief stretch out asleep,
like a catafalque, on the pastel double bed
of the box's top, both wearing pretty nightcaps.

THE SHIP POUNDING

Each morning I made my way
among gangways, elevators,
and nurses' pods to Jane's room
to interrogate the grave helpers
who tended her through the night
while the ship's massive engines
kept its propellers turning.
Week after week, I sat by her bed
with black coffee and the *Globe*.
The passengers on this voyage
wore masks or cannulae
or dangled devices that dripped
chemicals into their wrists.
I believed that the ship
traveled to a harbor
of breakfast, work, and love.
I wrote: "When the infusions
are infused entirely, bone
marrow restored and lymphoblasts
remitted, I will take my wife,
bald as Michael Jordan,

333

back to our dog and day." Today,
months later at home, these
words turned up on my desk
as I listened in case Jane called
for help, or spoke in delirium,
ready to make the agitated
drive to Emergency again
for readmission to the huge
vessel that heaves water month
after month, without leaving
port, without moving a knot,
without arrival or destination,
its great engines pounding.

FOLDING CHAIR

Jane's last public outing
was our cousin Curtis's
funeral, dead at three days
in his mother's arms.
I carried a folding chair
and Jane held on tight
as we crept over ice
through the year's coldest
wind to the baby's hole.
Jane sat shaking, in tears,
pale and swaddled under down
and wool. Our neighbors
and cousins nodded, smiled,
and looked away. They knew
who would gather them next.

Her Intent

She concentrated her intent
on letting go. Florists' vans
pulled into the driveway four
or five times a day. I covered
the dining room table, kitchen
counters, and two castiron
Glenwoods with lilies
and bouquets of spring blossoms.
Jane wouldn't allow
roses or daisies or tulips
into the bedroom;
flowers and music were life.
I could not play her Messiaen,
nor Mendelssohn, nor *Black*
and Blue, nor Benita Valente
singing "Let Evening Come."

"I want," she said, "to tell you
something important. I want . . .
I want . . . spinach!" Angrily
she shook her head back and forth.
Eyesight departed after speech.

Without

we lived in a small island stone nation
without color under gray clouds and wind
distant the unlimited ocean acute
lymphoblastic leukemia without seagulls
or palm trees without vegetation
or animal life only barnacles and lead
colored moss that darkened when months did

hours days weeks months weeks days hours
the year endured without punctuation
february without ice winter sleet
snow melted recovered but nothing
without thaw although cold streams hurtled
no snowdrop or crocus rose no yellow
no red leaves of maple without october

no spring no summer no autumn no winter
no rain no peony thunder no woodthrush
the book was a thousand pages without commas
without mice oak leaves windstorms
no castles no plazas no flags no parrots
without carnival or the procession of relics
intolerable without brackets or colons

silence without color sound without smell
without apples without pork to rupture gnash
unpunctuated without churches uninterrupted
no orioles ginger noses no opera no
without fingers daffodils cheekbones
the body was a nation a tribe dug into stone
assaulted white blood broken to shards

provinces invaded bombed shot shelled
artillery sniper fire helicopter gunship
grenade burning murder landmine starvation
the ceasefire lasted forty-eight hours
then a shell exploded in a market
pain vomit neuropathy morphine nightmare
confusion the rack terror the vise

vincristine ara-c cytoxan vp-16
loss of memory loss of language losses
pneumocystis carinii pneumonia bactrim
foamless unmitigated sea without sea

delirium whipmarks of petechiae
multiple blisters of herpes zoster
and how are you doing today I am doing

one afternoon say the sun came out
moss took on greenishness leaves fell
the market opened a loaf of bread a sparrow
a bony dog wandered back sniffing a lath
it might be possible to take up a pencil
unwritten stanzas taken up and touched
beautiful terrible sentences unuttered

the sea unrelenting wave gray the sea
flotsam without islands broken crates
block after block the same house the mall
no cathedral no hobo jungle the same women
and men they longed to drink hayfields no
without dog or semicolon or village square
without monkey or lily without garlic

AFTER LIFE

It took two hours
for the Visiting Nurse
to arrive and certify
that Jane was dead.
It took another hour
for Marion and Charlie
to come from Chadwick's
with the van, the canvas
stretcher, and the gurney.
When one day he saw her
walking Gussie on New Canada
Road, or heard her voice
calling him "Perkins!"

across a parking lot,
he had confirmed her death
with his eyes,
his fingers, and his lips.

~

The afternoon Jane died,
six-year-old Allison and he
pushed through the toolshed
to stroll outside
and look at the daffodils,
but stopped short to see
the crayoned cardboard
tacked over the freezer
with capital letters in blues,
reds, and greens: WELCOME
BACK JANE FROM SEATTLE!

~

As he started up-town
to see her laid out
in her white salwar kameez,
he worried how she would look,
made up. Halfway there,
he U-turned; he had
forgotten to wear his glasses.

~

Andrew had brought Emily,
six years old,
who kept returning
to look at Jane, so still
in the silky coffin,
and the next day confided
to Alice Mattison,
"We saw Jane's actual body."

~

When Alice Ling finished
praying over Jane's coffin,
three hundred neighbors
and poets stood in spring
sunshine. Then Robert
started to sing "Amazing
Grace." Out of the silence
that followed he heard
his own voice saying,
"We have to go, dear."

∽

That night he turned
his children out of the house
with difficulty, and was
alone again with her absence.
Before bed he drove
to the graveyard to say goodnight,
and at six A.M. dropped by
as if he brought her coffee.

∽

Driving the highway, the day
after the funeral,
he felt suddenly overtaken
by a weight of shame
that reminded him of waking,
years ago in Ann Arbor,
knowing that the night
before, drunk, he had done
something despicable.

∽

It was true, what he thought,
although pitiless. If he could say
now, "Jane has leukemia,"
he would feel such contentment.

∽

339

In a nightmare that May,
Jane died in their house
far in a sunless forest.
The townspeople were sad
because she died
and because the sheriff
was coming to arrest him.
He had put out everything
of spirit and energy
taking care of Jane
and had neglected
the old women who starved
in their wooden cottages.

           ∾

Every day he watched
the young green snake
on the granite step
by the porch's end
who sunned herself
in desolate noontime
and slipped like liquid
into her hole
after she lifted her head
to see his face.

           ∾

For half a year at least
Jane's thick nearsighted
glasses lay on the table
by the bed, and the wristwatch
they bought at a jeweler's
in Rome on their sixteenth
anniversary—put there when
she could still see, when
what time it was mattered.

           ∾

After a year he tried
to tell himself: Everyone
dies. Some die at three
days, and some
at forty-seven years.
How many have perished
in this long house,
or on the painted bed?
His grandmother and mother
were born in this place.
Only Jane's death
continues to prosper.

RETRIEVER

Two days after Jane died
I walked with our dog Gus
on New Canada Road
under birchy green
April shadows, talking
urgently, trying
to make him understand.
A quick mink scooted past
into fern, and Gus
disappeared in pursuit.
The damp air grew chill
as I whistled and called
until twilight. I thought
he tried to follow her
into the dark. After an hour
I gave up and walked home
to find him on the porch,
alert, pleased to see me,
curious over my absence.
But Gus hadn't found her

deep in the woods; he hadn't
brought her back
as a branch in his teeth.

The Painted Bed

"Even when I danced erect
by the Nile's garden
I constructed Necropolis.

"Ten million fellaheen cells
of my body floated stones
to establish a white museum."

Grisly, foul, and terrific
is the speech of bones,
thighs and arms slackened

into desiccated sacs of flesh
hanging from an armature
where muscle was, and fat.

"I lie on the painted bed
diminishing, concentrated
on the journey I undertake

to repose without pain
in the palace of darkness,
my body beside your body."

13 Letters Without Addresses

Letter with No Address

Your daffodils rose up
and collapsed in their yellow
bodies on the hillside
garden above the bricks
you laid out in sand, squatting
with pants pegged and face
masked like a beekeeper's
against the black flies.
Buttercups circle the planks
of the old wellhead
this May while your silken
gardener's body withers or moulds
in the Proctor graveyard.
I drive and talk to you crying
and come back to this house
to talk to your photographs.

There's news to tell you:
Maggie Fisher's pregnant.
I carried myself like an egg
at Abigail's birthday party
a week after you died,
as three-year-olds bounced
uproarious on a mattress.
Joyce and I met for lunch
at the mall and strolled weepily
through Sears and B. Dalton.

Today it's four weeks
since you lay on our painted bed
and I closed your eyes.
Yesterday I cut irises to set
in a pitcher on your grave;
today I brought a carafe
to fill it with fresh water.
I remember bone pain,
vomiting, delirium. I remember
pond afternoons.
                    My routine
is established: coffee;
the *Globe*; breakfast;
writing you this letter
at my desk. When I go to bed
to sleep after baseball,
Gus follows me into the bedroom
as he used to follow us.
Most of the time he flops
down in the parlor
with his head on his paws.

Once a week I drive to Tilton
to see Dick and Nan.
Nan doesn't understand much
but she knows you're dead;
I feel her fretting. The tune
of Dick and me talking
seems to console her.
                    You know now
whether the soul survives death.
Or you don't. When you were dying
you said you didn't fear
punishment. We never dared
to speak of Paradise.

At five A.M., when I walk outside,
mist lies thick on hayfields.
By eight the air is clear,
cool, sunny with the pale yellow
light of mid-May. Kearsarge
rises huge and distinct,
each birch and balsam visible.
To the west the waters
of Eagle Pond waver
and flash through popples just
leafing out.
            Always the weather,
writing its book of the world,
returns you to me,
Ordinary days were best,
when we worked over poems
in our separate rooms.
I remember watching you gaze
out the January window
into the garden of snow
and ice, your face rapt
as you imagined burgundy lilies.

Your presence in this house
is almost as enormous
and painful as your absence.
Driving home from Tilton,
I remember how you cherished
that vista with its center
the red door of a farmhouse
against green fields.

Are you past pity?
If you have consciousness now,
if something I can call

"you" has something
like "consciousness," I doubt
you remember the last days.
I play them over and over:
I lift your wasted body
onto the commode, your arms
looped around my neck, aiming
your bony bottom so that
it will not bruise on a rail.
Faintly you repeat,
"Momma, Momma."

                    Three times
today I drove to your grave.
Sometimes, coming back home
to our circular driveway,
I imagine you've returned
before me, bags of groceries upright
in the back of the Saab,
its trunk lid delicately raised
as if proposing an encounter,
dog-fashion, with the Honda.

MIDSUMMER LETTER

The polished black granite
cemented over your head
reflects the full moon of August
four months from the day
your chest went still.
For you, the gloom of August
was annual; you watched
the red leaves on Huldah's maple
burn down your summer's day.

Kate MacKay had me to supper
in Grafton, to read your poems
to our Hitchcock nurses.
Mary hooted when I read "The Shirt."
Walking to the car, I was happy
under the summer night, harsh
with stars.

          Nan died Wednesday.
Remember, when we visited her,
how you painted her nails pink
and she spread her fingers out,
unable to speak but grateful.
Alone after fifty-five years,
Dick is heartsick.
              We scattered
your mother's ashes in Eagle Pond
at the same spot where, a dozen
years ago, we watched your father's
float and sink. When your brother
cast Polly's into a scud of wind,
they opened in a glinting swarm
and plunged into water.

               I flew
to Washington for the Council.
It was desolate to return
through the Manchester airport
where we left the plane in triumph
last February. Remember,
after we drove to the farm,
how Gus sniffed you carefully,
as if you might be an impostor,
and when you checked out,

sang half an hour
beside you, his voice trilling
like a countertenor's.

I can't play your CDs or tapes.
In Symphony Hall I sat beside you,
witnessing as your spirit
hovered like a hummingbird.
Every day I look at the words
cut into stone, which you wrote
when I was supposed to die:

I BELIEVE IN THE MIRACLES OF ART BUT WHAT
PRODIGY WILL KEEP YOU SAFE BESIDE ME

Most days I wake at five-thirty
to work on these poems.
Then I turn to the taxes, read mail
and answer it—one thing
after another. But last week,
being photographed, I sat
still and speechless for ninety minutes
posing by daylilies and barns
and my idle mind entered
the coffin, where even the white
of your salwar kameez
was absolute blackness. My mind
made a jingle, rhyming
"ants" with "lips."

                    Philippa brought
the children from Concord
to wade in Eagle Pond. Allison
showed me a wild strawberry plant.
Abigail snatched at minnows

and laughed. For an hour
I watched them play, my tall grave
daughter beside me.

            The hour
we lived in, two decades
by the pond, has transformed
into a single unstoppable day,
gray in the dwelling-place
of absence. Tonight I sat
in nighttime silence by the open
window and heard the peepers' soprano
and the bass bullfrogs'
percussion repeating the August
nocturne we went to bed by.
I'll never read Henry James
aloud to you again. We'll never laugh
and grunt again as your face
turns from apparent agony
to repose, and you tell me
it registered 7.2
on the Richter scale.

            Last night
before sleep I walked out
to look at the cold summer moon
as it rose over Ragged Mountain.
I slept six hours,
then woke in the dark morning
to see it huge in the west
as if this were any August.

Letter in Autumn

This first October of your death
I sit in my blue chair
looking out at late afternoon's
western light suffusing
its goldenrod yellow over
the barn's unpainted boards—
here where I sat each fall
watching you pull your summer's
garden up.

             Yesterday
I cleaned out your Saab
to sell it. The dozen tapes
I mailed to Caroline.
I collected hairpins and hair ties.
In the Hill's Balsam tin
where you kept silver for tolls
I found your collection
of slips from fortune cookies:
YOU ARE A FANTASTIC PERSON!
YOU ARE ONE OF THOSE PEOPLE
WHO GOES PLACES IN THEIR LIFE!

As I slept last night:
You leap from our compartment
in an underground railroad yard
and I follow; behind us the train
clatters and sways; I turn
and turn again to see you tugging
at a gold bugle welded
to a freight car; then you vanish
into the pitchy clanking dark.

Here I sit in my blue chair
not exactly watching Seattle
beat Denver in the Kingdome.
Last autumn above Pill Hill
we looked from the eleventh floor
down at Puget Sound,
at Seattle's skyline,
and at the Kingdome scaffolded
for repair. From your armature
of tubes, you asked, "Perkins,
am I going to live?"

              When you died
in April, baseball took up
its cadences again
under the indoor ballpark's
patched and recovered ceiling.
You would have admired
the Mariners, still hanging on
in October, like blue asters
surviving frost.

              Sometimes
when I start to cry,
I wave it off: "I just
did that." When Andrew
wearing a dark suit and necktie
telephones from his desk,
he cannot keep from crying.
When Philippa weeps,
Allison at seven announces,
"The river is flowing."

Gus no longer searches for you,
but when Alice or Joyce comes calling

he dances and sings. He brings us
one of your white slippers
from the bedroom.

            I cannot discard
your jeans or lotions or T-shirts.
I cannot disturb your tumbles
of scarves and floppy hats.
Lost unfinished things remain
on your desk, in your purse
or Shaker basket. Under a cushion
I discover your silver thimble.
Today when the telephone rang
I thought it was you.

At night when I go to bed
Gus drowses on the floor beside me.
I sleep where we lived and died
in the painted Victorian bed
under the tiny lights
you strung on the headboard
when you brought me home
from the hospital four years ago.
The lights still burned last April
early on a Saturday morning
while you died.

            At your grave
I find tribute: chrysanthemums,
cosmos, a pumpkin, and a poem
by a woman who "never knew you"
who asks, "Can you hear me Jane?"
There is an apple and a heart-
shaped pebble.

Looking south
from your stone, I gaze at the file
of eight enormous sugarmaples
that rage and flare in dark noon,
the air grainy with mist
like the rain of Seattle's winter.
The trees go on burning
without ravage of loss or disorder.
I wish you were that birch
rising from the clump behind you,
and I the gray oak alongside.

LETTER AT CHRISTMAS

The big wooden clock you gave me
our first Christmas together
stopped in September.
The Bristol Watch Maker
kept it six weeks. Now it speeds
sixty-five minutes to the hour, as if
it wants to be done with the day.

When I try talking with strangers
I want to run out of the room
into the woods with turkeys and foxes.
I want to talk only
about words we spoke back and forth
when we knew you would die.
I want never to joke or argue
or chatter again. I want never
to think or feel.

Maggie Fisher
mailed pictures of the baby.

On Thanksgiving I brought Dick
from Tilton to Andrew's for dinner.
Peter grinned; we hugged Ariana
and conversed with Emily.
For three hours we played,
teased, laughed together.
Suddenly I had to drive home.

Yesterday I caught sight of you
in the Kearsarge Mini-Mart.

The first snow fell seven months
from the day you died.
We used to gaze at the early snow
where it heaped like sugar
or salt on boulders, barn roofs,
fence posts, and gravestones.
No one plows Cemetery Road;
I will miss visiting you
when snow is deep.

          In Advent
for twenty years you opened
the calendar's daily window;
you fixed candles in a wreath
for church; you read the Gospels
over again each year:
The Child would be born again.

Most years we woke up by six
to empty our stockings.
You gave me Post-Its, paperclips,
shortbread, #1 pencils,
and blank books. I gave you
felt pens, paperclips, chocolate,

and something libidinous
in the toe.

        I remember
only one miserable Christmas.
You were so depressed
that the spidery lace of a shawl
and a terra-cotta Etruscan woman
only left you feeling
worthless, stupid, and ugly.
Melancholy still thickens
its filaments over the presents
I gave you that morning.

Even last December
when our petrochemical three-foot
balsam stood on a glass
tabletop in that gimcrack Seattle
apartment, you strung it
with tiny lights, interrupting
your task to vomit. Bald
as Brancusi's egg, with limbs
as thin as a Giacometti strider,
you sat diminished
in a soft chair, among pumps
and bags. I programmed
the Provider for twelve hours
of hyperalimentation. Wearing
plastic gloves, I set up
the Bard-Harvard infusion
device to deliver ganciclovir.

Before your November transplant,
you had ordered me
loafers from L. L. Bean.

From another catalogue you bought
flowery green-and-white sheets.
I gave you a black MoMA
briefcase and cashmere sweats
from Neiman Marcus.
You preened, rubbing the softness
against your face.

                    Your feast
last year was applesauce
for pills, Ensure Plus,
and an inch square of bread
and jelly. I read you
from Luke's Gospel, then John's;
and then we fell silent
as the Child was born—
adored, clung to, irreparable.

            ∾

This first Advent alone
I feed the small birds of snow
black-oil sunflower seed
as you used to do. Every day
I stand trembling with joy
to watch them: Fat mourning doves
compete with red squirrels
for spill from rampaging nuthatches
with rusty breasts
and black-and-white face masks.

This year late autumn darkness
punishes me as it used
to punish you. For decades,
when December night closed in
midafternoon and you suffered,

I hunched by the reddening
Glenwood, finding the darkness
a comfort. Feeding your birds
consoles me now. If you
were writing this letter,
what would you turn to now?
Maybe you'd look at the mouse
that Ada offers.

              This year
there's no tree for Gus to sniff
and Ada to leap at, dislodging
an ornament from your childhood.
I toss the dead mouse outside
on Christmas afternoon
and wash my hands at the sink
as I look at Mount Kearsarge
through the kitchen window
where you stood to watch the birds.
Often I came up behind you
and pushed against your bottom.
This year, home from unwrapping
presents with grandchildren
and children, sick with longing,
I press my penis
into zinc and butcherblock.

LETTER IN THE NEW YEAR

New Year's Eve I baby-sat
the girls in Concord, napping
on the sofa. In Seattle
last year we slept through
as usual, except that your sugar

went crazy from prednisone.
I pricked your finger
every four hours all night
and shot insulin.

       The year
of your death was not usual
and this new year is offensive
because it will not contain you.

For six months Gus flung himself
down in the parlor all day,
sighing enormous sighs.
Now he lies beside me
where I sit in my blue chair
eating bagels in the morning,
watching basketball by night,
or beside our black-and-gold bed
where I read and sleep.
Ada curls on my other side.
I'm what they've got;
they know it.

       Stepping outside,
I check the weather to tell you:
The sun is invisible, still
ascending behind Ragged
but west of the pond its rays
pass overhead to light
the snow on Eagle's Nest.
The moon blanches in a clear sky,
with one cloud scudding
to the south over Kearsarge,
which turns lavender at dawn.
Time for the desk again.

I tell Gus, "Poetryman
is suiting up!"

                    The bulletin
this January is snow.
New Canada is a "One Lane Road"
along the old pasture's woodlot.
The hills collapse together
in whiteness squared out
by stone walls that contain
wavery birches and boulders
softened into breasts. White
yards and acres of snowfield
reflect the full moon,
and at noontime the sky
turns its deepest blue
of the year. I puff as Gussie
and I walk over packed snow
at zero, my heart quick
with joy in the visible world.

Do you remember our first
January at Eagle Pond,
the coldest in a century?
It dropped to thirty-eight below—
with no furnace, no storm
windows or insulation.
We sat reading or writing
in our two big chairs, either
side of the Glenwood,
and made love on the floor
with the stove open and roaring.
You were twenty-eight.
If someone had told us then
you would die in nineteen years,

would it have sounded
like almost enough time?

This month Philippa and her family
moved into a house they built
on wooded land in Bow.
Each girl has her own room.
I gave Abigail a bookcase
and Allison a grown-up oak desk.
As I read them storybooks
on the sofa, I thought of you
making clothespin dolls
with Allison, to put on a show;
you were supporting actress.

When you were dying, you fretted:
"What will become of Perkins?"
The children telephone
each morning. Sometimes our friends
visit and raise you up.

I meet Galway and Bobbie
in Norwich; Bobbie consoles me,
wearing your Christmas
cashmere sweats. Liam and Tree
bounce and exaggerate
the way we four did together.
When Alice took Amtrak
and Concord Trailways to visit
before Christmas, we watched
the Sunday school pageant.

Sometimes I weep for an hour
twisted in the fetal position
as you did in depression.

Hypochondriac, I fret over Gus
and decide he's got diabetes.
In daydream I spend afternoons
digging around your peonies
to feed them my grandfather's
fifty-year-old cow manure.
Next week maybe I'll menstruate.

I want to hear you laugh again,
your throaty whoop. Every day
I imagine you widowed
in this house of purposeful quiet.
You would have confided in Gus
and reproached Ada, lunched
with friends in New London,
climbed Kearsarge, wept,
written poems, and lain unmoving,
eyes open, in bed all morning.
You would have found
a lover, but not right away.
I want to fuck you
in Paradise. "The sexual
intercourse of angels," Yeats
in old age wrote his old
love, "is a conflagration
of the whole being."

MIDWINTER LETTER

I wanted this assaulting winter
to end before January ended.
But I want everything to end.
I lean forward from emptiness

eager for more emptiness:
the next thing! the next thing!

The thaw arrived as the front loader
departed: warm sun, slush, then
forty-eight hours of downpour.
Snowdrifts decomposed by the house.
Walker Brook tore ice blocks
loose with a clamor
that worried Gus as we walked
beside the filthy flesh
of old snow.

        I parked
on Route 4 by the graveyard,
wearing my new Christmas boots
that your brother's family gave me,
and hiked to your grave.
The snow was a foot deep, but stiff,
and I sank down only a little.
Gus danced and skittered, happy,
but not so happy as I was.

One day the temperature dropped
to zero, so icy I couldn't
walk Gus, and my knees hurt
like my mother's. Following
your advice, I took Advil.
I forgot to tell you: My tests
are good, no cancer, and my sugar
is stable. Sometimes for a week
I have trouble sleeping,
especially after a nightmare
when you leave me for someone else,

One weekend Andrew's family
stayed over for the night.
All three of the children
sat on my lap while I read stories
—and Emily liked my meatloaf.
Sometimes I read these letters aloud
to our friends.

       When you wrote
about lovemaking or cancer,
about absences or a quarrel,
I loved to turn up in your poems.
I imagined those you'd make
after I died; I regretted
I wouldn't be able to read them.

Although it's still light
at five P.M., the feeder goes unattended.
The woodpecker has done
with my suet for the day.
Red squirrels doze in their holes.
Chickadees sleep in the barn
or uphill in hemlock branches.
I want to sleep like the birds,
then wake to write you again
without hope that you read me.
If a car pulls into the drive
I want to hide in our bedroom
the way you hid sometimes
when people came calling.

Remembered happiness is agony;
so is remembered agony.
I live in a present compelled
by anniversaries and objects:

your pincushion; your white slipper;
your hooded Selectric II;
the label *basil* in a familiar hand;
a stain on flowery sheets.

Letter after a Year

Here's a story I never told you.
Living in a rented house
on South University in Ann Arbor
long before we met, I found
bundled letters in the attic room
where I took myself to work.
A young woman tenant of the attic
wrote these letters to her lover,
who had died in a plane crash.
In my thirtieth year, with tenure
and a new book coming out,
I read the letters in puzzlement.
"She's writing to somebody *dead*?"

There's one good thing
about April. Every day Gus and I
take a walk in the graveyard.
I'm the one who doesn't
piss on your stone. All winter
when ice and snow kept me away
I worried that you missed me.
"Perkins! Where the hell
are you?"

        In hell. Every day
I play in repertory the same
script without you, without love,

without audience except for Gus,
who waits attentive
for cues: a walk, a biscuit,
bedtime. The year of days
without you and your body swept by
as quick as an afternoon;
but each afternoon took a year.

At first in my outrage
I daydreamed burning the house:
kerosene in pie plates
with a candle lit in the middle.
I locked myself in your study
with Gus, Ada, and the rifle
my father gave me at twelve.
I killed our cat and our dog.
I swallowed a bottle of pills,
knowing that if I woke on fire
I had the gun.

                    After you died
I stopped rereading history.
I took up Cormac McCarthy
for the rage and murder.
Now I return to Gibbon; secure
in his reasonable civilization,
he exercises detachment
as barbarians skewer Romans.
Then Huns gallop from the sunrise
wearing skulls.

                    What's new?
I see more people now. In March,
I took Kate and Mary to Piero's.
At the end of the month ice dropped

to the pond's bottom, and water
flashed and flowed
through pines in western light.
The year melted into April
and I lived through the hour
we learned last year you would die.
For the next ten days, my mind
sat by our bed again
as you diminished cell by cell.

Last week the goldfinches
flew back for a second spring.
Again I witnessed snowdrops
worry from dead leaves
into air. Now your hillside
daffodils edge up, and today
it's a year since we set you down
at the border of the graveyard
on a breezy April day. We stood
in a circle around the coffin
and its hole, under pines
and birches, to lower you
into glacial sand.

              When I dream
sometimes your hair is long
and we make love as we used to.
One nap time I saw your face
at eighty: many lines, more flesh,
the good bones distinct.

It's astonishing to be old.
When I stand after sitting,
I'm shocked at how I must stretch
to ease the stiffness out.

When we first spoke of marriage
we dismissed the notion
because you'd be a widow
twenty-five years, or maybe
I wouldn't be able to make love
while desire still flared in you.
Sometimes now I feel crazy
with desire again
as if I were forty, drinking,
and just divorced.

Ruth Houghton had a stroke.
Her daughter sent me the album
of photographs Roger took
in his documentary passion—
inside and outside our house,
every room, every corner—
one day in September, 1984.
I howled as I gazed at that day
intact. Our furniture
looked out of place, as if vandals
had shoved everything awry.
There were pictures on the walls
we put away long ago.
The kitchen wallpaper shone
bright red in Roger's Kodacolor;
it faded as we watched
not seeing it fade.

14 *Throwing Away*

Weeds and Peonies

Your peonies burst out, white as snow squalls,
with red flecks at their shaggy centers
in your border of prodigies by the porch.
I carry one magnanimous blossom indoors
and float it in a glass bowl, as you used to do.

Ordinary pleasures, contentment recollected,
blow like snow into the abandoned garden,
overcoming the daisies. Your blue coat
vanishes down Pond Road into imagined snowflakes
with Gus at your side, his great tail swinging,

but you will not reappear, tired and satisfied,
and grief's repeated particles suffuse the air—
like the dog yipping through the entire night,
or the cat stretching awake, then curling
as if to dream of her mother's milky nipples.

A raccoon dislodged a geranium from its pot.
Flowers, roots, and dirt lay upended
in the back garden where lilies begin
their daily excursions above stone walls
in the season of old roses. I pace beside weeds

and snowy peonies, staring at Mount Kearsarge
where you climbed wearing purple hiking boots.
"Hurry back. Be careful, climbing down."
Your peonies lean their vast heads westward
as if they might topple. Some topple.

After Homer

When I drove home
from Manchester airport
after two nights
away, Jane ran out
from the screen door
with Gussie cavorting
behind her. I felt
like the wanderer
returning after twenty
years to his wife
and his dog.
        Stiff,
old, and alone,
I murder the suitors
all night each night
as they roister
in the stone hall.

Her Garden

I let her garden go.
      let it go, let it go
How can I watch the hummingbird
      Hover to sip
      With its beak's tip
The purple bee balm—whirring as we heard
      It years ago?

      The weeds rise rank and thick
      let it go, let it go
Where annuals grew and burdock grows,
      Where standing she

At once could see
The peony, the lily, and the rose
Rise over brick

She'd laid in patterns. Moss
let it go, let it go
Turns the bricks green, softening them
By the gray rocks
Where hollyhocks
That lofted while she lived, stem by tall stem,
Blossom with loss.

SUMMER KITCHEN

In June's high light she stood at the sink
With a glass of wine,
And listened for the bobolink,
And crushed garlic in late sunshine.

I watched her cooking, from my chair.
She pressed her lips
Together, reached for kitchenware,
And tasted sauce from her fingertips.

"It's ready now. Come on," she said.
"You light the candle."
We ate, and talked, and went to bed,
And slept. It was a miracle.

WOOL SQUARES

I sort through left-behind
Boxes that keep

375

A muddled heap
Of woman's work. I find
Wool squares she used to knit
While I sat opposite.

"Leftover life to kill,"
        Young Caitlin said
        With Dylan dead,
Yet lived with an ill will
Forty posthumous years
Of rage, fucking, and tears.

At seventy I taste
        In solitude
        Starvation's food,
As the land goes to waste
Where her death overthrew
A government of two.

Pond Afternoons

        When early July's
Arrival quieted the spring's black flies,
        We spent green afternoons
                Stretched on the moss
Beside dark Eagle Pond, and heard across
Its distances the calling of the loons.

        The days swam by,
Lazy with slow content and the hawk's cry.
        We lost ambition's rage,
                Forgot it all,
Forgot Jane Kenyon, forgot Donald Hall,
And sleepily half glanced at a bright page.

Day after day
We crossed the flaking railroad tracks and lay
In the slant August sun
To nap and read
Beneath an oak, by the pond's pickerelweed.
Then acorns fell: These days were almost done.

Hours Hours

Mornings we wrote, in separate domains.
Midday we napped and loved, and rose from bed
Back to the desk or garden. Then we read
Aloud from James or Keats, my turn or Jane's.

Some days were rankled by the unforeseen.
I quarreled with a friend. Another died.
When things went wrong, I sighed, I paced and sighed,
Until we found our way back to routine.

In June the black flies stung as Eagle Pond did
When the sharp smarting light assailed our eyes
On afternoons of our old enterprise
When the twin solitudes still corresponded.

The Wish

I keep her weary ghost inside me.
"Oh, let me go," I hear her crying.
"Deep in your dark you want to hide me
And so perpetuate my dying.
        I can't undo
        The grief that you
Weep by the stone where I am lying.
        Oh, let me go."

By work and women half distracted,
I endure the day and sleep at night
To watch her dying reenacted
When the cold dawn descends like twilight.
    How can I let
    This dream forget
Her white withdrawal from my sight,
        And let her go?

Her body as I watch grows smaller;
Her face recedes, her kiss is colder.
Watching her disappear, I call her,
"Come back!" as I grow old and older,
    While somewhere deep
    In the catch of sleep
I hear her cry, as I reach to hold her,
        "Oh, let me go!"

ANOTHER CHRISTMAS

Our first Christmas together
at Eagle Pond I bought
a chain saw to cut the tree
from our woodlot. Puffing
with accomplishment I set
an emaciated hemlock kitty-
corner from the Glenwood stove.

"What will become of Perkins?"
Jane asked when she could still
speak. Two years later
I miss her teasing voice
that razzed my grandiloquence:

"Perkins, dim your lights."
"Somebody cover Perkins's cage."

All year I could do anything
I wanted, any time of day
or night, travel anywhere, buy
anything. Therefore I sat
in my blue chair doing nothing
and trying to feel nothing.
On this second Christmas

I fix, decorate, and cherish
a visible vacancy kitty-
corner from the Glenwood.
Sometimes I dream awake.
Sometimes I see her face
in its strong-featured beauty
with her eyes full of pity.

SWEATER

The second June afterward,
I wrapped Jane's clothes
for Rosie's Place
but I keep on finding
things I missed—
a scarf hanging from a hook
in the toolshed, a green
down vest, or a sweater
tossed on the swivel chair
by her desk where
her papers pile untouched,
just as she left them

the last time she fretted
over answering a letter
or worked to end a poem
by observing something
as careless as the white
sleeve of a cardigan.

Distressed Haiku

In a week or ten days
the snow and ice
will melt from Cemetery Road.

I'm coming! Don't move!

∽

You think that their
dying is the worst
thing that could happen.

Then they stay dead.

∽

Will Hall ever write
lines that do anything
but whine and complain?

∽

The mouse rips
the throat of the lion,
the Boston Red Sox win
a hundred straight games,

and the dead return.

THROWING THE THINGS AWAY

A mouse flitters across
the floor of the old parlor
and disappears among cartons.
On the carpet lie stacked
a thousand books,
acquired in excitement, now
given away unread. I find
a picture that hung
over the sofa for ten years,
and discover another cache
of Jane's dresses and jackets.
Here's an album of snapshots
she took in China.

        ∽

        I open a box
that emptied a bureau drawer
in my mother's Connecticut
attic, and an intact day
from nineteen forty-two
leaps like a mouse surprised
eating a letter: a balsa
model of a Flying Fortress;
a ten-inch 78 of Connee
Boswell singing "The Kerry
Dancers"; a verse play,
The Folly of Existence;
the unbearable photographs
of young parents who cannot
know what will happen.
Exposed, a discovered body
crumbles into motes
revolving in deadly air.

        ∽

By wavery piles of tapes and CDs,
near the TV, I find an electric
grinder, wedged in, labeled,
"To grind Indian spices *only*."
Her underline. Why have I never
seen it, years after her death?
How did it get there? Maybe Jane
carried the grinder as the phone
rang, and set it down
to hear about bloodwork.

∾

                    A friend
fills boxes of books to mail
to a Sioux reservation.
At a chest of drawers packed
with linen, she stands beside me
holding a trash bag. I lift
pillowcases, sheets, napkins,
doilies, and tablecloths,
and shake out weightless dry
housefly carcasses. Most
of the fabric is rotten or holey
or bloodstained. Sometimes
she says, "This one is hand
done. This one is old." We keep
the pretty pieces, fancywork
of farm women who sat at night
underneath the parlor's
kerosene lamp, their fingers
scuttling in the yellow light
as quick as mice.

∾

                    To the dump
with Bing Crosby and Dinah Shore,

with my mother's unfinished
tatting and her Agatha Christies.
To the dump with my father's
colorless Kodachrome slides
of their cross-country trip
together. To the dump
with bundles of linen
and the gooseneck lamp Jane
wrote poems by. To the dump
with the baseball and its eaten-
away glove, with my father,
dead forty years, with my mother
who lasted until ninety, with
Jane, with generations of mice,
with me—tidying, opening
boxes, throwing the things away.

THE PERFECT LIFE

Unicorns envy their cousin
horses a smooth forehead.
Horses weep for lack of horns.

Hills cherish the ambition
to turn into partial
differential equations,

which want to be poems, or dogs,
or the Pacific Ocean,
or whiskey, or a gold ring.

The man wearing the noose
envies an other who fondles
a pistol in a motel room.

> Wake when dog whimpers. Prick
> Finger. Inject insulin.
> > Glue teeth in.
> > Smoke cigarette.
> > > Shudder and fret.
> Feed old dog. Write syllabic
>
> On self-pity. Get Boston *Globe*.
> Drink coffee. Eat bagel. Read
> > At nervous speed.
> > Smoke cigarette.
> > > Never forget
> To measure oneself against Job.
>
> Drag out afternoon.
> Walk dog. Don't write.
> > Turn off light.
> > Smoke cigarette
> > > Watching sun set.
> Wait for the fucking moon.
>
> Nuke lasagna. Pace and curse.
> For solitude's support
> > Drink Taylor's port.
> > Smoke cigarette.
> > > Sleep. Sweat.
> Nightmare until dog whimpers.

Nursing her I felt alive
in the animal moment,
scenting the predator.
Her death was the worst thing
that could happen,
and caring for her was best.

After she died I screamed,
upsetting the depressed dog.
Now I no longer
address the wall covered
with many photographs,
nor call her "you"
in a poem. She recedes
into the granite museum
of JANE KENYON 1947–1995.

I long for the absent
woman of different faces
who makes metaphors
and chops onion, drinking
a glass of Chardonnay,
oiling the wok, humming
to herself, maybe thinking
how to conclude a poem.
When I make love now,
something is awry.
Last autumn a woman said,
"I mistrust your ardor."

This winter in Florida
I loathed the old couples
my age who promenaded

in their slack flesh
holding hands. I gazed
at young women with outrage
and desire—unable to love
or to work, or to die.

Hours are slow and weeks
rapid in their vacancy.
Each day lapses as I recite
my complaints. Lust is grief
that has turned over in bed
to look the other way.

KILL THE DAY

> Work, love, build a house, and die.
> —*The One Day*

When she died it was as if his car accelerated
off the pier's end and zoomed upward over death water
for a year without gaining or losing altitude,
then plunged to the bottom of the sea where his corpse
lay twisted in a honeycomb of steel, still dreaming
awake, as dead as she was but conscious still.
There is nothing so selfish as misery nor so boring,
and depression is devoted only to its own practice.
Mourning resembles melancholia precisely except
that melancholy adds self-loathing to stuporous sorrow

and turns away from the dead its exclusive attention.
Mania is melancholy reversed. Bereavement, loss,
and guilt provide excitement for conversion
to dysphoria, murderous rage, and unsleeping joy.
When he rose from the painted bed, he alternated or cycled
from dedicated hatred through gaiety and inflation

to the vacancy of breathing in-and-out, in-and-out.
He awakened daily to the prospect of nothingness
in the day's house that like all houses was mortuary.
He slept on the fornicating bed of the last breath.

He closed her eyes in the noon of her middle life;
he no longer cut and pruned for her admiration;
he worked for the praise of women and they died.
For months after her chest went still, he nightmared
that she had left him for another man. Everything
became its opposite and returned to itself.
As the second summer of her death approached him,
goldfinches flew at her feeder like daffodils
with wings and he could no longer tell her so.
Her absence could no longer be written to.

He emptied her shelves, dressers, and closets,
stacking rings and bracelets, pendants and necklaces.
He bundled sweaters and jeans, brassieres and blouses,
scarves and nightgowns and suits and summer dresses
and mailed them to Rosie's Place for indigent women.
For decades a man and a woman living together
learned each other for pleasure, giving and taking,
studying every other day predictable ecstasy
secure without secrecy or adventure, without romance,
without anxiety or jealousy, without content

except for the immaculate sexual content of sex.
The toad sat still for the toad's astounding moment,
but the day wasted whatever lived for the day
and the only useful desire obliterates desire.
Now the one day extended into multiple encounters
with loneliness that could not endure a visitor.
Machinery corroded in the barn no longer entered,
and no smoke rose from the two opposite chimneys.

It is naïve to complain over death and abandonment,
and the language of houses praised only itself.

Bone's Orchard bragged of breakfast and work, church
with neighbors on Sunday, gardening, the pond, and love
in the afternoon. The day ignored that it undertook
mere interruption on the trudge to fathomless loss.
"The days you work," said O'Keeffe, "are the best days."
Work without love is idle, idleness doing its job
for the velvet approbation of kings and presidents
without art's purpose to excite a lover's pleasure.
He turned into the ash heap damp in the Glenwood,
the burnt shape and constitution of wretchedness

in his ludicrous rage that things are as they are.
When she died, at first the outline of absence defined
a presence that disappeared. He wept for the body
he could no longer reach to touch in bed on waking.
He wept for her silver thimble. He wept when the dog
brought him a slipper that smelled of her still.
In another summer, her pheromones diminished.
The negative space of her body dwindled as she receded
deeper into the ground, smaller and fainter each day,
dried out, shrunken, separated from the news of the day.

When the coffee cup broke, when her yellow bathrobe
departed the bathroom door, when the address book
in her hand altered itself into scratchings-out,
he dreaded an adventure of self-hatred accomplished
by the finger or toe of an old man alone without
an onion to eat between slices of store-bought bread.
There was nothing to do, and nothing required doing.
Her vanishing constructed a blue synagogue
in a universe without solace or a task for doing.
He imagined that on shelves at his workroom's end

lay stacked two hundred and sixty-seven tiny
corpses, bodies of her body, porcelain mannequins.
In this dream or story he had neglected to bury them;
it was something still to do, something to be done.
In the second year, into the third and fourth years,
she died again and again, she died by receding
while he recited each day the stanzas of her dying:
He watched her chest go still; he closed her eyes.
Without birthdays, she remained her age at death.
The figurine broke that clutched its fists

as she did dying. In the pantry there were cans
and boxes and jars she bought in the supermarket
seven years ago. He walked through the vacancies,
burying her again. He had imagined an old man
alone in this white house, looking in the mirror.
Looking in the mirror now, he was old and alone.
He felt solitude's relief and intolerably lonely.
He envied whatever felt nothing: He envied oak
sills and the green hill rising and the boulder
by the side of the road and his dead love rotting

in her best white dress inside Vermont hardwood.
It was useful to set his name on her black granite,
but imminent or eventual cellular junction provided
the comfort of stone: to keep her safe beside him.
Visions of pleasure departed when she departed.
The condition of contentment or satisfaction
remains unattainable because of affect's agreement:
Whatever the measure of joy in the day's day,
no pleasure carries with it one part in ten million
of agony's vastation in loss and abandonment.

Therefore the condition of being alive is intolerable,
with no reason for endurance except that DNA

continues itself in order to continue itself.
Agreeing to love each other, they perfected a system:
Love is the exchange of a double narcissism,
agreement of twin surrender, the weapons laid by,
the treaty enforced by habitual daily negotiation.
What would he do if he could do what he wanted?
The day prevented him from doing what he wanted.
Now he woke each morning wretched with morning's

regret that he woke. He woke looking forward
to a nap, to a cigarette, to supper, to port measured,
to sleep blessed sleep on the permanent painted bed
of death: Sleep, rage, kill the day, and die.
When she died, he died also. For the first year
his immediate grief confused him into feeling alive.
He endured the grief of a two-month love affair.
When women angry and free generously visited
the frenzy of his erotic grief, melancholia
became ecstasy, then sank under successful dirt.

Without prospect or purpose, who dares to love meat
that will putrefy? He rejoiced that he was meat.
How many times will he die in his own lifetime?
When TWA 800 blew out of the sky, his heart ascended
and exploded in gratitude, finding itself embodied
and broken as fragments scattering into water.
Then little green testicles dropped from the oaks
on New Canada Road again, another August of death,
and autumn McIntoshes rotted on the dwarf trees
already pecked by the loathsome birds of July.

Each day identified itself as a passage to elsewhere,
which was a passage to elsewhere and to elsewhere.
What did she look like now? Dried and slackening maybe.
Do the worms eat her? He supposed that they ate her.

Now he dreamed again of her thick and lavish hair,
of her lush body wetting and loosening beside him.
He remembered ordinary fucking that shone like the sun
in their household solar system, brighter than Jesus,
than poetry, than their orchard under the mountain—
the crossing place of bodies that regarded each other

with more devotion the more they approached her death
until they were singular, gazing speechless together
while she vanished into open eyes staring all night.
In the day's crush and tangle of melted nails,
collapsed foundation stones, and adze-trimmed beams,
the widower alone glimpsed the beekeeper's mask
in high summer as it approached the day they built,
now fallen apart with bark still on its beams,
nine layers of wallpaper over the dry laths—
always ending, no other ending, in dead eyes open.

Razor

You sat in the booth
across from me in shadow
and your wide brown eyes
softened and flared
as you spoke remembering
the sickly adored
father of your girlhood—
how you brought him tea
and his newspaper, how
you stood beside him
while he shaved, your head
as high as the washbowl,
and lathered your face
the way he did, and shaved

using your little finger
as a Gillette Safety Razor.

Your voice in an ardor
of old tenderness
lightened the darkness
of the bar at midnight.
You pigtailed my hair
and in your room rubbed
moisturizer from a jar
to smooth my wrinkles.

CONVERSATION'S AFTERPLAY

At dinner our first night
I looked at you, your bright green eyes,
In candlelight.
We laughed and told the hundred stories,
Kissed, and caressed, and went to bed.
"Shh, shh," you said,
"I want to put my legs around your head."
Green eyes, green.

At dawn we sat with coffee
And smoked another cigarette
As quietly
Companionship and eros met
In conversation's afterplay,
On our first day.
Late for the work you love, you drove away.
Green eyes, green.

CHARITY AND DOMINION

As we lay together after,
my forefinger modeled
your fair strong cheekbones
and you took my thumb
into your mouth, sucking it
carefully, licking its tip.

Tickle the trembling skin
of an arm or a leg
and even the little
skin hairs keep on coming.

I understood your charity
and dominion. I felt
like a fish flapping
on a boat's deck, and gasped
to the pretty stranger,
"I almost want to say that
I love—" You shook your head
fiercely and burst out:
"But it would be a lie!"

I admired your resolve,
your redeeming conviction
that rapture was trivial,
as you laughed all night
like a milkmaid in a meadow,
petticoats flung upward.

Sun

Both of us felt it: That day was an island,
strewn with rocks and lighthouses and lovers,
in the generous ocean. On the mainland,
people went about their business, eating
the *Times*, glancing through coffee and oatmeal,
as we walked the gangway into an original dream
of attentiveness, as if a day's pleasure
could concentrate us as much as suffering,
as if the seawall were a banquet without
surfeit, as if we could walk hand in hand
with no one nearby, as if silence and blue
wind became an Atlantic cove to float in,
and the air centered itself in small purple
butterflies flitting among the weed flowers.
In the darkening city we returned to,
our privacy completed the cafés of strangers.

Vlllanelle

Katie could put her feet behind her head
Or do a grand plié, position two,
Her suppleness magnificent in bed.

I strained my lower back, and Katie bled,
Only a little, doing what we could do
When Katie tucked her feet behind her head.

Her torso was a C-cup'd figurehead,
Wearing below its navel a tattoo
That writhed in suppleness upon the bed.

As love led on to love, love's goddess said,
"No lovers ever fucked as fucked these two!
Katie could put her feet behind her head!"

She curled her legs around my neck, which led
To depths unplumbed by lovers hitherto.
Katie could tuck her feet behind her head
And by her suppleness unmake the bed.

LOVE POEM

When you fall in love,
you jockey your horse
into the flaming barn.

You hire a cabin
on the shiny *Titanic*.
You tease the black bear.

Reading the *Monitor*,
you scan the obituaries
looking for your name.

AFFIRMATION

To grow old is to lose everything.
Aging, everybody knows it.
Even when we are young,
we glimpse it sometimes, and nod our heads
when a grandfather dies.
Then we row for years on the midsummer
pond, ignorant and content. But a marriage,
that began without harm, scatters

395

into debris on the shore,
and a friend from school drops
cold on a rocky strand.
If a new love carries us
past middle age, our wife will die
at her strongest and most beautiful.
New women come and go. All go.
The pretty lover who announces
that she is temporary
is temporary. The bold woman,
middle-aged against our old age,
sinks under an anxiety she cannot withstand.
Another friend of decades estranges himself
in words that pollute thirty years.
Let us stifle under mud at the pond's edge
and affirm that it is fitting
and delicious to lose everything.

15 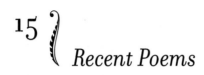 Recent Poems

You climbed Hawk's Crag, a cellphone in your baggy shorts,
and gazed into the leafing trees and famous blue water.
You telephoned, in love with the skin of the world. I heard you
puff as you started to climb down, still talking, switching
your phone from hand to hand as the stone holds required.

You sang show tunes sitting above me, clicking your fingers,
swaying your shadowy torso. We attended to each other
in a sensuous dazzle as global as suffering
until gradual gathering spilled like water over the stone dam
and we soared level across the long-lived lake.

     ∾

                           But how
can one flesh and consciousness adhere to another,
knowing that every adherence ends in separation? I longed
for your return, your face lit by a candle, your smile
private as a kore's under an inconstant flame—and dreamt
I stared into the flat and black of water, afraid to drown.

     ∾

It is half a year since we slept beside each other all night.
I wake hollow as a thighbone with its marrow picked out.
In falling snow, a crow pecks under the empty birdfeeder.

     ∾

When the house lights go out in wind and heavy snow,
the afternoon already black, I lie frightened in darkness
on the unsheeted bed. No one comes to my door.
Old age concludes in making wills and trusts and inventories,
in knees that buckle going downstairs. Wretched in airless
solitude, I want to call you,
                              but if you hear my voice
you will unplug your telephone and lie awake until morning.

ꙮ

I remember you striding toward me, hands in jean pockets,
each step decisive, smiling as if you knew that the cool
air kept a secret, but might be cajoled into revealing it.

THE ANGELS

In the cold mist of a November
morning, pickups park deep
in fallen leaves while hunters
file singly into the woods,
looking for deer that browse
in abandoned apple orchards
by cellarholes.
                    God watches
them move under oak and hemlock
like fleas in a dog's pelt,
so many of them, tiny among
the trees. The master declares:
"It makes no difference, a thousand
angels or one; there
is no number in eternity."

The Master

Where the poet stops, the poem
begins. The poem asks only
that the poet get out of the way.

The poem empties itself
in order to fill itself up.

The poem is nearest the poet
when the poet laments
that it has vanished forever.

When the poet disappears
the poem becomes visible.

What may the poem choose,
best for the poet?
It will choose that the poet
not choose for himself.

Surveyor and Surface

The surveyor climbs a stone wall into woods
scribbled with ferns, saplings, and fallen oaks

where weltering greens trope themselves into stacks
of vegetation. An ash forces itself around a rock

as a fist grasps a paperweight. Hemlocks rise
among three-hundred-year-old sugarmaples that hoist

an archive of leaves, preserves of pitiless survival.
Birches knocked down by wind, and popples chewed

by beaver, twist over and under each other
as trunks deteriorate into humus, becoming

polyseeded dirt loosening with the lively
pokeholes of creatures that look him back—possum,

otter, fox. Here the surveyor makes his mark;
he slashes a young maple and constructs a particular

stone cairn at an abstract angle; he tacks to a stake
a metal plate with his name and the day's date

and departs the unaltered wood where cellular life
presses upward from underground studies to read

the sun and copy the mottoes of dirt: "Never think
of a surface except as the extremity of a volume."

North South

When I stop by the grave in fall,
the chrysanthemums I set there
in August have frozen. Someone
has left two shimmering glass
baubles on the black granite.

My name and the year of my birth
mock me, carved on the stone.
I rise from the carseat slowly
and hobble to the grave
of a woman who does not age.

∾

Walking in the Amazon's Belém,
I stepped in front of a bus

and leapt clear. In Boston I stared
into the blazing warehouse,
eager for fire, terrified to burn.

∾

Nuthatches and chickadees
eat cells of black-oil sunflower seed,

swapping their perches, gorging
their stomachs full. I feel hunger

for their hunger, for the appetite,
so swiftly satisfied, of little ones.

∾

Let the year stay dark all year,
dark June and July. Long days of sun
present themselves as measure,
but the only measure is darkness.

∾

The day is a dog with failing hindquarters:
It can no longer chase the thrown stick.

∾

Sky clears into sky, small clouds scudding,
the mountain lofty in morning light, the pond

shining through popples. I enter the province
of words, domain without clocks or despair.

∾

My friend of forty-five years
refuses to catch my eye.
Across the road dead hens
cackle, dead roosters crow.

∾

For several days I have felt
neither ecstatic nor suicidal.

The cat stretches awake, yawning,
after a dream of sparrows.

Clouds gather against blue sky,
it rains, the mountain continues.

It seems that I might wake up
tomorrow and turn to my work.

Where was this greeny field
last week? Ask me tomorrow.

THE MYSTERIES

The god of monkeys leaps from branch
to branch. The god of horses neighs.
The god of dogs bays at the moon.

∾

If it happens once, it will happen again.

∾

I built a chamber underground,
crawled inside for five months,
and in the sixth month rose
with my thighs turned to tubers.

∾

I appeared at the same hour
in Prague and New Hampshire.

∾

In differing they agree with themselves,
the connection always *in verso*—
like the bow and the arrow. Warmth cools,
cold heats, wet dries, parch moistens.

∽

Among the divinities, she is Lord,
and wisest in measure, who inhabits
the temple of limb-loosening love.

OLIVES

"Dead people don't like olives,"
I told my partners in eighth grade
dancing class, who never listened
as we foxtrotted, one-*two*, one-*two*.

The dead people I often consulted
nodded their skulls in unison
while I flung my black velvet cape
over my shoulders and glowered
from deep-set, burning eyes,
walking the city streets, alone at fifteen,
crazy for cheerleaders and poems.

At Hamden High football games, girls
in short pleated skirts
pranced and kicked, and I longed
for their memorable thighs.
They were *friendly*—poets were mascots—
but never listened when I told them
that dead people didn't like olives.

Instead the poet, wearing his cape,
continued to prowl in solitude

405

intoning inscrutable stanzas
as halfbacks and tackles
made out, Friday nights after football,
on sofas in dark-walled rec rooms
with magnanimous cheerleaders.

But, decades later, when the dead
have stopped blathering
about olives, obese halfbacks wheeze
upstairs to sleep beside cheerleaders
waiting for hip replacements,
while a lascivious, doddering poet,
his burning eyes deep-set
in wrinkles, cavorts with their daughters.

After Horace

(Odes 3.15)

Ibycus, man of property,
Chloris's husband, stop chasing young
women. Now that you're
almost ready for the grave, give up

fucking around. It won't do
to try passing for one of the randy studs
and darken their young sky
with Viagra's lechery. Your grandson Nathus

runs after pretty girls, as well
he might, pursuing them into their villas.
Like a satyr piping his lust,
he's a billygoat in his desire for Phloe,

         but as for you, at your age,
it's time to sit and snore. Forget love songs,
         Ibycus. Stop lusting over
the Swimsuit Issue, while you drink Bud all day.

EA

After fifty years we meet to take
a cup of tea on your seventy-fifth birthday.
Your body is still slim, lips red
and full, eyes sunken in a crush of skin.

For a moment, I remember us
nineteen and naked on an Oriental rug
in the Lexington living room—your smooth
narrow body, pale thighs pumping,

sexual damp on pubic hair, both of us
giddy and wild and frightened with desire—
and your father's hesitant voice calling
from upstairs, "Lillian? Lillian? Lillian?"

We finish our tea and embrace briefly.
Each of us knows: We are old people.
You drive me to my Marriott, holding tight
to the wheel as our eyes adjust to darkness.

SAFE SEX

If he and she do not know each other, and feel confident
they will not meet again; if he avoids affectionate words;

407

if she has grown insensible skin under skin; if they desire
only the tribute of another's cry; if they employ each other

as revenge on old lovers or families of entitlement and steel—
then there will be no betrayals, no letters returned unread,

no frenzy, no hurled words of permanent humiliation,
no trembling days, no vomit at midnight, no repeated

apparition of a body floating face-down at the pond's edge.

TENNIS BALL

I parked by the grave in September, under oaks and birches,
and said hello again, and went walking with Gussie

past markers, roses, and the grave with plastic chickens.
(Somebody loved somebody who loved chickens.)

Gus stopped and stared: A woman's long bare legs
stretched up at the edge of the graveyard, a man's body

heaving between them. Gus considered checking them out,
so I clicked my fingers, as softly as I could, to distract him,

and became the unintending source of *coitus interruptus*.
Walking to the car, I peeked. She was restarting him, her

head riding up and down. It was a fine day, leaves red,
Gus healthy and gay, refusing to give up his tennis ball.

943

They toughened us for war. In the high school auditorium
Ed Monahan knocked out Dominick Esposito in the first round

of the heavyweight finals, and ten months later Dom died
in the third wave at Tarawa. Every morning of the war

our Brock-Hall Dairy delivered milk from horse-drawn wagons
to wooden back porches in southern Connecticut. In winter,

frozen cream lifted the cardboard lids of glass bottles,
grade A or grade B, while Marines bled to death in the surf,

or the right engine faltered into Channel silt, or troops marched
—what could we do?—with frostbitten feet as white as milk.

JSAGE

When I was sick at seventeen she was a nurse's helper
at St. Raphael's—sixteen, naïve, slender, pretty, and lived

in a three-decker house. After they sent me home,
I telephoned her and for three years we dated, Friday

and Saturday nights—kissing, rubbing, repeating how much
we loved each other, naming our children, and painfully

not going all the way. In my second year of college,
I broke it off, and we parked weeping instead of kissing.

Driving home, I heard a line, "I walked all through you,"
and excoriated myself: I used her misery for a poem.

When my wife died fifty years later, I wrote about Cytoxan,
TBI, emesis, and white death. I could not stop writing.

WHITE CLAPBOARD

When we tore out the chimney
of the original Cape, one brick
read *1803*. Two centuries ago
teams of oxen piled their cargo
alongside the Grafton Turnpike
for the bearded crew
to butter and shape, lifting—
from the scooped-out root cellar,
among oak beams squared
with an adze—a tree of bricks
to warm four rooms and a loft
where many births endured
eight decades into many deaths,
and the Cape extended its white
clapboard into the long house
where once again a cherished
childhood, brittle with age, falters
to drowse among familiar things.

WITNESS'S HOUSE

From the scratchy sleep of old age,
a ghost-gray whippoorwill wakes me
with her three-step song.
When I woke in this room as a boy,
my grandmother Kate brought me coffee
at dawn, her long gray hair
already braided over her soft face
while my grandfather Wesley milked
the sisterhood in the barn.
                    One by one
they atrophy, knees and hipjoints,

ears and eyes, leg muscles and fingers.
Hair departs from the head
and dark tight hairs from the body,
leaving a whiteness of old thighs
and calves, smooth as a girl's
but with blue veins, the wreckage
and comfort of a body contracted
to frailty.
          We wheelbarrowed milkcans
to Route 4, where they perched
for the dairy truck as the new day rose
past Ragged Mountain, over Kearsarge.
We hayed with Riley the horse under a sun
that never moved from its noon.
                       Sundays,
great-aunts and -uncles visited,
stepping from their Model A's
with vivacious red wrinkled faces,
neck wattles and liver spots.
They waved thin hands to conduct
the familiar stories, and stood
slowly, in sections, to stretch and yawn
before walking.
          At bedtime Wesley
gummed bread and milk
while Kate drank Moxie and we listened
to Edward R. Murrow on the Emerson
radio, shaped like a cathedral,
who told us that London was burning.
At ninety my grandmother gave up
her sheep and her chickens, to live
seven years in a diminishing house.
When she died, I entered
her oilclothed kitchen to grow old
living alone like Kate, looking out

the same window at the same acres,
where in midafternoon the western sun
paints the unpainted wood of the barn,
ruin of gray and gold. A lamp
stays lit all night
in the witness's house.
                    Sunrise
is lavender, orange, and pink, latticing
a sky as gray and hard as ice
in the new cold. I scrape the windshield,
feeling a bite in my elbow, and drive
to town for the *Globe.* In the rearview
mirror the sky over Kearsarge is pink,
lavender, and orange as I drive home,
happy, to black coffee and news
of cities and fire, under the standing lamp.

GOSPEL

Hatred is wise beyond its years.
Hatred is intent, clever, and patient,

sophisticated and implacable.
When hatred enters the garden

it consumes every rose and cabbage,
every ear of corn, every hollyhock.

Hatred is diligent, it is cellular,
it is replicable. If we cut off

hatred's head, ten new murders
grow from the pod of its head.

And now abideth hatred, *invidia*,
and *Schrecklichkeit*, ripening black fruit

for the bounty of empire's orchard,
and the chiefest of these is hatred.

WE BRING DEMOCRACY TO THE FISH

It is unacceptable that fish prey on each other.
For their comfort and safety, we will liberate them
into fishfarms with secure, durable boundaries
that exclude predators. Our care will provide
for their liberty, health, happiness, and nutrition.
Of course all creatures need to feel useful.
At maturity the fish will discover their purposes.

FISHING FOR CATS, 1944

Sometimes we counted freight trains a hundred cars long,
carrying searchlights, wings, and fuselages to Montreal.

My grandfather and I found Luther's leaky old rowboat,
its oars shipped, across the railroad by Eagle Pond.

We pushed it into dark water, carrying sticks for poles
and the Bokar coffee can of worms I collected

digging with a spade in loam at the hayfield's edge.
We pinned the pink wriggly creatures onto small hooks

and he told me stories while we caught bony perch
to feed the barn cats at home. Only the old mother cat,

her teats hanging down to the barn floor, survived Chevys
and Model A's on Route 4, to breed more litters of kittens.

When I dug holes to bury the young ones, dead in the gutter,
I didn't care. For Sunday dinner we killed a setting hen

and laughed as she ran in circles with her head cut off.
In the Boston *Post* we read that the skies over Europe

were black all day with American boys bombing Germany.

THE HUNKERING

In October the red leaves going brown heap and scatter
over hayfield and dirt road, over garden and circular driveway,

and rise in a curl of wind disheveled as schoolchildren
at recess, classes just starting and summer done, winter's

white quiet beginning in ice on the windshield, in hard frost
that only blue asters survive, and in the long houses that once

more tighten themselves for darkness and hunker down.

NOTE

This book selects from poems written over sixty years. Sometimes I have changed titles or revised lines. I include one poem from *The Alligator Bride*, a selection of 1978, which I omitted from *Old and New Poems*, a selection of 1990. Mostly I have cut from the earlier volumes. In *The One Day*, I have dropped several stanzas from the final section. Some collections ended with notes, which I now find superfluous.

Index of Titles and First Lines

Titles are set in italic type.

417